Radicalism at the (

Radicalism at the Crossroads

*African American Women
Activists in the Cold War*

Dayo F. Gore

NEW YORK UNIVERSITY PRESS
New York and London

NEW YORK UNIVERSITY PRESS
New York and London
www.nyupress.org

First published in paperback in 2013

References to Internet websites (URLs) were accurate at the time of writing.
Neither the author nor New York University Press is responsible for URLs
that may have expired or changed since the manuscript was prepared.

Library of Congress Cataloging-in-Publication Data

Gore, Dayo F.
Radicalism at the crossroads : African American
women activists in the Cold War / Dayo F. Gore.
p. cm.
Includes bibliographical references and index.
ISBN 978–0–8147–7011–5 (pb : alk. paper)
ISBN 978–0–8147–3236–6 (cl : alk. paper) — ISBN 978–0–8147–3278–6 (e-book)
1. African American women political activists—History—20th century.
2. Women radicals—United States—History—20th century. 3. African American
radicals—History—20th century. 4. Radicalism—United States—History—20th century.
5. Feminism—United States—History—20th century. 6. Communism—United States—
History—20th century. 7. United States—Race relations—History—20th century. I. Title.
E185.615.G668   2010
322.4'20820973—dc22   2010033744

New York University Press books are printed on acid-free paper,
and their binding materials are chosen for strength and durability.
We strive to use environmentally responsible suppliers and materials
to the greatest extent possible in publishing our books.

Manufactured in the United States of America
10 9 8 7 6 5 4 3 2 1

Contents

Acknowledgments

I began research for this book many years ago with a grainy microfilm copy of Paul Robeson's *Freedom* newspaper. In the course of this project's transformation from an intriguing archival find into a book, I have relied on the support and generosity of many individuals, friends, colleagues, archivists, and institutions. I can only begin to account for the full depth of my gratitude in these brief acknowledgments. I must first thank the women whose lifelong activism and commitment to creating a better world inspired this book. I am particularly grateful to Esther Cooper Jackson, Thelma Dale Perkins, and the late Vicki Garvin for taking the time to share their memories and insights with me. I am also extremely grateful to Miranda Bergman, Lincoln Bergman, and Sheila Gregory Thomas, for sharing with me their stories about and memories of their loved ones and to photographer Norma Holt for use of her images.

Research and writing for this project have been made possible by the generous support of several grants and fellowships including a research grant from the Schlesinger Library on the History of Women in America; a yearlong fellowship from the International Center for Advanced Studies Project on the Cold War at New York University; a National Endowment for the Humanities summer seminar grant; a Scholars-in-Residence fellowship, funded by the National Endowment for the Humanities, at the Schomburg Center for Research in Black Culture; and a timely course release supported by the Women, Gender, Sexuality Studies program at the University of Massachusetts at Amherst. I owe a particular debt of gratitude to Colin Palmer, the Director of the Schomburg's Scholars-in-Residence Program. It was at the Schomburg that I began to rethink and revise my work. Colin's intellectual engagement and generosity contributed to making my time at the center invigorating and productive. Many thanks also to Diana Lanchatanere, curator of the Schomburg's Manuscript, Archives, and Rare Book Division, who, during my time in residence and after, provided helpful suggestions and graciously answered questions.

For their guidance in negotiating archival material and images, I would like to thank Thomas Lisanti, Permissions Manager at the New York Public Library; David Kuzma, Reference Archivist, and Erika Gorder, Associate University Archivist at the Special Collections and University Archives, Rutgers University Library; Donna L. Levy, Librarian, and Erika Gottfried, Curator of Nonprint Collections at the Tamiment Library and Robert F. Wagner Labor Archives, New York University Libraries; and Teresa M. Burk, Research Services Archivist in the Manuscript, Archives, and Rare Book Library, Emory University.

I have benefited immeasurably from the insights and generosity of many teachers and scholars in the field, particularly Robin D. G. Kelley, Lisa Duggan, Tricia Rose, Marilyn Young, and Frederick Cooper, who as my dissertation committee provided crucial direction and constructive criticism during the early stages of this research. They continue to offer guidance and powerful models of politically engaged scholarship. I am also grateful to Gerald Horne, whose prodigious research and scholarship have done much to reinvigorate the study of the black left during the 1950s. His comments on a chapter of this book and his advice regarding publication came at particularly useful moments. I would also like to thank James Campbell, whose enthusiasm for history and intellectual exchange inspired me as an undergraduate student in his freshman seminar on African American history. After years without contact, I have been heartened by his renewed support of my work.

The book has been greatly improved by those who have generously read portions or all of the manuscript and offered sage comments. They include Jamila Gore, Christina Hanhardt, Peniel Joseph, James Smethurst, Jeanne Theoharis, Rebeccah Welch, and Komozi Woodard. I am also grateful to the anonymous reviewers at New York University Press and Duke University Press, who provided much appreciated feedback and detailed suggestions for improving the manuscript. Debbie Gershenowitz at New York University Press believed in this project even when it still needed considerable work. Her encouragement and editorial attention have been exceptional. Gabrielle Begue shepherded the book through its many phases with skill, and Despina P. Gimbel's attention to detail and patience during the final stages of the manuscript were much appreciated.

This book and my own thinking have also benefited enormously from a community of scholars also engaged in studying black women's radicalism and the black left during the 1940s and 1950s. I would like to thank Martha Biondi, Ruth Feldstein, Erik S. Gellman, Jennifer Guglielmo, Mary Helen Washington, Erik McDuffie, Barbara Ransby, James Smethurst, and Judith Smith, who have, through research leads, their own scholarly examples, conversations, and shared conference panels, helped to make this a richer historical study.

Throughout this project, I have been sustained by both newly formed and longstanding bonds of collegiality and friendship. I owe many, many thanks to my activist communities in New York City, particularly those I met through the Audre Lorde Project, CAAAV: Organizing Asian Communities, and People's Justice 2000. Their friendship, dedication, and political vision helped to keep me grounded and focused on the larger project of liberation. A special thanks is also due my fellow CANS members; Betsy Esch, Kimberly Gilmore, and Michael LaCombe for helping me to resist all the naysaying. I am also grateful to Nerissa Balce, Richard Chu, Margo Crawford, Celina Denkins, Eva Hageman (thanks for the research help), Lili Kim, Tuyet Le, Asha Nadkarni, Mireille Miller-Young, Sherie Randolph, Sujani Reddy, Micol Seigel, and Andy Terranova, for providing keen insights and encouragement when needed and sanity-saving distractions and humor when necessary. My many conversations with Christina Hanhardt, a trusted friend and fellow traveler in academic life, helped me to see my work in a broader political and intellectual context. I would also like to thank Jeanne Theoharis for her friendship, counsel, and intellectual generosity. The final edits for this manuscript were completed under particularly trying circumstances. I cannot express how appreciative I am to Shamaila Khan, Hector Adames, and Carla Bernardes for stepping in when work demanded my attention and to Deborah Fox and Lamar Miller for welcoming me into their home.

Finally, I owe immeasurable thanks to my family, whose love, encouragement, and support have seen me through it all. My parents, James Gore and Juliet Jenkins Gore, have each, in their own way, instilled in me a love of history and political debate, as well as a stubborn commitment, sometimes to their own vexation, to charting my own life path. My mother's stories about her great-grandfather and her own journey from Newport News to Detroit in the 1960s sparked my initial curiosity about "what happened back then," and my father's keen eye for racial politics allowed me to see the importance of these issues in our everyday lives. For their love, humor, and the occasional reality checks, I thank my brothers and sisters, Cheryl, Demetreus, Gabriel, Keesonga, and Jamila, as well as the extended Gore family, Angie, Daiquan, Grace, Jaden, Nicole, Nyemah, Serena, and Zachery.

My most heartfelt love and gratitude goes to Arianne Miller for her unwavering love and belief in me. As this book has traveled along its path, she has read too many drafts to count and has always offered honest and insightful comments. She has celebrated my accomplishments, encouraged me in the face of setbacks, and listened to the minute details of my research, all while completing her own research and writing. Her creativity, passion, and perseverance continue to amaze and inspire.

Abbreviations

AFL—American Federation of Labor
ALP—American Labor Party
ANT—American Negro Theatre
AWP—American Women for Peace
AYC—American Youth Congress
CRC—Civil Rights Congress
CP—Communist Party USA
CPA—Communist Political Association
CAW—Congress of American Women
CIO—Congress of Industrial Organizations
CNA—Committee for the Negro in the Arts
CAA—Council on African Affairs
DPOWA—Distributing, Processing and Office Workers of America
HUAC—House Committee on Un-American Activities
ILD—International Labor Defense
NAACP—National Association for the Advancement of Colored People
NCASF—National Council of American-Soviet Friendship
NCFIF—National Committee to Free the Ingram Family
NNC—National Negro Congress
NNLC—National Negro Labor Council
NWAC—Negro Women's Action Committee
PCC—Parent Community Committee
SACB—Subversive Activities Control Board
SNYC—Southern Negro Youth Congress
STJ—Sojourners for Truth and Justice
UOPWA—United Office and Professional Workers of America
USCPFA—U.S.-China Peoples Friendship Association
WIDF—Women's International Democratic Federation
WCEJ—Women's Committee for Equal Justice

Introduction

The Freedom Train is rolling and Negro women are not in the
second car or in the third car, but they're right up there in the
first car. (APPLAUSE) And more than that—the drivers [*sic*]
seat on the Freedom Train of the Negro people is a double
seat—it's got room for the male—and the female (LAUGH-
TER and APPLAUSE). And this is the kind of movement
this is, and this is the kind of role we're gonna fight for and
we're gonna get . . . we're going to get our freedom and we're
going to roll over anybody and everybody who's in our way.
(APPLAUSE)

—Pearl Laws, National Negro Labor Council convention, 1951[1]

The work of black women radicals overflowed from the pages of the
newspaper *Freedom*.[2] The author Alice Childress's regular fictional column,
"Conversations from Life," employed humor and pointed political insights in
chronicling the everyday struggles, labor, and resistance of Mildred, a black
domestic worker. A photo of the labor activist Vicki Garvin, smiling alongside her article "Labor Council Links Fight of Negro and Unions," took center stage as part of a two-page spread detailing the founding convention of
the National Negro Labor Council (NNLC). The organization hoped, with its
November convention, to mobilize black workers in the fight for civil rights
and labor rights.

On another page, a headline announced "Women Voice Demands in
Capital Sojourn." This headline introduced a set of articles by staff writer
and future playwright Lorraine Hansberry on the Sojourn for Truth and
Justice, a meeting in Washington, D.C., of more than 130 "representative"
black women, demanding redress from the U.S. Department of Justice for
the "wives, mothers and victims of race hatred." The protest had been initiated by a group of black women radicals that included the actress and
author Beulah Richardson (Beah Richards), the activists Yvonne Gregory
and Louise Thompson Patterson, and Alice Childress. At the bottom of the

page appeared a picture of Mrs. Rosa Lee Ingram, a black sharecropper who, along with her two sons, had been sentenced to life imprisonment in 1948 for "defending herself from a would-be rapist-murderer." Framed as a fight against "legal lynching," Ingram's battle garnered support from women active in the NNLC and served as "the symbol of the Sojourn itself."[3] The range of black women's activism covered in this October 1951 issue illustrates black women's central role in sustaining radical resistance and "united action" during the early Cold War.[4]

In 1960, almost ten years later, some four years after *Freedom* ceased publication, Vicki Garvin again appeared alongside a powerful group of black women radicals, this time picketing on the sidewalk outside an F. W. Woolworth store in Manhattan. In February the Congress of Racial Equality (CORE) called for a boycott of Woolworth to support the wave of student sit-ins sweeping through the South. Participation in the picket marked one of the first protests by the recently formed Negro Women's Action Committee (NWAC), which counted Garvin, Louise Thompson Patterson, and longtime Communist Party (CP) activist Maude White Katz among its members. These black women, "having persevered in [the] past," again committed themselves "anew to march forward . . . in supporting our youth in whatever form and manner possible" and in "undertaking specific projects." In May 1960, hoping to solidify the organization's mission, Garvin and White Katz circulated a statement declaring that "now the time has come for still another *organized* movement and demonstration of our will and determination to claim our real heritage and to bequeath to the coming generation the full citizenship so long denied our people."[5] The statement not only celebrated the important skills and insights these women had garnered from their shared histories of radical resistance: it also acknowledged the responsibility they felt to pass these lessons on to a new generation.

Such sketches of persistent activism, drawn from the pages of *Freedom* and from the later work of the NWAC, belong to a rich and complex (yet little-known) history of black women's radicalism and post–World War II politics. Drawing on a range of underutilized archival sources, *Radicalism at the Crossroads* documents a network of black women leftists who became politicized in the 1930s and in the 1940s and defiantly maintained communist affiliations in the midst of a politically repressive "red scare" of the 1950s. These women articulated a forceful demand for black women's equality at a time when an idealized vision of women's domesticity and "separate spheres" dominated gender discourse and advocated for the rights of black defendants years before African Americans' challenges to institutionalized racism and economic injustice would claim the national stage. Furthermore, many of the women sustained these politics well into the 1970s.

This dynamic community of women included established CP organizers such as Louise Thompson Patterson, Maude White Katz, Marvel Cooke, and Claudia Jones; authors Beulah Richardson, Lorraine Hansberry, and Alice Childress; and lesser-known activists such as Vicki Garvin, Yvonne Gregory, Thelma Dale Perkins, and Halois Moorhead. Not all of these women could be counted as active members of the CP, yet they were part of a black left that worked in a number of CP-affiliated organizations whose national offices were based in New York. They also coalesced around two of the most well-known black radicals of the twentieth century, the celebrated artist Paul Robeson and the renowned intellectual W. E. B. Du Bois.

All of these women were supportive of a "left-wing" politics.[6] They shared a critique of U.S. capitalism as exploitative of workers and highlighted the role of white supremacy in buttressing a range of inequalities. Their analysis also carried with it a commitment to advancing women's equality and an internationalist vision of the black freedom struggle. The key tenets of their radicalism were expressed in a range of CP-affiliated organizing efforts aimed at sustaining and reframing leftist politics in the United States during the early Cold War years. These women served as contributing writers, staff, and members of the editorial board of Paul Robeson's *Freedom* newspaper, and they made crucial contributions to numerous campaigns led by the Civil Rights Congress (CRC). They also served as invaluable leadership and on-the-ground organizers in the NNLC and as founders of the Sojourners for Truth and Justice (STJ), an all-black women's civil rights organization that formed after the 1951 Sojourn for Truth and Justice protest.[7] Many of these women also sharpened their skills as writers and artists by producing powerful cultural work in support of a variety of political campaigns and organizations.

These women radicals found a common ground based on bonds built over years of shared activism and struggle. Many of the women had encountered each other in the 1930s during the political heyday of the U.S. left, either in the milieu of Harlem politics, through CP connections, or within the broader liberal-left coalition of the Popular Front such as the National Negro Congress (NNC). For example, some of the women writing for *Freedom*, such as Gregory, Dale Perkins, Moorhead, and Garvin, had worked together during World War II in the New York–based NNC and had helped to publish

Congress View.[8] They also lent a radical edge to the "Double V" or victory campaign led by the African American press, which argued for the victory of democracy at home and abroad, thus using the international issue of war to draw attention to America's racist practices, particularly segregation in the Jim Crow South. Yet, within more mainstream African American politics, the "Double V" campaign often operated to buttress American nationalism and signaled the early shifting tide against black communists.[9]

By the 1950s, the number of activists willing to work with CP-affiliated organizations had shrunk dramatically. Many black women activists, from Mary McLeod Bethune, national leader and founder of the National Council of Negro Women, to the more radical-leaning Ella Baker, conceded to the pressures of Cold War anticommunism and distanced themselves from communist associations.[10] Faced with thinning ranks, a number of active CP members relocated to major cities like New York. Here black women radicals found themselves among a vital group of black leftists invested in building the black freedom struggle and open to black women's efforts to develop a radical politics that centered both race and gender.

These women's political contributions do not, however, fit the neat frameworks of a local community study, an organizational or Communist Party history, or even a series of individual biographies. Their lives and activism, as well as their political alliances, often expanded beyond such boundaries. Their politics were not dictated by, nor did they always mesh with CP policies. "I didn't feel that the party was the only organization out there doing these things," recalled Dale Perkins. "I supported them [the CP] and their right to exist . . . but it didn't necessarily mean that I had to beat the drums for the Communist Party and I didn't."[11] Moreover, their activism was neither developed nor contained within any one specific organization or issue. During the early Cold War years, black women who remained active in the CP milieu addressed a wide array of political issues and participated in numerous activities, from founding organizations and producing insightful political commentary to leading direct-action protests. Therefore, their stories of resistance, community, and longevity emerge more fully within the points of contact and exchange across their ongoing activism rather than in specific organizational histories or individual biographies.

To better capture these multiple avenues of interactions and to provide "a detailed historical record" of black women's political practices, *Radicalism at the Crossroads* presents a collective political biography of this group.[12] Their social location, subjectivity, and experiences as black radical women fighting, often but not always from the margins, for a greater voice in shaping left politics provided the foundation of their common cause. As theorists and activists, they demanded that left-leaning organizations embrace an intersecting analysis that centered race and gender, as well as economics. They enacted a vision of liberation and resistance anchored at these points of intersection. Indeed, their shared political work took shape at the crossroads of the fights for black liberation, women's equality, workers' rights, and the U.S. left.

From this viewpoint, one can read these black women radicals as "protofeminists," which the political theorist Joy James defines as "historical women . . . who preshadowed contemporary black feminist radicalism" and "provided models and strategies for resistance."[13] A detailed examination of these women's political thought and activism forces one to reconsider both the impact of anticommunist attacks on the U.S. left and the influence and longevity of black women's radical resistance. Their experiences of organizing for political and social change join other stories of Cold War resistance in forcing a reconsideration of historical narratives that have long framed the early postwar years, in particular the 1950s, as a period of pervasive political repression and conformity wedged between the radical upheaval of the 1930s and the explosive social movements of the 1960s.[14]

The sustained organizing and strategic analysis of CP-affiliated black women activists challenge dominant understandings of black left and CP politics during this period. For example, their political commitments and transnational visions undermine the commonly held belief that the narrowing Cold War landscape successfully contained all African Americans' demands for equality within the frame of American liberalism. As Cold War politics defined racial equality as central to U.S. democracy, and as postwar labor restructuring forced issues of gender and work to center stage, black women radicals found themselves uniquely positioned to speak to both discourses. A resolution on Negro women at the founding convention of the National Negro Labor Council perhaps best exemplifies this conjuncture by proclaiming that "the progress of the American workers and the Negro people can best be measured by the status of Negro women."[15]

In this context, these women's radical engagement with race and gender debates was a crucial tool that enabled them to negotiate the rising tide of conservatism and to claim space to articulate the intersections of black liberation and women's equality, simultaneously. From Claudia Jones, who issued a call, in 1949, for "An End to the Neglect of the Problems of the Negro Woman!," to Beulah Richardson, whose poetry exposed racialized womanhood and defended a black women's right to self-defense, black women emerged as significant participants in transnational struggles over the meanings of U.S. democracy, equality, and citizenship.

The ideas and affiliations that defined these women's radicalism also reveal the limitations in drawing sharp divisions between CP-influenced ideologies and tactics, civil rights strategies, and black nationalist politics. Historians of the U.S. left have argued heatedly over individuals' CP membership, Soviet influence in local activism, and the degree to which U.S. communists denounced the Soviet Union for the brutal policies of the Stalin era. Debates within the literature on the black freedom struggle have been most sharply defined by Harold Cruse's caustic critique of black communists as dupes of the CP and by what mainstream accounts continue to mark as a distinct turn from the nonviolent demands for integration voiced by the civil rights movement to the more boisterous cries for black power and self-defense. The inclusive political visions of black women radicals, however, illustrate that these ideological differences were not always unyielding, restrictive, or incompatible. Their ability to build strategic alliances across a range of ideological camps complicates much of the scholarship on the U.S. left, which has chronicled radical activism as if it could be explicated by individual ideological debates or defined entirely by organizational affiliations.[16]

Amplifying the full range of political thought and activism embraced by black women working within CP-affiliated organizations also presents an alternative depiction of black women's activism. Increasingly, historical studies include black women activists as central participants in the black freedom struggle. Yet, even as they acknowledge black women's contributions, these studies tend to emphasize their work as locally based grassroots activists, as the "ground troops" of the movement, and as "bridge leaders" in the community.[17] Such a singular focus has helped to solidify a vision of black women as behind-the-scenes organizers, making invisible the national and international aspects of their activism and precluding a full account of their intellectual and philosophical contributions to black radicalism. Unearthing the political activism of these women illuminates their contributions as national leaders, intellectual architects, and strategists in building the black freedom struggle, U.S. radicalism, and feminist politics.

Finally, the multi-issue activism and intersectional analysis of these black women radicals provided an important foundation and accessible legacy for the social and political movements that would emerge later. In their demands for federal protection of civil rights, advocacy of black self-determination, and calls to address the intersecting forces of race, class, and gender, they articulated a politics during the 1950s that resonated with many of the demands and ideas fundamental to the civil rights, black power, and women's movements in the 1960s and 1970s. The points of continuity in these struggles were not coincidental but were explicitly cultivated by seasoned black women radicals as they sought to share their skills and insights in the emerging social movements. The founding of *Freedomways*, in 1961, under the managing editorship of Esther Cooper Jackson, reflects one such effort by this older group of black leftists to connect with and support a younger generation of black radicals.[18] Envisioned as a revival of Paul Robeson's *Freedom*, the new journal relied on a number of women with longtime connections to the communist left, including Beulah Richardson, Thelma Dale Perkins, Maude White Katz, and Shirley Graham Du Bois. Moreover, centering the persistent activism of the community of women who worked on *Freedom* and found inspiration in Robeson's politics suggests that Robeson's staunch resistance to Cold War anticommunism can be read not simply as the cause of his tragic fall but also as an important model of mentorship and political fortitude for these black leftists as well as for generations to come.

Cold War Stories: Rethinking the Long Black Freedom Struggle and Red Feminism

Despite these black women's prescient political analysis and wealth of activism, few mainstream historical accounts of the Cold War period include a detailed study of their work. For too long, dominant conventional narratives have presented the 1950s as a period of decimation and defeat for the U.S. left, in which rampant anticommunism silenced black leftists and radical activism. Likewise, these narratives portrayed the era as a time of rising domesticity and the rolling back of changes wrought by World War II, as well as a period of prosperity and conformity in which national leaders successfully contained African Americans' and women's political demands.[19] In challenging this conventional historiography of the 1950s as a period of pervasive political repression and conformity, this book joins a new wave of scholarship excavating the early Cold War period.

Since the 1990s, a series of works ranging from anthologies to local studies have begun to disrupt conventional readings of black activism and the Cold War political landscape.[20] Much of this scholarship highlights the longevity of what the historian Martha Biondi calls a "Black Popular Front" operating in both the national and international arenas well into the late 1940s.[21] Studies tracing black labor organizing in the South, black radical theorists, and the anti-imperialist politics of the black left have revealed the "roots" of these politics in the "contested left of the 1930s."[22] In exploring a range of postwar black organizing this new scholarship revises the historical periodization that ignores Cold War black radicalism and uncovers its connections to later decades of activism, including African American civil rights activism after 1955.

Much of this scholarship has also begun to highlight the U.S. left as a key incubator for black liberation and feminist politics by demonstrating the ways in which radical activists influenced a number of significant political shifts from the 1940s on. These insights are reflected in a range of historical studies, including Kate Weigand's *Red Feminism: American Communism and the Making of Women's Liberation* (2001), Martha Biondi's *To Stand and Fight: The Struggle for Civil Rights in Postwar New York* (2003), and Nikhil Pal Singh's *Black Is a Country: Race and the Unfinished Struggle for Democracy* (2005).[23] Unearthing the legacy of Popular Front leftists, this new work has complicated conventional histories of both postwar U.S. feminism and the black freedom struggle by reconsidering the roots and lengthening the time frame of these movements. Such studies lend additional force to Singh's convincing argument that, despite the onset of the Cold War and political tensions, one can trace "a more or less consistent tradition of radical dissent" from the 1930s onward.[24]

While this reframing has helped to make more visible the activism of black women during these periods, few studies detail their contributions in full. Much of the scholarship on the black left and women's activism tends to cast black women radicals as background figures in a larger story or as silenced by the power of anticommunism, with little examination of their activism and theoretical contributions.[25] In addition, scholars often trace the continuity of radical ideas and politics through the activism and writings of more established intellectuals, activists, and cultural figures, as well as those who were able to "reinvent themselves and continue in the movement" under a different banner.[26] This tendency conceals the activity of black women radicals who, while well known in the black left, rarely achieved mainstream prominence as intellectuals or public figures. Even when they did rise to such status, as did Lorraine Hansberry and Beulah Richardson (as Beah Richards), their leftist roots went unacknowledged. Moreover, as I suggested earlier, an emphasis on those figures who chose to reinvent themselves obscures the careers of black women radicals such as Vicki Garvin, who continued to act from a communist-inspired politics. The women of NWAC and the founders of *Freedomways* were political long-distance runners who continually invested in black radicalism as they carried their ideas, strategies, and lessons from early Cold War activism into a variety of political spaces during the 1960s and 1970s.

A sustained historical account of the political thought and activism of this community of black women radicals adds to the larger project of revisioning the Cold War period and the roots of postwar radicalism. It also provides a powerful record of these women's significant contributions to the articulation of an expansive political vision that engaged the black freedom struggle and women's rights organizing. Furthermore, as exemplified in the pages of *Freedom*, their continued commitment to left politics allowed them to claim valuable space and resources to craft a politics centering black women's experiences. These options proved possible, in part, as the early postwar years produced a period of openings, as discourses around the political and cultural meanings of race and gender took center stage, and closings, as the acceptability of radical politics narrowed. At certain moments, such as the founding of the NNLC and the Rosa Lee Ingram case, black women claimed a greater voice in shaping U.S. left politics. A few black women even moved into leadership positions as anticommunism forced black men out. For example, Vicki Garvin was appointed executive secretary of the New York chapter of the NNLC to replace the labor activist Ferdinand Smith, who was deported in 1951.

This is not to suggest that black women radicals escaped repression. Many women endured intense surveillance by the Federal Bureau of Investigation and were called to testify before the House Committee on Un-American Activities (HUAC); these included Vicki Garvin, Thelma Dale Perkins, and Marvel Cooke.[27] They suffered when close allies "named names" and saw their organizations infiltrated.[28] Nevertheless, by engaging dominant discourses, creating multiple spaces in which they could carry out their work, and building tight-knit networks, many of these women were still able to organize around a radical political agenda during the height of McCarthyism.

In fact, black women lent incisive direction to building an expansive radical politics within a number of CP-affiliated organizations. They expressed the ways in which sexualized racism and gender politics informed "legal lynching" in the U.S. court system; they exposed the race and class bias in debates over women's roles in U.S. society; and they mobilized an expansive labor politics to defend workers' rights. Such engagement addressed not only concerns traditionally framed as within the domain of (black) women activists, such as sexual assault, and women's interracial unity, but also concerns considered more broad, including the theoretical framing and organizing strategies that were integral to sustaining left politics and the black freedom struggle during the 1950s. In each of these efforts, they provided a crucial intersectional analysis of how race, gender, and economic structures operated together to reshape the postwar landscape. Beulah Richardson's poem "The Revolt of Rosa Ingram" perhaps most succinctly captures the broad reach of their intersectional politics. Locating the cause of Ingram's violence in unequal structures of power, Richardson declares:

> 'Tis the lawless laws of this land / that killed this man!
> . . . It's starving children, lonesome and scared
> and people being bombed to death in their beds.
> It's burned down houses / a woman fighting for her life
> cause some people think she's got no rights...
> It's separate this / and separate that. / It's me first and you get back.
> . . . no wonder he couldn't understand / my body belongs to me.[29]

By engaging widespread conversations about race and gender in U.S. democracy, these activists announced their own visions of equality. They argued for the importance of black women as powerful voices of resistance because they could speak to multiple and interconnected forms of oppression. Moreover, as exemplified by their support for a model of interracial solidarity advocated by the CP and the CRC, as well as for the racial self-determination that framed the work of the STJ and the NNLC, these black women radicals defy neat categorizations and convenient ideological labels.[30] Finally, as indicated by black women's participation in the Sojourn for Truth and Justice, in Washington, D.C., and in numerous national and international conferences, most of these women traveled extensively for their activism. Although some had come of age in New York, others settled in the city as it became an important base for the black left during the early Cold War years. Nonetheless, all of these women continued traveling to build and maintain political ties in the South and the world. Their mobility, coupled with their organizing experience and their internationalist politics, helped to solidify their contributions as leaders and strategists with national and transnational reach. Therefore, while this book acknowledges the severe impact of anticommunist assaults on black radicalism and on institutions within the organized left, it also emphasizes black women's ability to maintain militant resistance. Their experiences challenge not only the idea of a decimated left but also the accepted wisdom that anticommunism proved profoundly debilitating to black radical politics.[31]

These women's experiences provide an important addition to an emerging, but still underrepresented, area of study specifically focused on black women's radicalism in the postwar period.[32] As Carole Boyce Davies's recent work on Claudia Jones attests, "the study of black communist women remains one of the most neglected among contemporary examinations of black women."[33] This proves especially true for black women communists during the early Cold War. Much of the groundbreaking scholarship in this area has understandably focused on individual biographies of well-known CP-affiliated black women.[34] Such studies, while important, can produce a view of these women as exceptional or outlying figures. In addition, several of these works reproduce dominant narratives of a Cold War decline and absence, by providing few details of these women's activism during the 1950s or glossing over the ways they sustained their radical activism well into the 1960s and 1970s.[35]

A growing wave of articles and studies, such as Mary Helen Washington's important work on Alice Childress and several other women writers connected to *Freedom*, has begun to present a more complete picture of black women's collective activism and to highlight the ways such politics continued to shape later organizing work.[36] Taken together, the variety of emerging scholarship on black women communists provides an important beginning in detailing these women's lifelong activism within the broader historical context of U.S. radicalism and the black freedom struggle. Yet, as Washington notes, there is still much to be done "to historicize the role and contributions of black women on the Left."[37] In fact, no book-length study specifically focuses on the activism and political thought of this diverse community of black women radicals as they operated in multiple spaces associated with the CP in the 1950s. Building on recent scholarly efforts, *Radicalism at the Crossroads* seeks to present a more complete and detailed history of CP-affiliated black women activists during the early Cold War years.

Centering Black Women Radicals and Revealing an Alternative Narrative

In situating CP-affiliated black women within the growing body of scholarship that is excavating early Cold War activism, uncovering the varied legacies of the "old left," and beginning to address the contributions of black women radicals, *Radicalism at the Crossroads* provides four significant interventions that help to reframe black radicalisms and U.S. postwar activism. First, this book joins a powerful counternarrative to the idea that the U.S. left was decimated by Cold War anticommunism. Black women radicals' incisive politics of resistance, in conjunction with determination, an expansive political vision, and the support of figures such as Paul Robeson, enabled them to cultivate their activism in the midst of government repression and anticommunist pressures. Second, the work details the radical "protofeminist" politics of black women as they asserted "the centrality of racial-sexual struggles and analyses often passed over in mainstream discourse."[38] Third, it advocates for a broader conception of black women's activism by highlighting black women radicals' contributions in national leadership, both as political strategists and as on-the-ground organizers, during the 1950s and well into the 1970s. Last, this book provides convincing evidence of the continuity of black women radicals' political thought and activism into the 1960s and 1970s, as well as of their influence on and connection with the periods emerging political movements.

The story of black women radicals' activism and the impact of their political theorizing takes shape in the next five chapters. Chapter 1 provides a prelude to the larger story by tracing the continuity between the radical politics of the 1930s and that of the 1950s. Examining the roots of their affiliations with the organized U.S. left, the chapter details the ways black women—including Vicki Garvin, Yvonne Gregory, Maude White Katz, Thelma Dale Perkins, Marvel Cooke, and Claudia Jones—were radicalized within the milieu of 1930s Popular Front politics. It also traces the political and life paths that brought these women into New York's black left. The chapter also outlines how they negotiated the shifting politics of postwar America and began to carve out space for themselves within a range of left organizations, particularly those with ties to the Communist Party.

The next three chapters focus on black women radicals' leadership and political strategies in specific organizing campaigns and debates during the early Cold War years. Chapter 2 analyzes the writings of black women radicals who engaged public conversation over dominant constructions of black womanhood and gender relations in the United States. This chapter examines the debates about the black family and heterosexual relationships that emerged in the black-owned publication *Negro Digest*, as well as the calls for addressing women's equality by white women in the CP. These debates provide a backdrop for examining black women's discussion of such issues in various publications, speeches, and their own cultural work, as they intervened to include black women's experiences in theorizing "the woman's question" and "the Negro question" within a range of left spaces. In analyzing this political contestation, this chapter pays particular attention to the ways in which black women radicals critiqued white women's privilege, discussed constructions of black women's sexuality, and articulated a black feminist politics.

Chapter 3 turns to an examination of a protracted civil rights campaign. It describes the political strategies and organizing that shaped black women radicals' activism in the celebrated fight to free Rosa Lee Ingram, a black woman convicted, along with two of her sons, of murdering a white man in rural Georgia. The chapter highlights black women's leadership in organizing to win the Ingrams' freedom and in publicly asserting black women's right to self-defense and control over their bodies. These women situated their activism within the postwar context, as well as within black women's long history of sexualized violence. Working through the Civil Rights Congress, the Women's Committee for Equal Justice, and the all-black women's organization Sojourners for Truth and Justice, Yvonne Gregory, Beulah Richardson, and other women crafted a political analysis that sought to broaden the scope of civil rights activism. Through such efforts, these women fought to assert black women's leadership and vision in shaping postwar civil rights politics.

Chapter 4 draws on the work and writings of Marvel Cooke and Vicki Garvin to explore how black women analyzed—and resisted—the dual impact of gender and race discrimination in the labor market during the early Cold War years. The chapter details the journalism of Marvel Cooke, who chronicled the experiences of black women domestic workers by revisiting the "Bronx Slave Markets" in the pages of the New York newspaper *The Daily Compass*. It also follows the political development of Vicki Garvin, as her commitment to labor activism took her from Smith College, where she became one of the first black women in the college to earn a master's degree in economics, to wartime work at the National Labor War Board and to leadership in the National Negro Labor Council during the 1950s. Their labor activism, which went beyond the traditional bounds of trade union organizing, illustrates how black women radicals helped to develop a more expansive view of labor activism that addressed the full range of experiences of black women workers.

The final chapter traces the extension of these women's radical activism and political vision beyond the 1950s. It outlines the key strategies that allowed many of them to continue their work for such a long time, and it highlights the connections and alliances that sustained them throughout these years. The chapter begins with the emergence of the NWAC and the founding of *Freedomways* journal, which began publication in 1961 as a revival of Paul Robeson's *Freedom* newspaper. It goes on to detail Maude White Katz's work in parent-led school protests in New York and her contributions to Toni Cade Bambara's *The Black Woman*, Vicki Garvin's travels abroad, and black women radicals' participation in the campaigns to free Angela Davis and Joan Little. Thus, this chapter also explores a range of local, national, and transnational activism and cultural work that black women radicals took up as the political landscape expanded, and they sought to connect with a new generation of activists and contribute to the radical politics taking shape during the 1960s and 1970s.

That the political activism of these women survived Cold War anticommunism to find resonance with newly emerging social movements of the 1960s and 1970 is only part of the story I seek to tell in this book. Another important part of the story concerns the ways in which these black women radicals, in a moment dominated by McCarthyism, came together to articulate an expansive radical politics that placed black women at the center. These politics not only helped to create a range of important radical organizations and lasting strategies but—perhaps more significant—created a network of black women affiliated with the U.S. left who would remain lifelong activists and allies.

It was the 1930s that helped to form the political commitments and community that would prove central to their longevity. For black women on the left, Popular Front politics of the 1930s and a burgeoning black left provided an important training ground just as the emerging postwar discourses around gender and race produced key openings in terms of national debates over democracy and equality. As chapter 1 explores black women radicals' early political grounding in the U.S. left and growing ties to the Communist Party, it also highlights central concerns that shaped their political vision and activism for the next half-century. Thus, this period provides a crucial base for understanding the activism, strategic insights, and theorizing that would come into full bloom during the 1940s and 1950s as black women worked in a wide range of radical spaces, from their contributions to *Freedom* newspaper, the campaign to free Rosa Lee Ingram, and their defense of black womanhood to advocating for workers' rights and transnational solidarity.

Forging a Community of Radical Intellectuals and Activists

Black Women, the Black Left, and the Communist Party USA in the 1930s and 1940s

> I never was a great student of Marxism. I read what I had to read but that wasn't really what attracted my attention, more the right people. The people I respected were a part of the trade union movement and I thought that was the way to go. . . . they [the Communist Party] played a major role in all that. They demonstrated by action that they believed in equality of opportunity.
>
> —Thelma Dale Perkins, October 2007

In 1926, ten-year-old Victoria "Vicki" Holmes (Garvin) moved with her mother, father, and younger sister from their hometown of Richmond, Virginia, to New York City. Although Garvin's parents had stable employment in Richmond—her father, Wallace Holmes, as a plasterer in a black trade union and her mother as a domestic worker—they hoped that a move north would provide better opportunities and education for their daughters.[1] The Holmeses settled in Harlem, joining millions of migrants and immigrants in one of the largest waves of black migration to the urban North. That same year, twenty-three-year-old Marvel Jackson (Cooke) also arrived in New York City. Born in 1903 and raised in Minneapolis, Cooke grew up in a progressively minded and solidly middle-class family. Her father, Madison Jackson, worked as a Pullman porter but also maintained numerous business connections, and her mother, Amy Woods, spent much of her married life caring for her family. After graduating from the University of Minnesota, Cooke, through family connections, found employment in the city with the preeminent black scholar W. E. B. Du Bois and initially settled in Brooklyn with a cousin. Cooke's path to New York, driven by her desire to live in a diverse black community, reflected an option open to only a select number of black migrants from established families.[2]

Although separated by a twelve-year age difference, Garvin and Cooke would develop their radical politics and lifelong alliances within the political and cultural vibrancy of the Harlem Renaissance and the upheaval of the Great Depression. As they struggled to negotiate the emerging economic crisis, both Vicki Garvin and Marvel Cooke found community and employment opportunities in the explosion of mass-based organizations, left politics, and organized protests that dominated New York's urban life during the 1930s. While one often thinks of Harlem as a center for artists and writers, the city also nourished a black radical politics that set the stage for the wave of social movements that would reshape postwar America.

Harlem's electric mixture of culture and politics and both women's sharpening political analysis led them to become active members of the Communist Party USA (CP). By the late 1940s and early 1950s, Vicki Garvin would emerge as a key union activist in the United Office and Professional Workers of America (UOPWA) and the National Negro Labor Council (NNLC), and Marvel Cooke would become a progressive journalist working for the black-owned *New York Amsterdam News* and *People's Voice*, as well as for New York's *The Daily Compass*. Through their work, both women developed into significant leaders in the black left and became powerful voices in helping to sustain a radical politics amid anticommunist attacks.

Garvin's and Cooke's early experiences of migration, urban life, and left activism represent some of the common threads in the routes to politicization traveled by most of the other black women radicals at the center of this book. These women, including Thelma Dale (Perkins), Louise Thompson (Patterson), Claudia Jones, Alice Childress, Yvonne Gregory, Maude White (Katz), and Esther Cooper (Jackson), were influenced greatly by 1920s black migration and 1930s radicalism, yet they would rise to political leadership and emerge as key theorists during the less celebrated years of the early Cold War. Moreover, whether as official members or so-called fellow travelers within affiliated organizations, all of these women circulated within a CP milieu. Through their involvement in Popular Front politics and the CP, they gained training and resources that allowed them to work as full-time paid activists. They furthermore solidified lifelong connections that shaped their activism and political vision.

In tracing the politicization process of these activists, this chapter uncovers some of the strategies of 1930s radicalism—including its emphasis on direct-action organizing, interracial working-class politics, and sharp critiques of the U.S. government—that would continue to play out within black women's activism and writings for years to come. The chapter also begins to outline some of the longstanding limitations, opportunities, and tensions black women encountered organizing within the CP and the U.S. left more broadly. These key depression-era and Popular Front experiences would greatly inform their political and personal investments in left organizations and the CP during the late 1940s and early 1950s.

Throughout the 1930s, these black women activist-intellectuals learned to negotiate and challenge much of the troubling race and gender politics that emerged from a white-dominated left, including the influence of white supremacy and sexism in shaping politics and practices, a lack of theorizing around race, gender, and class as intersecting categories, and the continued marginalization of black women, especially as organizational leaders and theorists.[3] Such lessons proved fruitful in the ensuing decades as black women were, at times, able to mobilize significant space and resources in support of their own organizing efforts. Thus, a focus on the 1930s provides a framework for understanding not only the roots of black women's radicalism but also the ways their experiences with Popular Front activism provided them with important skills in sustaining a radical vision. These skills would serve them well when faced with Cold War anticommunism. Moreover, this chapter sets the stage for understanding the ways U.S. left and Communist Party politics and power shifted as the Popular Front era gave way to the early Cold War.

The Great Depression, African American Radicalism, and the U.S. Left

The Great Depression marked a decade of profound change that altered an entire generation of Americans struggling to survive in the midst of economic chaos. African American communities in particular were already coping with an upheaval of their own following one of the largest migrations in U.S. history. Sparked by the industrial buildup to World War I, the Great Migration included, by the war's end, the movement of more than 1.5 million blacks to urban centers in the North and the South. Although the majority of African Americans continued to reside in southern states, this migratory surge would last well into the postwar era and would reshape U.S. political and cultural life.[4]

In addition to Garvin and Cooke, a number of other black women radicals participated in this wave of migration. Born in Charleston in 1916, Alice Childress migrated along the common south-to-north trajectory. After her parents divorced, Childress relocated with her mother in 1925 to live with her maternal grandmother, Eliza Campbell White, in Harlem. Reflecting the transnational impact of migration, in 1924, the nine-year-old Claudia Vera Cumberbatch (Jones) emigrated with her three sisters and her aunt from Port of Spain, in Trinidad, to join her parents in New York. Meanwhile, Maude White (Katz), born in 1908 and raised in McKeesport, Pennsylvania, just outside Pittsburgh, would leave her family home as a teenager, after a progressive school teacher encouraged her to continue her political development by moving to Chicago to live with an older sister. Yvonne Gregory also participated in the northward migration. Born in Washington, D.C., in June 1919, to Thomas Montgomery Gregory and Hugh Ella Hancock, both middle class and college educated, she moved at the age of five with her family to Atlantic City, New Jersey.[5] Louise Thompson Patterson followed a less conventional migratory path. At the age of four, she and her family moved west from Chicago to Seattle and then to California; Thompson Patterson returned east only after graduating with a B.A. from the University of California at Berkeley, in 1924.[6] Despite the diversity of their experiences and the range of cities they called home, these black women radicals, through their migration stories, reveal movement and travel as an important force shaping their development.

The impact of migration was evident in the vibrant intellectual and artistic communities that these women joined as they made new lives in major urban cities, part of an increasingly diverse and militant political scene. The 1920s image of the New Negro came to represent many of these shifts as organizations and journals, from Du Bois's *The Crisis* and the National Association for the Advancement of Colored People (NAACP) to Marcus Garvey's Universal Negro Improvement Association and A. Philip Randolph's black socialist journal *The Messenger*, articulated the emerging power of black resistance. The process of continued movement helped to sustain connections between urban migrants and their southern communities. It also expanded the reach and intensity of white supremacy and black civil rights struggles and the influence of institutions seeking to address such issues. These political and cultural changes would continue to develop well into the 1930s, albeit under very different conditions.

African Americans—among the first to face the economic crisis of the Great Depression—suffered disproportionately throughout the economic downturn, especially those who relied on southern agricultural industries. Throughout the depression era, the rate of black unemployment averaged almost double the national rate, and for African American women the percentage was even higher. African Americans struggled to retain even the most menial employment in a shrinking labor market.[7] In an investigative report titled "The Bronx Slave Market," Marvel Cooke and Ella Baker chronicled the struggles of black women domestic workers who were reduced to selling their services as day laborers on street corners in New York during the depression. Vicki Garvin's father's diminishing job opportunities forced him to take on menial work, including a job as a delivery boy, while her mother turned to bargaining for wages as a domestic in the brutal day laborer market. Garvin vividly recalled her father's humiliation because of his inability to support his family, as well as her own resentment over her family's financial hardship and her intense embarrassment at having to collect food aid for her family from the local school.[8]

The intensified struggles of Garvin's father, who even before the downturn had had great difficulty finding employment in a trade where the color line closed him out of the all-white construction unions, and of her mother, who often faced low wages and disrespectful treatment by white employers, exemplified the increased pressure on black workers during the Great Depression. For Claudia Jones, the growing depression coincided with the death of her mother and her own battle with tuberculosis. By 1935, Jones, a stellar student, had to give up her college aspirations and enter the workforce. Working at a laundry factory, in a millinery shop, and as a sales clerk, she experienced firsthand the struggles with low wages, job insecurity, and harsh labor conditions suffered by the black working class during the depression. The difficulty of earning a livable wage affected both working-class blacks and the burgeoning class of educated workers. Even Marvel Cooke, who in 1928 moved from working as Du Bois's literary editor at *The Crisis* to being editorial secretary at the *New York Amsterdam News*, found it difficult to make ends meet on her initial salary of eighteen dollars a week.[9]

In addition to economic devastation, the depression also brought about an increase in racism and racial violence.[10] Black organizations tracked a rise in lynching and in the hostility of white workers and unions, which increasingly viewed black workers as unworthy competitors for scarce resources. Faced with such dismal prospects, many African Americans drew heavily on a long legacy of protest in times of crisis. Organized agitation became for many black people a cornerstone of their strategies for political and economic survival during this decade. Black communities participated in a range of protests, including "don't buy where you can't work" campaigns, supported union organizing, particularly among the often overlooked domestic and farm workers, and petitioned government institutions for inclusion in New Deal relief programs.[11]

As African Americans, and the nation, began to search for ways to understand the economic and social crisis, radical organizations in the United States found themselves in an opportune position to provide an alternative analysis for those who were willing to listen. This proved particularly true of the Communist Party, which had invested in a sharp critique of America's economic order. During this period, the left gained an important foothold in urban black communities. Thousands of African Americans, men and women, in search of answers, action, and resources found support among Marxist-based organizations. Many left organizations, including the Socialist Party (SP) and the CP, began to explore ways to attract greater numbers of African Americans, who were increasingly viewed as an unorganized segment of society with revolutionary potential. The black women at the center of this study represented an important cross-section of those African Americans drawn to Marxist politics during the 1930s. Despite these women's varied personal experiences, the political vibrancy of urban life and their own lived experiences encouraged them to look beyond mainstream answers.

What about the left attracted African Americans during the 1930s? Historians point to a number of factors. First and foremost, Marxist-based organizations, from the Socialist Party to the Communist Opposition "factions," armed with their critiques of capitalism, provided intelligent analyses of the economic crisis and clear (if untested) visions for reordering society on the basis of an expansive union movement and workers equality.[12] This emphasis on building a strong union movement appealed to both black and white workers, as well as to women workers, and was exemplified by the growth of such unions as the International Ladies Garment Workers Union of the American Federation of Labor (AFL) and the United Electrical, Radio, and Machine Workers Union, which was part of the Congress of Industrial Organizations (CIO). The emphasis on interracial unions proved particularly attractive to black workers, for whom the union color bar served as a continued barrier to securing better employment. Second, these organizations took up concrete and visible activism, including rent strikes, battles for black civil rights, and struggles within federal aid programs like the New Deal Works Progress Administration (WPA), to provide some relief from existing conditions. Participation in such activism often allowed black women access to resources and institutions that were rarely open to them in other forums.[13] Such a concerted response to the collapse of the world economy in 1929 seemed to redeem the Marxist-based critiques of American capitalism and to force all progressive organizations to develop strategies for responding to the crisis.

Migration, Education, and Travel: The
Making of Urban Women Radicals

A generation of black women radicals came of age politically within this context of black migration, increased cultural and political militancy, the reorganization of the U.S. left, and economic crisis. Each of these social forces would shape the life experiences, choices, and political identities of these young women. For example, Claudia Jones's path to radicalism was defined in large part by her early entry into the workforce and by her immersion in Harlem politics. As Jones reshaped her life around daily work instead of school, she also found other outlets for her creative talents. When not working to support her family, Jones participated in local political and cultural events. She performed with the National Urban League's theater troupe and regularly followed street-corner discussions led by representatives of a wide range of political opinions.

Jones was particularly impressed by the CP-supported International Labor Defense's (ILD) national campaign to defend the Scottsboro Boys, nine young black men unjustly arrested and sentenced to execution for the rape of two white women near Scottsboro, Alabama. Since 1931, the ILD had pushed beyond the NAACP's emphasis on legal strategies to build a mass-based and uncompromising campaign in defense of the young men. Working closely with family members, the defense campaign drew national and international attention to the racial bias in Jim Crow justice and elicited unprecedented support from black communities throughout the nation. Jones was not alone in her affinity for the CP because of its strenuous defense of the young men, as the campaign attracted numerous black activists to the CP. In 1936, after being active in the campaign for less than a year, Claudia Jones joined the Young Communist League (YCL), the youth division of the CP. She worked as a staff writer for the organizational paper the *Daily Worker* and edited the YCL's newspaper. By the late 1940s, Jones would emerge as one of the highest-ranking black women activists and theorists within the CP. As a member of the CP's National Committee and as secretary of the National Women's Commission, she would stand as a forceful advocate of black working-class liberation and black women's leadership.[14]

Garvin's family also had a difficult time finding the improved opportunities and education they had been seeking when they first decided to migrate to New York. Despite, or perhaps because of, this lack of opportunity, the Holmeses prioritized education and supported their daughters through high school and college.[15] At the age of sixteen, Garvin graduated from Wadleigh

High School, in Harlem, and began classes at Hunter College full time. Politically active at both schools, Garvin helped to found the Dunbar Circle, a black history club at Wadleigh, and served as president of a similar club, the Toussaint L'Ouverture Society, at Hunter. While at Hunter, she also encountered a range of radical student organizations, including a very active Young Communist League.[16] Having witnessed her parents' economic hardship, Garvin found that her growing interest in black history and politics provided her with some key tools of analysis to explore the ways racial and class structures helped to produce such conditions. Garvin also gained a deeper political understanding through her employment as a sweatshop laborer during her summers off from school and through her work with Harlem-based community organizations. She attended lectures on black history and youth programs led by the left-leaning preacher and future congressman Adam Clayton Powell Jr. at Abyssinian Baptist Church, the same church her family attended. In fact, Garvin joined her first picket line in Powell's "don't buy where you can't work" protest, which fought to gain employment for black workers in the shops along 125th Street in Harlem.[17]

After college, Garvin deepened her involvement with CP politics by working as a switchboard operator for the CP-affiliated American League for Peace and Democracy, a broad-based antiwar and antifascist group, and by becoming an active union member in the left-led United Office and Professional Workers of America (UOPWA). She would also participate in the political campaign that elected the left-leaning Vito Marcantonio to the U.S House of Representatives in 1938, as well as in Powell's campaigns for government office. After helping to organize an academic conference on the Wagner Act, Garvin was offered a scholarship to attend Smith College by the radical economist Dorothy Douglas. From 1940 to 1942, Garvin lived in Northampton, Massachusetts, and attended graduate school at Smith. As the only graduate student in economics, she worked closely with Professor Douglas, studying Marxist theory and labor economics.[18] It was at Smith that Garvin gained a full introduction to Marxism, and she emerged with what she called a "qualitative change" in her viewpoint on politics and the world. Despite her new perspective and her longstanding affiliations with radical activists, Garvin would not officially join the CP until 1947, when she fully committed herself to a life fighting for radical change.[19] Throughout the late 1940s and 1950s, Garvin was a key player in New York's black left.

Marvel Cooke would also become a leading activist in the Communist Party after becoming immersed in the diverse community of black artists, intellectuals, and activists that helped to make Harlem such a dynamic and energetic space in the 1920s and 1930s. Cooke's family had long been engaged in progressive politics, especially her father, who had supported the early campaigns of the socialist Eugene V. Debs for president. After growing up in the only black family in a predominantly white suburb of Minnesota, where she experienced numerous racial slights, Cooke was determined to live and work with a black community. "I'd seen Harlem," recalls Cooke, "it wasn't south but it was black and I decided I wanted to live in Harlem."[20] Harlem also connected her with an increasingly radical black politics. In taking up work as an editorial secretary at the *Amsterdam News* in 1928 and then, from 1931 to 1940, as a writer, Cooke joined one of the leading black-owned newspapers and deepened her ties to an important group of black leftists and intellectuals who wrote or worked for the paper, including Roi Ottley, Ann Petry, and Adam Clayton Powell Jr. The work also kept Cooke abreast of the CP as the *Amsterdam News* reported on, criticized, and at times supported numerous CP-led activities, from its role in the Scottsboro case to antidiscrimination boycott campaigns and internecine party politics.[21]

It was while working at the *Amsterdam News* that Cooke voted with the paper's editorial staff to unionize under the American Newspaper Guild. In 1935, she joined the picket lines that successfully unionized the paper. The strike's success proved a major catalyst in Cooke's activist life. Later in the year, Cooke became an official member of the CP, recruited by Benjamin Davis, a close friend and one of the most prominent black leaders in the party. Cooke also committed herself to working within the black community. It was shortly after the strike that she co-authored, with the future civil rights activist Ella Baker, an exposé on black women domestic workers, and became an active supporter of the efforts of the newly formed Domestic Workers Union (DWU) to organize these black women day laborers.[22] Cooke would then go on to become a vocal progressive journalist, working as an editorial manager at Adam Clayton Powell Jr.'s *People's Voice* from 1942 to 1946 and, in the 1950s, as the first African American reporter at the New York-based *Daily Compass*.

As the early life histories of Jones, Garvin, and Cooke illustrate, there was not one singular path to communist political affiliation. Yet, there were common themes and experiences that these women shared along the way. Education, both formal and political, substantially shaped their life paths, just as it was a major factor in African American migration overall. Although some black women radicals came from families with wealth, most grew up in working families with limited economic resources. Still, most of their parents shared a common emphasis on giving their daughters a full education. In fact, many black women radicals completed high school and college, and a few even pursued graduate degrees. Such high levels of educational attainment placed them among a growing but still small group of college-educated black women.

Formal education was clearly a motivating force in Vicki Garvin's political life, as graduate school deepened her understanding of Marxist theories. Education would also prove central to Thelma Dale Perkins's political development. Born in 1916 and the youngest of four, Dale Perkins grew up in the integrated Anacostia neighborhood of Washington, D.C. Her family life proved economically stable, with her father, John Henry Dale, working for the postal service and her mother, Lucille Emma Patterson, only occasionally taking up employment outside the home. While Dale Perkins traces her early political outlook to her participation as a Sunday school teacher in the A.M.E. Church, her first organizing experiences occurred in high school after she was invited to an all-white youth discussion group that introduced her to interracial radical politics. In 1932, Dale Perkins began college at Howard University. There, with the support of such radical faculty as Doxey Wilkerson and W. Alphaeus Hunton, she became more heavily involved in student activism. She worked with the university's Liberal Club and the American Youth Congress (AYC), which was the leading national student organization of the period, and also helped to found a local chapter of the Negro Youth Congress. She completed her degree in 1936 but, finding few job opportunities, continued on with graduate study at Howard University, earning a master's in social work and carrying out research with the renowned black sociologist E. Franklin Frazier.[23] Although not a committed student in the classroom, as a social science major Dale Perkins emerged from Howard with a thorough grounding in African American history, firsthand experiences with D.C. politics, and a rich network of activist connections in D.C. and beyond. All would serve her well in her future work.

As the eldest daughter of a Howard University English professor, Yvonne Gregory found that her life trajectory was shaped by formal education. Her talents as a writer were noticed at an early age. After moving to Atlantic City, Gregory was awarded a fellowship to attend Northfield Seminary for Young Ladies, a boarding school located in northern Massachusetts. In 1938, Gregory would travel from boarding school in Massachusetts to undergraduate study at Fisk University in Nashville, Tennessee. Unable or unwilling to adjust to the restrictions placed on students at the southern university, she left after a year to continue her undergraduate studies at the University of Michigan in Ann Arbor. By 1941, Gregory would return to the east coast to begin graduate study at New York University.[24]

Beyond these traditional routes of formal education, black women radicals also gained a broad and more explicitly political education through a number of schools and training centers run by Marxist organizations, such as the Brookwood School, the CP's Workers School, and the Jefferson School of Social Science. Although she resigned from the CP in 1951 because of its racial politics, almost thirty years after Audley "Queen Mother" Moore revoked her membership, she still credited the party with teaching her "an analysis of imperialism and of socialism":

> Well, one of the things the Communists did teach me was the difference between a quantitative change and a qualitative change, you see. They taught me the science of society. I'll give them that, while I give them hell on other things that they did wrong, you see.[25]

Even Vicki Garvin, who obtained much of her training in Marxist theory as a graduate student, credited the CP's courses on basic Marxism with providing valuable tools for practical political use.[26]

Perhaps Maude White Katz's trip to the Soviet Union in 1927 to study at the University of the Toilers of the East, or KUTVA, best exemplifies the unique opportunities for political education that were available to some black women through the CP. White Katz had been recruited to the party after her high school teacher took her to hear the Marxist economist Scott Nearing speak in Pittsburgh, and she became immersed in CP activism while living in Chicago. A year after arriving in Chicago, White Katz was offered the opportunity to study in the Soviet Union. During her three years in the Soviet Union, she not only became versed in Marxist philosophy, communist history, and theoretical debates about "the national question" but also became immersed in a community of young black and Third World radicals that included the future Kenyan leader Jomo Kenyatta and African American communists Harry Haywood and William Patterson.[27] White Katz would return to the states in 1930 to apply her training to union organizing in the needle trade industry, and she briefly served as the editor of the *Harlem Liberator* before relocating to Cleveland in 1934 to work as a party organizer and social worker.

Neither traditional nor political education insulated black women radicals from economic hardship, but they did provide a certain level of mobility and at times a shield from some of the harshest forms of racial and gender discrimination. These women's training allowed them access to skilled office work and other professional jobs, particularly those available within an expanding left, progressive organizations, and federal government programs such as the Works Progress Administration. Yet, for these educated black women, opportunities for respectable, more mainstream employment proved limited during the Great Depression and were clearly less attractive than the opportunities provided by more politically oriented work.

Migration and travel also served as a major influence in the lives and political work of these women radicals. As a result, many of the black women radicals who were living in New York City during the 1930s had arrived from elsewhere, be it a southern state or the Caribbean. [28] Whether moving with their families or traveling on their own, women radicals counted New York as just one of several cities where they would find a connection with Popular Front politics and have access to a range of political experiences and a diverse network of radical activists. For example, when Louise Thompson Patterson arrived in New York City, in 1928, as an Urban League Fellow, this proved only one of many stops in her travels. They had already led her to study at the University of California at Berkeley and the University of Chicago and work in Los Angeles, California; Pine Bluff, Arkansas; and Hampton, Virginia. Thompson Patterson's time living and working as a college teacher in the South exposed her to the harsh realities of "separate and unequal education" and the degrading and racist force of white paternalism masked as support.[29] After joining the CP and marrying William Patterson, in New York, in 1938, Thompson Patterson would relocate again, this time back to her hometown of Chicago.[30]

While New York City stood out as the most central location for such radicalizing encounters, it was not the only site that provided black women with grounding in left theories and Popular Front radicalism. Thelma Dale Perkins, who moved to New York in 1943, had already embraced a life of radical activism, traveled extensively, and faced government harassment for her political work. Dale Perkins credits her participation in an early American Youth Congress conference in Lake Geneva, Wisconsin, with profoundly changing her outlook as she bonded with black and white students of diverse economic backgrounds from throughout the nation.[31] By 1939, Dale Perkins had already secured a reputation as a leading youth organizer. She served as a representative of both the AYC and the recently formed Southern Negro Youth Congress (SNYC), a black-led youth group that became a key political force in the South, as well as the D.C. chapter of the National Negro Congress (NNC).[32] She also secured a job in the Federal Securities Administration and was an active voice in the Social Service Employees Union. Listed in the Dies Committee's 1939 reports on the AYC as the regional representative of the SNYC, Dale Perkins was eventually forced out of her federal job as a result of her politics.[33] Facing continued harassment because of her activism, she decided to move to New York to work for the NNC, a broad-based network of progressive black organizations that included the student-led SNYC.[34] Dale Perkins arrived in New York in the early part of 1943 and entered a new phase in her political life, immersing her fully into the city's black left as she connected with a community of black women radicals and a host of progressive organizations.[35]

Esther Cooper Jackson also settled in New York long after she had become a seasoned activist and a member of the CP. Indeed, much of her early travels and many of her educational experiences in the South and the Midwest proved crucial to shaping her political pursuits. Cooper Jackson encountered a vibrant range of campus-based organizing and peace activism while attending Oberlin College in Ohio. After graduating, in 1938, she moved to Nashville, Tennessee, to earn a master's degree in social work at Fisk University, where she became part of a radical community of activists and soon officially joined the CP. This new political commitment would lead Cooper Jackson to Birmingham, Alabama, to join the work of SNYC. [36] Thus, black women radicals traveled not simply as part of an effort to gain better education or even job opportunities. They moved also in hopes of attaining greater personal freedom, building connections, and sustaining relationships.

Whether through school, work, activism, or travel, black women radicals coming into adulthood within the vibrant political swirl of 1930s activism gained a varied and lasting education in radical politics. They also found new perspectives and tools for analyzing world politics (and their own lives), and membership among a community of radicals who believed they could help remake the world. However, neither leaving the South nor the political and cultural vibrancy of the 1930s allowed these women to completely avoid all social barriers and political limitations, particularly those defined by the intersecting structures of race, gender, and economic inequalities. In fact, encounters and frustrations with limiting gender and racial politics would continue to be a sticking point for many of them, even as they found engaging political homes within an increasingly welcoming U.S. left.[37]

Black Women Radicals and the Communist Party USA

Black women radicals took full advantage of the resources available to them within the U.S. left, including access to employment, political communities, and education, as they worked among numerous radical organizations. Indeed, by the late 1940s, many of them had developed some affiliation with the CP. In part, this reflected the fact that, by the 1930s, the Communist Party had emerged as the dominant Marxist organization of the period and far surpassed all other organizations in its recruitment and work among African Americans. Although membership numbers are not completely reliable, over a year span between 1929 and 1930 black membership rose from under a few hundred to about one thousand, or almost 11 percent of total CP enrollment.[38] The increase in membership reveals only a part of the CP's influence, since most black activists of this period at one time or another worked with or encountered party members. The historian Mark Naison aptly illustrates this point by stating that, for many African Americans in New York City "who came of age in the Depression, especially those of an activist bent, the party helped to define a generational experience." The CP made an indelible mark on these activists, "whether they joined it, fought it, learned from it or measured themselves against it."[39]

What made the CP such a dynamic organization? The party distinguished itself from other communist groups working in African American communities through its continual commitment to connect with black people and its greater organizing efforts. These connections can be traced to the CP's relationship in the early 1920s with the African Blood Brotherhood (ABB), a black revolutionary organization founded by Cyril Briggs that blended black self-determination and Marxist-Leninist politics. The CP recruited from the leadership of the ABB and in 1924 formed the American Negro Labor Congress to continue its work within black communities.[40] During the depression, the CP built on these efforts with two major policy directives: the 1928 "Resolution on the Negro Question" and the acceptance of black cultural expression as part of a "revolutionary tradition" of class resistance, a practice officially sanctioned in 1935 as part of the CP's Popular Front strategy. The resolution upheld African Americans' rights to self-determination as an oppressed nation in the South, emphasized the importance of organizing black workers as part of a revolutionary struggle, and called for fighting white chauvinism at every turn. Although it is much debated whether these new policies served the best interest of African Americans, they did have a profound impact on party organizing within black communities by placing such work at the forefront of revolutionary struggle.[41]

This period of shifting policies coincided with the expanding influence of CP-affiliated organizations such as the ILD and the CIO. As the political and cultural influence of the CP grew, it became an increasingly important voice within more mainstream public debates. Fueled by this acceptance, the CP embraced a "united front" strategy of building mass-based organizations and alliances with a broad range of progressive forces. This Popular Front or

"people's front" movement drew in numerous liberal and moderate supporters. The movement also produced a range of national organizations, from the
National Negro Congress founded in 1936, with the renowned black labor
leader and socialist A. Philip Randolph as president and CP member John
P. Davis as national secretary, to the New York–based American Labor Party
(ALP), which was formed by the American Federation of Labor and the CIO
to support the 1936 re-election of Franklin Roosevelt. This broad coalition
included a vibrant community of cultural workers and intellectuals. It also
specifically engaged transnational solidarity efforts and connected the international fight against fascism to the fight against racism in the United States.
This held particular resonance for black communities that mobilized in protest over fascist Italy's 1935 invasion of Ethiopia, one of the last noncolonized
African nations, and over U.S. inaction in the face of the invasion.

In fact, the growing fight against European fascism helped solidify a liberal-left alliance between the United States and the Soviet Union internationally and among communists, socialists, and liberals domestically. These
united-front organizations had local and regional variations throughout the
country and created space for a wide range of political ideologies and tactics. Both the NNC and the ALP brought together communists, socialists,
and progressive forces and proved key spaces for black women's activism.[42]
Between 1936 and 1939, the NNC in particular emerged as a powerful voice
for black equality and became a major organizing site for black CP members and progressive affiliates throughout the country. It was at a 1937 NNC
meeting that the future leaders of the SNYC came together and decided
to build an organization in the South, to be headed by African American
youth.[43] The NNC also supported a range of black women's organizing
campaigns, including the work of the New York–based Domestic Workers
Union.[44]

The CP's range of activities captivated a dynamic contingent of black
women radicals and drew them into its political orbit. Like Claudia Jones,
Audley Moore was also introduced to party activities by the campaign of
the CP-led ILD to free the Scottsboro Boys. Moore initially joined the ILD
believing that this also meant she had membership in the party. She would
not officially join the CP until two years later, in 1933.[45] Marvel Cooke entered
the orbit of communist organizing through her membership in the American Newspaper Guild and her activism during the victorious strike for union
representation at the *Amsterdam News*.[46] Although Esther Cooper Jackson joined the party while a graduate student at Fisk University, she would
become most active through her leadership in the Birmingham-based SNYC.

The party's new emphasis on African American communities fueled a growing sense "that genuine Black folk culture was at least implicitly, if not explicitly revolutionary" and was behind an increasing willingness to use black cultural forms and institutions to reach black audiences.[47] Robin D. G. Kelley has highlighted the significance of this cultural interplay as it helped to organize black workers in the South in the early 1930s, although it seemingly went against official party policy.[48] Numerous scholars have also highlighted the impact of these shifts in party politics on African American artists and CP culture in major urban centers well into the 1940s.[49] As these scholars demonstrate, from New York to Chicago, the growing emphasis on organizing black communities allowed black intellectuals and artists greater political leeway as they engaged the party. This proved especially true after the party instituted its Popular Front strategy in 1935, which emphasized more mainstream alliances. Louise Thompson Patterson, who would emerge as a leading figure in the CP in 1940s and 1950s, moved freely between CP space and the Harlem artist scene. Marvel Cooke's membership in the CP allowed her to bridge her employment as a writer for the *Amsterdam News* and later the *People's Voice*, her activism in support of the DWU and the NNC, and her participation in Harlem's cultural scene. This was exemplified by the *Amsterdam News's* coverage, most likely written by Cooke, of a musical benefit for the DWU that drew representatives from the NNC and the ILD.[50]

The CP's increased attention to organizing in black communities and its embrace of black culture were central to the party's success in developing a strong foothold in some African American communities. Many black cultural workers and activists gravitated to CP activities, which increasingly tied black cultural expression to activist campaigns. Early incarnations of this strategy were exemplified by the founding of the left-wing Harlem study group Vanguard and by a 1932 CP-sponsored trip to the Soviet Union by a group of young Harlem artists to make a film documenting black life in the United States. Party supporter Louise Thompson Patterson helped organize both efforts, which between them included a range of artists with varying degrees of support for the CP, from Langston Hughes and Henry Lee Moon to a significant number of black women, including the Harlem sculptor Augusta Savage and the writers Gwendolyn Bennett and Dorothy West.[51]

The growing emphasis on culture allowed the CP to count among its supporters or "fellow travelers" a plethora of black women cultural workers. This trend continued well into the 1940s as a variety of black-led and CP-affiliated campaigns continued to attract support from emerging artists. For example, both Elizabeth Catlett and Thelma Dale Perkins taught courses at the NNC-supported George Washington Carver School under the directorship of the Harlem writer Gwendolyn Bennett. Founded in 1943 as a "People's Institute," the school presented a range of practical courses, from "How to Make a Dress" and "How to Speak in Public" to courses on black history and politics, including one, led by Dale Perkins, titled "Race Prejudice: Its Origins and Remedies."[52] In addition, the American Negro Theatre (ANT), founded in 1940 by the playwright Abram Hill and the actor Frederick O'Neal as part of a more left-leaning black theater effort, provided an important training ground for new artists, served as a public platform for new material, and brought together black and white cultural producers. Initially located in the basement of the 135th Street branch of the New York Public Library, which had served as a center of black arts in Harlem since the 1920s, the ANT counted among its members a number of progressive artists who would develop successful careers.[53] Alice Childress, Sidney Poitier, Ruby Dee, and Harry Belafonte all launched their acting careers in the ANT. These artists not only became successful stage and film actors but also continued to help sustain a radical community of black cultural producers well into the 1970s.[54]

The CP's investments in black culture also made available valuable resources, including access to tools of mass communication and sometimes even paid work, on a scale and with a reach that few other institutions could or would provide to black women radicals.[55] Jones escaped factory work in the garment industry when she was hired to write for CP newspapers, and she gained a deep theoretical grounding through her involvement in the party's schools and training centers.[56] The party also offered to many black women cultural workers mass publication of their work through party publications and access to broader audiences through cultural events and even popular clubs like Café Society, where Billie Holiday first sang "Strange Fruit" and Lena Horne regularly performed.[57] The activist Thelma Dale Perkins remembers the Café as an important site for both black entertainers and the progressive community at large, for it provided one of the only integrated social clubs she attended while working in New York's progressive community.[58]

"Personal Politics" and the Communist Party USA

As suggested earlier, the CP's increased attention to theorizing the path to black liberation and embracing black culture created important political venues for black women's activism. However, this shift in political line was not always the primary reason for these women's attraction to the party, nor did it always address the needs of black women already in the CP. While the new attention to black liberation attracted radicals like Audley Moore, who took note of the CP because she viewed its statement on self-determination as fitting within her framework of Garveyism and anti-imperialism, it repelled others. The Socialist Party supporter and future civil rights activists Pauli Murray felt an immediate "negative reaction to the principal Communist Party slogan directed to Negroes in the 1930s, 'Self-Determination for the Black Belt,'" believing that the policy emphasis on African Americans as an oppressed nation ignored black southerners' rights as U.S. citizens and offered only "another form of racial segregation."[59]

In addition, the CP's celebration of black "folk" culture and the attendant proletarian interracialism often carried with it a masculinist edge that served as a common language for building bonds between white and black men, and even black men and white women, but often excluded black women.[60] As the literary scholar William Maxwell states, "the triangular rhetoric of Communist interracialism therefore casts cross racial alliances as a homosocial affair of white and black proletarians [men] conducted by means of white women who function locally as integration's conduits" but that left black women "either absent or distant, indistinct constituents of a racial minority gendered male."[61] Thus, while the party stressed the importance of interracial alliances, these attempts at racial unity were most often enacted with black men, leaving black women as marginal figures in the process.

In general, left social spaces reflected the culture of the CP's majority-white membership and party leaders who had little idea how to put into practice the politics of interracialism. This regularly produced exclusionary social gatherings or awkward social situations that both black and white members found uncomfortable, as well as political pronouncements that rarely addressed the real challenges of interracialism and at times even increased racial tensions. Maude White Katz experienced firsthand how the fight against white supremacy took shape through personal and political interactions while working as an organizer in the Needle Trades Workers' Industrial Union. Intent on addressing the exploitation of subcontracted pressers, who were mostly black women, White Katz encountered strong resistance and outright racism from unionized workers. These conflicts came to a head not on the shop floor but at the union's social events, where white workers often refused to admit new black union members. Although most white CP members preferred to turn a blind eye to these situations, White Katz demanded that the party take action to challenge white supremacy as a core barrier to building black-white unity.[62]

Perhaps the most oft-cited example of black women addressing personal interactions as a political question concerned the issue of interracial dating. In arguing that black women often "do not feel that they fit in, do not feel as much a part of it [the party] as even our Negro men comrades," women members pointed to the party's culture and social interactions, where heterosocial relations between black men and white women proved much more common than those between white men and black women.[63] In this context, interracial dating and marriage between black men and white women became a visible example of interracial unity and a volatile example of black women's exclusion.[64] This must have been exacerbated, one suspects, by the ways in which black womanhood was often measured against white womanhood and found lacking, as well as by the long history and the lived experiences of sexualized racism that produced the lynching of black men for the alleged rape of white women, while white men rarely faced any consequences for raping black women.[65]

Speaking to the often hidden gender and sexual politics that underlay the left's push for interracialism, black women radicals highlighted the difficulties such seemingly personal interactions produced as the party tried to recruit and retain black women activists. Louise Thompson Patterson, herself a recent recruit to the CP's Harlem section, addressed these issues in an article published in the party's internal paper, the *Party Organizer,* special issue on party building. In the article, she argues for the need to use "some sort of human approach" when recruiting black women:

> For example I think that often when we have affairs, dances etc., if we went around we would find young Negro girls who would be glad to attend. If they got there and found they were given consideration; danced with— not made wallflowers—we would find that these are the things that count. These are the things that hold a lot of Negro women back from the party. They are not so political, but they do mean a great deal.[66]

Such concerns would continue to be raised by black women CP members in the postwar period as they sought to challenge white supremacy and sexism within the CP. In addition, they would seek to politicize the "personal" as it emerged in their activism concerning civil rights and their efforts to organize labor and to combat anticommunist attacks.

Certainly, these racialized and gendered tensions within the CP, and the left more broadly, strained black women's participation. Louise Thompson Patterson's clear critique of the limits of CP social circles led her to consciously build a social life among black leftists and artists both within and outside these spaces, even as she would go on to marry William Patterson, an outspoken party member. Yet, such conflicts were not the sum total of black women radicals' experiences within the CP's social milieu. The social world of left organizations proved a complicated negotiation, creating varying degrees of support as well as isolation for black women radicals.

Black women did build significant personal relationships that clearly sustained their commitment to radical politics and organizations. Although there is limited evidence to suggest that these social circles served as vibrant spaces for a significant number of single black women in the party, and even less to suggest that they were welcoming spaces for same-sex desire, several black women did meet and partner with fellow activists within the CP and the black left more broadly. Vicki Garvin married a fellow black activist, Clinton Arthur Garvin, in part because she felt that she shared a greater political connection with him than she did with her first husband. The artist Elizabeth Catlett met and married a fellow artist, Charles White, within Chicago's progressive black arts community. Both would move to New York in 1942 and serve as staff artists for the NNC newsletter before the end of their brief marriage. Both Claudia Jones and Maude White Katz would marry white men affiliated with the party. Jones married Abraham Scholnick in 1940, and White Katz married Arthur Katz in the late 1940s.[67] Thus, despite the structural challenges of social interactions, a number of black women within the orbit of the Communist Party developed fulfilling and long-lasting intimate relationships through their political activities.

Indeed, most black women radicals were able to find meaningful communities among fellow black women activists, within the black left more generally, or among individual like-minded comrades. Marvel Cooke found a welcoming social community in Harlem that exposed her to a heterosocial black world vastly different from that which she had encountered while attending college in her home state of Minnesota. Initially engaged to Roy Wilkins, future head of the NAACP, Cooke would later date the Harlem writer Eric Walrond and eventually married a Caribbean immigrant and Columbia graduate named Cecil Cooke. Working at the *Amsterdam News* and later at the *People's Voice*, Cooke built a wide array of friendships and enjoyed close ties to such luminaries as Du Bois, Ben Davis, and Eslanda Robeson, whom she interviewed in 1935 for the *Amsterdam News*. Cooke also built a professional and personal friendship with the writer Ann Petry, who worked at both newspapers and shared a similar background, having grown up in a majority-white community.[68]

Yet Marvel Cooke built her most lasting friendships with those within the party, including Richard and Gladys Carter, both white CP members, and the black writer and fellow Minnesotan Lloyd Brown. Having grown up in a predominately white community, Cooke likely found the interracial social world of the CP familiar territory. But she insisted that the real source of affinity with CP members rested in the fact that they "feel the way I do about the way this country is going, whether they're black or white." Cooke traced her strong bond with the Carters to their shared work within the labor movement, pointing out that "we were together in some struggles we had at the Newspaper Guild. We just developed a very close friendship."[69]

These bonds of political and personal relationships would continue during the war and in some ways intensified in the postwar period as the CP and black leftists came under increasing attack and the community of activists shrank. Thelma Dale Perkins, who moved to New York City in 1943 to serve as acting administrative secretary for the NNC during its later years, fondly recalls the warm welcome she found among the community of black leftists in New York. She specifically remembered the support given by Vicki Garvin and Marvel Cooke, who helped Dale Perkins to find housing and get settled in New York. She was immediately drawn into the mixture of politics and culture that attracted black radicals to New York. Cooke most likely introduced Dale Perkins to Café Society, since soon after her arrival they attended at least one Café Society event together, along with the emerging artist Elizabeth Catlett. Their attendance at the event was noted in the society page of the *Amsterdam News*.[70]

Over the years, Dale Perkins would develop a particularly lasting friendship with Vicki Garvin as they worked together in the NNC and later at *Freedom* newspaper.[71] Garvin's apartment provided a convenient rest stop for Dale Perkins following late nights in Harlem, and she regularly socialized with Garvin and her husband, Arthur, after their marriage, in 1947. In addition, Garvin served as the witness during Dale Perkins's marriage to Larry Perkins in 1954, whom, perhaps not surprisingly, Dale Perkins first met in the office of *Freedom* newspaper.[72] Yet, their initial friendship developed while both women were single and outlasted many of the organizations they helped to sustain. Garvin and Dale Perkins provided key support for each other during the height of McCarthyism, as they shared strategies for finding employment, surviving personal struggles, and remaining political active well into the 1970s. As suggested by Dale Perkins and Garvin's relationship and discussed in subsequent chapters, such friendships and communities would become increasingly important as Popular Front alliances gave way to Cold War anticommunism.

Radical Politics and World War II

The range of Popular Front strategies embraced by the Communist Party represented an effort to build unity with other left organizations and a concentrated strategy to Americanize their own politics. It also reflected the increased willingness of black activists to build alliances with majority-white left organizations. Such alliances would be profoundly reshaped as the United States mobilized for war. For example, Popular Front unity and antifascist mobilizations encountered a major roadblock when the CP, in response to the 1939 Nazi-Soviet Pact, suddenly shifted positions, taking an antiwar stance and refusing to challenge wartime fascism. Although the policy was short-lived and ended by 1941, it produced some lasting distrust within Popular Front coalitions.[73] Still, most on-the-ground progressive and left forces supported a strong antifascist stance and praised U.S.-Soviet cooperation as part of the allied forces.[74] Wartime mobilization and activism helped to restructure the location and economic roles of black citizens and women as war industries increased the migration of African American southerners to urban industrial cities, and the rhetoric of "woman power" and Rosie the Riveter opened up many industries to women workers. Perhaps less noted is the ways in which these shifts in mainstream society also took place among radical organizations. For example, just as men's enlistment in the armed forces opened up job opportunities for women in the workplace, it also provided openings for women in left organizations.[75]

During the war years, increasing numbers of black women rose to key leadership positions in left organizations while male activists enlisted in the war effort. In addition to James Jackson of the SNYC and Ed Strong of the NNC, the war mobilization had enlisted such emerging black radicals as the actor and communist fellow traveler Ossie Davis, the playwright Willie Branch, the artist Charles White, and Coleman Young, who would go on to become a leader in the National Negro Labor Council.[76] The rise of black women to leadership positions, including the appointment of Thelma Dale Perkins as executive secretary of the NNC and Esther Cooper Jackson as head of the SNYC, provides just a few clear examples of the impact of wartime mobilization on black women's positions within the U.S. left. These openings marked a major turning point in the ability of African American women to claim greater power in shaping the on-the-ground politics of the U.S. left.

Despite these gains, African American radicals' faith in the Popular Front strategies would be tested as the broad alliance took on a more mainstream tilt. As the war transformed both U.S. economic and political structures and international politics, some CP leadership envisioned and fought for an expansion of the liberal-left alliance, which they hoped would bring about a radicalization of American society.[77] However, inclusion within the New Deal coalition battling fascism came at increasingly higher and higher costs, as many affiliated with the CP accepted policies that curbed their militancy. Not only did the party stop supporting many of its more radical organizations and retreat from its commitment to fighting racial oppression, but also CP leadership endorsed a wartime no-strike pledge in the face of increased labor protests, supported the use of the Smith Act against Trotskyists, and turned a blind eye to the internment of Japanese Americans.[78] These policies, adopted in the name of wartime unity, rested upon a belief that such cooperation would bring together the left, labor, and government liberals, yielding a stronger postwar coalition in the United States —and internationally—between the United States and the Soviet Union.[79]

Not all left and progressive forces wholeheartedly embraced the call for unity and wartime cooperation, especially since many of these wartime concessions on strategy and political line tended to be conservative and shifted resources away from activists fighting for racial and gender equality.[80] Within the party, William Z. Foster and his supporters opposed any Popular Front analysis of world conditions that suggested a lessening of class conflict and U.S. imperialism.[81] In addition, many African Americans also resisted efforts to build unity at the cost of fighting for racial equality. This stance reflected a common viewpoint among African American activists, even those within the party, who maintained a more cautious approach to the war efforts as they weighed the calls for unity against the continued use of segregation as the nation recruited troops and workers for the war.

In response to these contradictions, African American radicals drew on wartime rhetoric of democracy and self-determination to challenge racial oppression. This took shape through activities like the "Double V" campaign, which called for victory against fascism abroad and Jim Crow at home; support of anticolonial struggles in Asia and Africa; and the March on Washington Movement (MOWM), led by A. Philip Randolph, which demanded an end to employment discrimination.[82] It was in this context that Claudia Jones led the fight against army segregation by penning a pamphlet in 1940 entitled "Jim-Crow in Uniform," which, following the CP's brief policy shift, articulated an antiwar stance as it pointed out the racism faced by black soldiers in the army and when they returned home. Thelma Dale Perkins also took up the fight against Jim Crow in her work with the NNC, yet she did so while supporting the war effort through her ties with black soldiers, including her

Thelma Dale (Perkins) on the cover of the December 1945 issue of the National Negro Congress's newsletter. (Tamiment Library and Robert F. Wagner Labor Archives, New York University Libraries)

older brother William.[83] Vicki Garvin's work as a wage stabilization officer in the National War Labor Board also reflected this strategy of supporting the war while fighting segregation and the exploitation of workers. She often worked with unions to secure the best wages for their members and urged representatives to support the Fair Employment Practice Committee (FEPC) to protect workers from racial and gender discrimination.[84]

As these black women moved into leadership in several key left organizations, they continued to articulate a common vision and often relied on their fellow women activists to help carry out the work and to actively support their organizing efforts. For example, between Dale Perkins's appointment, in 1943, and 1946, the NNC drew support from a number of leading black women activists. Vicki Garvin served as executive secretary and Halois Moorhead as recording secretary of the NNC's Manhattan Council.[85] In addition, Moorhead, Marvel Cooke, Elizabeth Catlett, Augusta Strong, and Yvonne Gregory all served on the editorial board or as regular contributors to the organizations publication, the *Congress View*. Black women radicals used these platforms to address a number of topics, from the emerging battle for a permanent FEPC and support for black women's wartime employment to efforts to ensuring job security for black women workers in the postwar period.[86]

This wartime activism also produced initiatives led by black women, such as Negro Women Incorporated (NWI). Founded in 1942 to "organize women for mass participation in the war effort," the group was led by Ann Petry and included a number of black women radicals in its activities. In 1944, NWI launched a fall event, "Negro Women Have a Vote—How Shall They Use It," to encourage black women to vote. The gathering included on its speakers list Marvel Cooke as a representative of the *People's Voice*, the Brooklyn activists and future Civil Right Congress leader Ada B. Jackson, and New York City Councilman and leading CP stalwart Ben Davis Jr.[87] Through such organizations, black women were powerful contributors to the outpouring of wartime activities produced by African American radicals, including work with united-front organizations like the NNC, support for anticolonial struggles and labor organizing, and political cultural productions. This period produced so much wartime activity that the historian Penny Von Eschen contends, "these black civil rights and anti-colonial activists represented a black Popular Front 'crafted by the left' but embracing the full range of black American activists."[88] While most scholars argue that the wartime upsurge of black radicalism subsided with the onset of Cold War anticommunism, a detailed look at black women's postwar activism reveals the ways this community of radicals continued to build on wartime gains as it pushed forward its own vision of radical politics and equality.

Cold War "Reconversion" and Resistance

Immediately following the war, America entered a process of "reconversion." Corporate and government officials viewed the process as a reordering of American economic production and politics and containment of the wartime political momentum gained by progressive forces. For working women and African Americans, "reconversion" often challenged their wartime gains, especially in labor and national politics. Postwar rhetoric, under the guise of attacking communism, championed a return to an idealized construction of the (white) woman as homemaker and a redefining of racism that sought to ignore its ties to a long history of economic and political oppression.[89]

For the U.S. left more generally, the postwar period marked a moment of unexpected decline, particularly in light of the high expectation that the wartime Popular Front coalition would be expanded. In 1944, the CP, seeking to build upon wartime liberal-left unity and to move more into the mainstream of U.S. politics, dissolved as a political party advocating socialism and reconstituted itself as the Communist Political Association (CPA) USA. However, the Popular Front ideal of a grand East-West alliance between the United States and the Soviet Union and continued liberal-left engagement began to evaporate as soon as the war ended.[90] As the West began to construct an Iron Curtain at home and abroad, U.S.-based Popular Front and radical activists increasingly became the target of anticommunist assaults and suffered profound organizational fissures. Earl Browder's decision to form the CPA reflected a clear misreading of the conditions in the United States and left the organization largely unprepared for the coming Cold War. In 1945, a year after the CPA was formed, Browder faced public criticism from Moscow for dissolving the party and was soon demoted for straying too far from the core principles of communism. Under the leadership of the newly appointed William Z. Foster, the American CP re-emerged with a sharper critique of the U.S. government and more explicitly Marxist-Leninist politics.[91] Such internal reordering in the CP could not stem the larger political tide. The crushing 1948 defeat of the Progressive Party presidential candidate, Henry Wallace, hastened the demise of the CP's leadership in more broad-based coalitions.[92] At the same time, activists from labor organizers to white-collar workers were feeling increasing pressure to renounce all radical politics and any affiliations to the left. A once-thriving Communist Party was in crisis.[93]

Neither Browder's efforts at Americanizing communism nor Foster's support for a more hard-line left politics could sustain a Popular Front movement or slow the onslaught of Cold War anticommunism. However, Foster's emphasis on returning to long-held CP critiques of the U.S. government both in the United States and internationally provided important support for party members who were committed to a radical politics centered on the struggle for gender and racial equality, and who had remained active in these movements throughout the war.[94] This proved particularly true for black women radicals, who experienced both shifting Communist Party politics and some of the fallout from anticommunist attacks as a mixed bag of both challenges and opportunities.

Although black women were deeply invested in a range of CP institutions, their political theorizing, especially their increasing articulation of a racialized and gendered class analysis, did not always fit within the CP's theories. In fact, they often found themselves on the periphery of party politics, particularly as the CP attempted to become more mainstream. As a result of this outsider status and their disagreements with many of the strategies for popularizing communist politics, most black women found a moment of opportunity in the upheavals within the CP and the attendant move toward more militant politics.[95] Therefore, as gender and race politics took center stage in the postwar period and a more hard-line politics took hold in the CP under William Z. Foster, there developed an increasing emphasis—often pushed by black women themselves—on not only attacking white supremacy but also addressing issues relevant to black women and promoting black women's leadership.[96] Moreover, as leading party activists such as Ben Davis, James Jackson, and William Patterson faced federal investigation and anticommunist attacks restricted the activism of two of the leading black intellectuals of the period, W. E. B. Du Bois and Paul Robeson, black women often moved into leadership positions in ongoing campaigns, including the fight to end such government prosecutions.

These openings for black women organizers, which allowed them to begin to shift from outsiders to significant leaders in CP-affiliated organizations, were not solely an outgrowth of circumstance. It reflected a concerted effort by these women to "raise the question of the role of Negro women." In 1943, as Thelma Dale Perkins took up her post in the NNC, she addressed this issue in an effort to push left organizations to have a better understanding of the "woman question in general and the lack of Negro women particularly." Dale Perkins also wanted left leaders to consider black women for roles "on the basis of [their] capacity for leadership." [97] Drawing on their wartime experiences and seeking to retain some of those wartime gains in a variety of organizations, black women radicals continued to demand greater leadership opportunities and political voice as the war came to an end.

The publication of Dale Perkins's article "Reconversion and the Negro People," carried in the October 1945 issue of *Political Affairs*, "a magazine devoted to the theory and practice of Marxism Leninism" and the unofficial theoretical journal of the CP, provides one example of the ways black women claimed space within these moments of upheaval and sought to set a tone for the period. Articulating a position similar to the one she took at the start of the war, Dale Perkins, in her article, outlined the unique struggles of black women workers, demanded that the CP develop a more "theoretical analysis of the Negro question," and called for "strengthening and broadening" African American leadership in all areas of the CP, not just those "restricted to work amongst Negroes only." In her view, the future rested in "maintaining the faith of the Negro masses."[98] Dale Perkins's suggestion for a strategic path forward and her sharp critique of CP practices set the stage for a continuing conversation among black women radicals about organizing strategies, tactics for building a theoretically relevant politics, and mobilizing the full force of African American and women workers. Dale Perkins's writing represented just the first of many salvos launched by black women that challenged the CP's political practices during the postwar period, as black women worked to sustain a radical left voice in the United States. Indeed, Dale Perkins continued these conversations even after she moved from the NNC in 1946, when it merged with the ILD to form the CRC. She took up leadership in the Congress of American Women and American Women for Peace during the late 1940s and early 1950s. And, in 1952, after advocating for a woman on the Progressive Party ticket, she served as associate director of the Progressive Party and campaign manager for Charlotta Bass during her run as the Progressive Party's vice presidential candidate. In each of these spaces, Dale Perkins continued to advocate for black women's leadership and to push for a more expansive understanding of black women's experiences and black liberation.[99]

Black women radicals increasingly relied on each other and a shrinking New York black left to sustain such activism in the midst of a growing crackdown on left leadership and the CP more specifically. The dynamic group of black women that had been coalescing around the CP since the 1930s came together in New York during the 1950s. Following a path taken earlier by Thelma Dale Perkins and reflecting a CP strategy of relocating active members under anticommunist pressure, many black women based in the South or in smaller left communities moved to central cities, with most settling in New York during the Cold War. For example, after anticommunist attacks forced the disbanding of the SNYC, Esther Cooper Jackson moved her activism for a brief period to Detroit, Michigan, and then settled in Brooklyn, New York, while her husband went underground. Maude White Katz and Louise Thompson Patterson also made the move to New York City during the 1950s. Thus, travel and relocation continued to serve as an important part of these women's political development well into the 1950s.

Although this strategy of relocation coincided with the dissolution of several organizations, it rarely meant an end to these women's political engagement. In fact, the presence of the renowned singer and actor Paul Robeson, who refused to denounce the CP or the Soviet Union, alongside such black left figures as W. E. B. Du Bois, former SNYC leader Louis Burnham, and W. Alphaeus Hunton, helped to make New York a particularly attractive site for black radicals. Whether they were seeking to weather the Cold War, to reconnect with allies, to build on wartime gains or to lend their support to black leaders under attack, these seasoned women radicals joined New York's black left out of their commitment to the fight for black liberation. In doing so, they helped to maintain, in the midst of Cold War anticommunism and a constricting black politics, space for black radicals interested in continuing the fight for civil rights, economic justice, and women's equality.

Throughout the 1950s, this radical community attracted a number of younger black women, as well as women activists who in other circumstances might have found a political home in more mainstream organizations. Beulah Richardson and Lorraine Hansberry were counted among these younger postwar activists who were attracted to New York's black left. Both women had traveled throughout the nation and had found radical allies elsewhere before connecting with the black left in New York City in the early 1950s. Born in Vicksburg, Mississippi, in 1926, Richardson spent her college years at Dillard University, in New Orleans. An effort to leave behind what she considered a stifling life in Vicksburg motivated her travels. Richardson recalls suffering racism "every day of my life" and found that, despite her mother's assertions that she could do whatever she wished, she felt constantly constrained and inhibited by Vicksburg's segregationist practices. For Richardson, attending school in New Orleans and taking up work as an actor provided a much needed escape.[100] Graduating, in 1948, with a bachelor's degree in drama, she worked in San Diego and Los Angeles. While in Los Angeles, Richardson connected with progressive activists and was involved in the L.A. chapter of American Women for Peace. She moved to New York City in 1951. Lorraine Hansberry spent much of her early life in the Midwest. She was born in 1930 and raised, the youngest of three children, in a progressive-minded upper-middle-class family on the South Side of Chicago. Hansberry attended college at the University of Wisconsin in Madison, where she was swept up in Henry Wallace's 1948 presidential campaign and became a member of the CP. In 1950, at the age of twenty, she moved from Madison to New York City and began working on the staff of *Freedom* newspaper.

These late arrivals were mentored in a Popular Front–like milieu of black leftists and CP activists. Richardson moved to New York at the urging of William and Louise Thompson Patterson, and Hansberry was drawn in through her CP affiliations. Through these connections, the lessons from the heyday of the 1930s served as a guidepost for both Hansberry and Richardson.[101] They benefited greatly from the close ties that had emerged between black women cultural workers and black radicalism during the 1930s and continued well into the 1940s and 1950s. Many of these women were first published in newspapers and journals staffed by CP members.

Lorraine Hansberry's first published poem "Flag from a Kitchenette Window" appeared in *Masses and Mainstream*, and Beulah Richardson's poem "A Black Woman Speaks" garnered national acclaim among progressives at a Chicago peace conference. Even more established artists such as Alice Childress also benefited from these resources; her collection of short stories *Like One of the Family* was originally published as a series in *Freedom* as "Conversations from Life."[102]

These women radicals were able to coalesce as a community of activists and even to mentor younger radicals because their leadership was not always evident or expected. Black men were the most visible leadership in CP-affiliated African American organizations, and the dominant gendering of leadership as male allowed most black women to remain relatively invisible during the early years of McCarthyism. This is not to imply that black women activists did not also come under attack or that their resistance did not come at great personal cost. Numerous black women faced federal investigation, lost their jobs, and were called in front of the House Committee on Un-American Activities (HUAC). However, as the historian Andrea Friedman, in her article on the activist Annie Lee Moss, makes clear, in the gender and racial discourse of Cold War anticommunism and American liberalism, "black women's political subjectivity was almost unimaginable."[103]

Conclusion

In the context of postwar radical organizing, a community of black women coalesced around the Communist Party and a number of mass-based organizations that worked alongside the party. These women, whose family histories and paths to politicization varied greatly, found a common bond in their experiences as black women politicized and active within the United States left during the 1930s and 1940s. Even as they embraced different relationships to the CP and at times had conflicting political positions, they continued to share a common goal of pushing the U.S. left to develop a more intersectional analysis that theorized the interconnected force of race, gender, and class in shaping the political landscape.

As the CP and a range of affiliated mass-based organizations came under increasing political and governmental pressure in the postwar period, black women radicals drew on the lessons learned, the strategies created, and the alliances formed during the height of 1930s radicalism and wartime mobilization to help define and bring to life their political vision, while helping to sustain a radical base of resistance. From the late 1940s well into the 1950s, this community of seasoned black activists provided central leadership in organizations such as the Civil Rights Congress, the National Negro Labor Council, and the Sojourners for Truth and Justice. They also gained a more visible presence in a range of left publications, from *Freedom* newspaper to *Masses and Mainstream* and the CP's theoretical journal, *Political Affairs*. In the context of Cold War politics, these women articulated an expansive vision of radicalism and provided a new base of support for a U.S. left operating within a more constrained political landscape, and increasingly alienated from its traditional networks. As detailed in the following chapters, during the 1950s, black women increasingly carried out much of the day-to-day organizing and political strategizing in a number of CP-affiliated organizations.

In Defense of Black Womanhood

Race, Gender, Class, and the Politics of
Interracial Solidarity, 1945–1951

I would that I could speak of white womanhood
as it will and should be
when it stands tall in full equality.
But then, womanhood will be womanhood
void of color and of class
and all necessity for my speaking thus will be past.
Gladly past.

—Beulah Richardson, 1951

An outstanding feature of the present stage of the Negro liberation movement is the growth in the militant participation
of Negro women in all aspects of the struggle for peace, civil
rights, and economic security.

—Claudia Jones, 1949

On July 1, 1951, Beulah Richardson, a young poet and activist, took
the stage at the Women's Workshop of the American People's Peace Congress, in Chicago. The workshop, organized by American Women for Peace
(AWP), had more than five hundred women in attendance as Richardson
read from her poem, "A Black Woman Speaks . . . of White Womanhood, of
White Supremacy, of Peace." Speaking "in searching honesty," she reported
to the majority-white audience "how it seems to me. White womanhood
stands in bloodied skirt and willing slavery." Richardson urged her audience to remember "white supremacy is your enemy and mine" and put forth
the challenge, "What will you do? Will you fight with me?" The conference
participants, who included a range of liberal, progressive, and openly communist women activists, gave Richardson a standing ovation. Her reading

became the talk of the meeting, sparking Congress delegates to adopt a statement on "Negro-white unity" and to award Richardson a conference prize.[1]

The enthusiastic response to Richardson's poem signaled the uneasy investments of progressive majority-white women's organizations in interracial organizing and contestation over the role of women in U.S. society. Mainstream debates were most notably defined by idealized visions of white middle-class motherhood and domesticity and warnings about the damaging effects of "bad" mothers.[2] Left-leaning majority-white women's groups attempted to subvert these confining constructions of womanhood by presenting alternative models of white motherhood and options for women outside the home.[3] From peace organizations like the Women's International Democratic Federation (WIDF) and the AWP to the work of Communist Party theorists such as Mary Inman and Betty Millard, white women on the left sought to expose the gender inequalities embedded in a discourse of domesticity and to claim greater space for women as mothers, activists, and valued political actors. However, because many of these subversions of mainstream discourse did little to challenge the ways race and class also defined this gendered discourse, they proved less successful in addressing the experiences of African American women and often exacerbated existing tensions that impeded the building of interracial unity among women radicals. From this vantage point, the Chicago audience's embrace of Richardson also represented one of the ways progressive majority-white women's groups negotiated black women's criticism of the U.S. left's continued failure to adequately theorize and organize around the intersections of race and gender.

This chapter examines the key interventions black women radicals, such as Thelma Dale Perkins, Beulah Richardson, Alice Childress, and Claudia Jones, as well as the network of black women they organized alongside, made in these gender debates. Committed to giving voice to the full complexity of black women's experiences in the United States, these women radicals crafted their own nascent feminist politics that called attention to the impact of social constructions of race and class on women's lives. In speeches, essays, and creative pieces, these women conveyed an intersectional analysis that recognized the importance of understanding women's experiences as they interacted with racial and economic structures. Such analysis made it clear that all women did not share the same gendered experience. Black women radicals not only made the differences among women visible but also revealed what the historian Elsa Barkley Brown argues are "the relational nature of those differences."[4] Moreover, their insights demonstrated the ways race operated as a "metalanguage" to mask differences among black women as well as complicating any bonds of womanhood that did exist across race. In defining her theoretical use of the term "race as a metalanguage," the scholar Evelyn Brooks Higginbotham argues that, "in societies where racial demarcation is endemic to their sociocultural fabric and heritage," race serves as a "global sign, a metalanguage" that "not only tends to subsume other sets of social relations, namely gender and class, but blurs and disguises, suppresses and negates its own complex interplay with the very social relations it envelopes."[5] Read through these theoretical lenses, black women radicals' explication of the ways gender identity was inextricably tied to race and class represented an innovative contribution to Cold War debates about American womanhood. This chapter not only documents the shared theoretical underpinnings of these women's work but also reveals the subtle differences in black women's theorizing about the intersections of race, gender, and class and the path to interracial organizing.

Black women radicals contributed their insights to arguments over motherhood, womanhood, and interracial solidarity in a range of spaces, including progressive organizations and magazines. As suggested by Richardson's work, these women proved particularly skilled at employing their cultural writing to address such concerns. In so doing, black women emerged as central figures in a number of progressive women's groups, including the WIDF, the Congress of American Women (CAW), and the AWP. They also provided radical voices on the question of women's and black liberation in a number of left-leaning publications, including the CP-affiliated journals *Masses and Mainstream* and *Political Affairs*. They used these public venues to deconstruct dominant images of black womanhood and to address central issues concerning black-white solidarity, the boundaries of feminist thought, and, to a lesser extent, gender relations within black communities. Their insights brought to the fore the ways both economic and racial inequalities limited the possibilities for a mass-based women's movement and weakened progressive politics more broadly. They also argued for viewing the fight against racial and economic oppression as a crucial component of the struggle for women's liberation and demanded greater attention to black women's unique place in these struggles. This outlook was clearly expressed in Claudia Jones's declaration that "the Negro woman, who combines in her status the worker, the Negro, and the woman," served as "the vital link" to a "heightened political consciousness," especially for the progressive women's movement.[6]

Constructing an Ideal

The U.S. mobilization for World War II sparked a profound restructuring of gender roles and heated discussions about women's contributions as citizens. The wartime efforts to fill industrial jobs vacated by enlisted men relied heavily on a rhetorical, as well as practical, mobilization of a female labor force that included increasing numbers of married and older women. From the representative image of "Rosie the Riveter" to a growing discussion of the ways women as mothers and wives could support the troops, U.S. women became key targets of wartime mobilization discourse. As the historian Cynthia Harrison writes, "World War II had infused discussion of women's roles with new energy."[7]

However, much of the wartime propaganda emphasized the temporary nature of an increasingly female workforce. As discussed in chapter 1, immediately following the war, the nation entered a process of "reconversion." This attempt to contain changes inspired by the war effort intertwined with mainstream economic shifts and efforts to define the political landscape by trumpeting the world dominance of U.S. capitalism and democracy. For women in the United States, postwar restructuring often challenged their wartime gains, especially in labor and national politics. The most conservative of this postwar rhetoric, under the guise of promoting stability and attacking communism, championed a "return" to an idealized construction of (white) womanhood, against which all women were to be measured.[8]

Increasingly, public conversations about womanhood focused on family and domesticity. Built upon the economic gains and nuclear family structure of the white middle class, this discourse influenced mainstream images of womanhood broadcast in women's magazines and movies, on television, and even in political debates. The cornerstone of the idealized woman emphasized female subordination, heterosexuality, and domesticity. It also encouraged women to help sustain domestic security by devoting themselves to their homemaking skills, supporting their husbands, and raising their children to be good citizens. Although these ideals did not reflect the real experiences of many women during the postwar period, the cultural and political force of the ideology resonated strongly across class and race boundaries, producing powerful expectations of what all American women ought to be and do.[9] As Elaine Tyler May writes, "It was the values of the white middle-class that shaped the dominant political and economic institutions that affected all Americans. Those who did not conform to this were likely to be marginalized, stigmatized, and disadvantaged as a result."[10]

Ruth Feldstein's study of race and motherhood in the postwar years illustrates the ways "representations of women as mothers developed in conjunction with debates about who was a healthy citizen and what was healthy democracy."[11] In such popular studies as Paul Wylie's *Generation of Vipers* (1942) and Marynia Farnham and Ferdinand Lundberg's *Modern Woman: The Lost Sex* (1947), white (middle-class) women were criticized for their frequent failures as mothers and blamed for producing inadequate male citizens, among other ills. Bad mothering and the ensuing social disorder it could produce became a major source of anxiety in the postwar context.[12]

Although both the idealized woman and the "bad" mother were clearly racialized as white in psychological studies as well as in popular media, black women did not escape the burden of these images and, indeed, were often already imagined as failing to live up to the ideal. Historically, financial necessity had forced most black women into the workforce. During the 1940s and 1950s, these circumstances remained, and black women were increasingly caught between the need to survive and the growing pressure to behave within "traditional" gender roles. Studies of black women's experiences during the postwar years highlight these contradictions. The scholar Paula Giddings points out the ways sociologists and black commentators "scolded" black women "for being too domineering and too insecure; too ambitious and too decadently idle all in the same breath."[13]

Black women were often framed in mainstream society as inadequate versions of (white) womanhood. The black counterpart to the "bad" white mother was the emasculating and dominating matriarch and the sexually deviant black woman. Long before Daniel Patrick Moynihan's controversial report *The Negro Family: The Case for National Action* (1965), the sociologist E. Franklin Frazier outlined the damaging effects of the black matriarch on black families in urban environments in his studies *The Negro Family in the United States* (1939) and *Negro Youth at the Crossways* (1940). Yet, Frazier's analysis of the urban "matriarchy" and the black family took on a more ominous tone in the hands of postwar sociologists and public policy experts, who sought to explain what they viewed as the problem of the "disorganized black family."[14] As the nation looked to the nuclear family—defined by white middle-class standards—as the site for ensuring social stability, black family structures were inevitably found lacking. Like their white counterparts, black women faced the brunt of the blame for failures within the family structure. Black women who succeeded in the workplace were more often than not seen as contributing to black men's inability to play the traditional male role of breadwinner. Yet, poor and single black mothers, too, were often marked as the source of disorganization and sexual deviance in black families.[15] In either context, dominant perceptions tagged black women, regardless of economic status, as the pathogens in the black family.

Despite the widespread efforts to contain discussions of U.S. womanhood within this narrow framework, progressives and working women fought to build upon wartime openings by broadening dominant conceptions of gender roles and discussions of women's capabilities.[16] Women activists seeking to take advantage of these postwar openings hailed from a range of political positions and held a variety of views on what defined women's issues and the road to women's liberation. Some sought to claim power by living up to the idealized images of womanhood. Middle-class women, both black and white, often took this route, arguing that, as mothers and wives, women should play a key role not only in family decisions but also in national politics. Other women activists drew on these ideals, but in the hopes of articulating a more radical feminist agenda.

Black women radicals provided key contributions to these debates. Often operating in multiple spaces and making use of a range of discourses, these women not only critiqued mainstream constructions of woman's roles but also pushed progressive forces to acknowledge the interconnectedness of working-class liberation, black people's liberation, and women's liberation. Through their emphasis on black women's lives, these women radicals highlighted the links between the fight for civil rights, workers rights, and women's rights and the battles against male and white supremacy. These political insights emerged from their continued engagement with and responses to a range of public conversations and writings.

The Negro Digest, Black Womanhood, and the Marriage Debate

One of the more notable conversations concerning marriage and the black family occurred in a series of articles published in the *Negro Digest* between 1947 and 1950. The *Negro Digest* served as one of the leading black periodicals of the period. Founded by John Johnson in 1942 and patterned after *Reader's Digest*, within a year of its initial release the periodical had gained a national circulation of more than fifty thousand a month. In part, the success of the magazine rested on its ability to speak to a broad range of concerns in African American communities and the nation.

During this period, *Negro Digest* published numerous articles that examined black heterosexual relationships and gender roles.[17] These articles provide a glimpse into how debates over black womanhood and the black family took shape among African American public intellectuals. Authored by a number of highly regarded black scholars, writers, and activists, the articles included such titles as "Why I Want a Negro Wife," "Are Black Women Beautiful?," and "Why Negro Women Leave." The most pointed differences of opinion emerged in a series of essays written by prominent left-leaning intellectuals, including the novelist Ann Petry's article "What's Wrong with Negro Men?," Roi Ottley's reply, "What's Wrong with Negro Women?," Pauli Murray's "Why Negro Girls Stay Single," and the sociologist St. Claire Drake's piece, "Why Negro Men Leave." While all of these writers had some affiliations with the Popular Front during the 1930s and 1940s, most did not carry lasting baggage from these alliances into the early Cold War years. As celebrated black intellectuals, they wrote articles that illustrated the impact of the postwar debates about gender roles within black communities, as well as the ways black intellectuals and the more established black press addressed women's equality.[18]

Ann Petry and Pauli Murray began the conversation with two articles that presented a feminist analysis of the black woman's roles in heterosexual relationships. Reflecting their own lived experiences and their analysis of gender politics in the United States, Petry and Murray challenged the dominant discursive construction of women as homemakers and wives. Refusing to accept gender as a singular category that explained black women's lives, both Petry and Murray criticized mainstream assessments for not taking into account the role of racial, economic, educational, and social status in influencing the choices black women did and could make. Each of the authors clearly defined how racism and economics shaped gender relations within black communities and made it almost impossible, and often undesirable, for most black women to live up to normative heterosexual ideals of marriage and family.

Ann Petry had emerged as a powerful voice addressing black women's experiences with the publication, in 1946, of her bestselling novel *The Street*.[19] Born in 1911, in Old Saybrook, Connecticut, Petry moved to New York in 1938 after marrying George David Petry. She worked for the *New York Amsterdam News* for three years and from 1941 to 1944 edited the women's page of the progressive newspaper *People's Voice*. As discussed in chapter 1, it was during this period that Petry befriended a number of black women radicals affiliated with the CP, including Marvel Cooke. Indeed, her acquaintance with the community of black writers and the black left in Harlem led her to embrace radical politics, if not organizational affiliations, and also helped to further her career. Between 1943 and 1945, several of her short stories, published in the *Crisis*, gained national attention, and she briefly joined the American Negro Theatre, appearing in the play *Strivers Row*.[20]

Written in the midst of her literary success, Petry's brief article, entitled "What's Wrong with Negro Men?," took a humorous perspective on the issues of heterosexual relationships. This tone differed greatly from that of Petry's acclaimed novel *The Street*, which examines, through the character of Lutie Johnson, the economic and sexual vulnerability of a working-class black single mother. In her article, Petry used parody to expose the ways that black men often "boasted about being progressive in politics . . . or the great qualities of women," but in private "his attitude about women comes straight out of the dark ages." Painting an over-the-top picture of a vain and demanding husband who imagines his wife as "the little woman" especially skilled at performing "purely womanly chores," Petry skewered black men who embraced dominant society's emphasis on prescribed gender roles.[21] She also argued that for black women to attempt to live up to prevailing ideals of women as homemakers and wives, particularly given the economic circumstance of most black families, meant accepting a life of constant work and exploitation.

Petry's article marked a sharp and rare critique of black manhood from a prominent black woman. This may account for the humorous tone the author employed throughout the article, which softened her critiques of male privilege and sexism. Nonetheless, Petry's assessment countered the dominant trend of blaming black women for problems within the black family. In particular, she challenged the myth of the emasculating black matriarch by portraying black men as the domineering and demanding partner in black marriages. Petry argued that this domineering male behavior reflected not the pathology of black heterosexual relationships, but rather the ways sexism bonds men across racial and economic differences. "In this respect," Petry writes, "he [the black man] is as medieval as his white brother."[22]

Pauli Murray's article "Why Negro Girls Stay Single" also examined the complexities of heterosexual relationships in black communities. Murray had a more strained relationship with the CP-affiliated black left than did Petry. A longtime supporter of the Socialist Party, Murray inclined more toward the anti-Communist left of A. Philip Randolph and the civil rights strategies of the NAACP. She had become politicized in New York amid the radical protests of the 1930s. Murray briefly joined the Lovestonite Communist Opposition faction, which was led by the former head of the Communist Party USA Jay Lovestone and which attracted other black women radicals, such as Ella Baker and former CP member Grace Campbell.[23] Yet, by 1947, Murray, a graduate of Howard University Law School, had gained some prominence after being named woman of the year by the National Council of Negro Women and *Mademoiselle* magazine.

Speaking from her own family history and from her personal experiences as an unmarried professional black woman, Murray defended professional women. She argued that the disproportionate number of single black women reflected broader social forces at work. For Murray, this "alienation of the sexes" stemmed from racial and social conditions in the United States. Black women's rebellion against the "framework of 'male supremacy' as well as 'white supremacy,'" which placed them "at the bottom of the economic and social scale," produced, in Murray's view, a generation of college-educated and professional black women but not a parallel cohort of black male peers. Yet, unlike most critics, who blamed black women for their successes, Murray instead pointed to the ways racism limited black men's economic development and underscored the barriers such limitations created in black male-female relationships. Moreover, Murray criticized the "general mis-education of the sexes" and "outmoded social tabus" that helped to create rigid gender roles and behavioral expectations within black communities.[24] For Murray, the tensions created within African American heterosexual relationships by racism, sexism, and economic pressure produced a "jungle of human relationships" that, in her words, "intensifies homosexuality and often results in a rising incidence of crimes of passion, broken homes and divorce."[25] Murray, in contending that there existed a higher level of disorganization in black heterosexual relationships than in comparable white relationships, embraced a common perspective among mainstream intellectuals, even as she highlighted broader social forces as the root cause.

Pauli Murray's framing of homosexuality as part of a list of aberrant behavior created by societal limitations takes on specific significance when read in light of her own conflicted struggles with same-sex desires and gender identity. While Murray clearly presented homosexuality as deviant, her articulations of same-sex relationships as an outgrowth of the limited options available to many black women reflected a bold pronouncement that, in a sense, validated those choices. It is especially evocative considering the Cold War homophobic discourse, which most often defined homosexuality as a psychological weakness that threatened both personal stability and the nation's ability to resist a communist incursion.[26] Moreover, her willingness to address the same-sex relationships as a social issue, given her personal history, hints at a profound shift from her earlier views of her own sexual desires and gender nonconformity as an intensely personal matter and a "biological problem" needing medical attention.[27] In this context, Murray's discussion of homosexuality among black women, albeit demeaning, represented a breach of the silence around same-sex desire that had shaped much of her public life. This suggests that the shifting postwar discourse around gender and race, as well as the challenges posed by radical women to dominant constructions of gender roles, provided an important opening for Murray to begin to reconceptualize her own experiences within a broader social context.[28]

Murray's and Petry's insights met with some resistance in the pages of the *Negro Digest*. Three years after the publication of Petry's article, the journalist Roi Ottley penned a reply in "What's Wrong with Negro Women?" Ottley, a nationally respected journalist, began his career in the 1920s at the *New York Amsterdam News*, as an active voice in articulating the concerns and experiences of black people in the United States. He served on the New York Support Committee of the National Negro Congress, carried out extensive research on black life in New York for the Works Progress Administration (WPA), and worked as the director of public relations for the CIO War Relief Committee. In 1943, Ottley published *A New World A-Coming: Black Life in America,* which provided the basis for a popular radio program of the same name. At the time of his article's publication, Ottley had just relocated to Chicago to work as a staff writer for the *Chicago Defender,* a leading black newspaper.[29]

Ottley framed his article as a report on black men's private conversations about black women, the kind heard only in the "clubs, lodge halls" or shared with "close friends and psychiatrists." Although careful to note that there are no "fundamental differences between Negro women and white women," Ottley asserted, "There are things which most Negro women have in common." He then pointed to a series of flaws, including the contentions that "many Negro girls have a false sense of values and standards," that "too few Negro women contribute to the race fight," and that, among a "certain class" of Negro women, "household duties and manners could stand vast improvement."[30] Despite Ottley's efforts to downplay a comparison between black and white women, by the end of the article it is the idealized white woman against whom black woman are being measured and found lacking. Therefore, while he acknowledges the ways social and economic factors created an idealized white womanhood, in his final estimation it is black women who need to be fixed with a "few improving touches here and there."[31]

St. Claire Drake, an established social scientist, also entered the debate with the brief article "Why Men Leave Home." Trained in anthropology at the University of Chicago, Drake contributed research to several significant social science studies on race, including Gunnar Myrdal's *American Dilemma.* By 1950, Drake, an activist and a professor at Roosevelt College, in Chicago, had co-authored, with Horace Cayton Jr., *Black Metropolis* (1945), a groundbreaking study of black life in Chicago.[32] In his piece for the *Negro Digest*, Drake sought to bring social scientific insight to the question of why black men are more likely to desert their wives than are white men. Drawing heavily from Frazier's *The Negro Family in the United States*, particularly the chapter "Roving Men and Homeless Women," Drake highlighted limited economic opportunities and racism as key factors in producing black male desertion.[33]

Yet, unlike Murray, for Drake the solution to disorganization and male desertion within the black family resided in allowing black men to live up to the "ideal picture of the American husband" and to become "solid middle class." Drake embraced proscribed gender roles and located the real problem in the inability of black families to live up to these standards, arguing that black women's steady employment had "weakened" black men's "position in the family."[34] Both Ottley's and Drake's articles speak to a common thread found among many black male intellectuals of the period who sought to disprove racial stereotypes about the black family and black manhood and who advocated for greater economic opportunities for black men, yet rarely addressed the issue of black women's exploitation or sexism in black communities. Thus, their proposed solutions often reinforced dominant gendered norms and male supremacy.

Defining Women's Equality and the "The Woman Question"

The viewpoints outlined in the *Negro Digest* articles represent one aspect of the political debate black women radicals engaged as they launched their defense of black womanhood. Petry's and Murray's articles presented a strong defense of black womanhood that also included a powerful indictment of male dominance aimed directly at gender relationships within black communities. Drawing on similar issues, these CP-affiliated women radicals also emphasized the role of economic and racial oppression in shaping black women's options and the structures of the black family. However, most of these women did not have the mainstream cachet to publish in popular journals such as *Negro Digest,* so their writings were aimed at a markedly different audience. They directed their defense of black womanhood to the U.S. left and particularly interracial women's organizations, in an effort to push for a more expansive gender politics. In these spaces, they directed their sharpest and most explicit critiques at white women's theorizing of the "the woman question" and the flaws within interracial organizing efforts. They also pushed the U.S. left to support a political and theoretical framework that addressed "the problems of the Negro woman."

During the 1940s and 1950s, CP-affiliated white women articulated a vision of women's oppression that not only challenged the CP political line, which defined women's primary oppression as workers, but also demanded that the CP take seriously the issue of male supremacy within party (and U.S.) culture. The historian Kate Weigand notes that, in framing these interventions, white women borrowed many tactics and lessons from the black freedom struggle and from black radicals' campaigns to push the CP to address issues of white supremacy and theorizing around what had come to be known as "the national question."[35] The demands to address racial inequality laid the groundwork for many of the emerging calls from within the CP for women's equality. Yet, progressive white women rarely moved beyond simply viewing "the national question" as a comparative model for women's equality. Thus their framing of the fight for women's equality and their modes of engaging questions of racial inequality also provided much of the fodder for black women radicals' critiques of the U.S. left. Indeed, the writings and political organizing of white women progressives, which often drew comparisons between race-and gender oppression, proved a provocative counterpoint to black women's intersectional analysis and calls for detailing the specificity of black women's lives.

Betty Millard's two-part series published in *New Masses* in December 1947 and January 1948 provides a clear example of white women radicals' theorizing of "the woman question." *New Masses*, which would be reestablished in 1948 as *Masses and Mainstream*, served as one of the leading journals for CP-affiliated writers, and Betty Millard proved a key voice in women's organizing. Active in the CAW, Millard wrote the two-part series "Woman against Myth" in honor of the one-hundred-year anniversary of the Seneca Falls Convention and the publication of the *Communist Manifesto*. The articles proved so successful that they were later issued as a pamphlet by the CAW.

Millard's essays addressed the continued "economic, legal, and political barriers against women," as well as the social and religious customs that "conspire to keep woman in her place." In celebrating the work of Susan B. Anthony and Elizabeth Cady Stanton and the insights of Marxism, Millard also emphasized the historical relationships between the "women's fight against oppression" and "that of labor and especially the Negro people." Although she acknowledged the importance of the fight for workers' rights and black equality, she presented these movements as completely distinct from the struggle for women's rights. This specifically emerged as Millard used white supremacy and the oppression of African Americans as an analogous framework for describing male supremacy and women's oppression.

She argued, "[W]omen are not lynched—as women. . . . For women there is generally reserved a quieter, more veiled kind of lynching."[36] Such theorizing not only ignored the intersections of race and gender but also implicitly privileged the experiences of white middle-class women.

This thinking is particularly visible in Millard's description of the public-private divide, which relegated women to the home, as the primary factor structuring women's oppression and in her suggestion that "intimate daily relationships" with men allowed all women access to the "seeming security" of an "inferior but 'protected' position."[37] With such claims, Millard effectively erased from her analysis of "women's oppressions" large swaths of black and working-class women, who had long been employed outside the home and found little "protection" in their "inferior position" as wives and mothers. Moreover, in the essay, Millard literally relegated black women's experiences to the margins as she limited to a footnote the insight that "the lynching of a Georgia Negro is the violent expression of a pattern of white supremacy; rape is a violent expression of a pattern of male supremacy, and when a Negro woman is raped by a white man these two aspects of our society merge."[38] For Millard, the rape of black women rated only as an exception to her main point, since such violence was often discussed as an attack on black women or African Americans and not on women as a distinct group. It was precisely this type of framing of "the woman question" and interventions in debates over American womanhood, which continually centered the experiences of nonracialized (white) women, that black women sought to challenge as they presented a more expansive and intersectional view of "the woman question."

Black Women Speak of Black Womanhood and Interracial Women's Organizing

As reflected in Millard's articles, peace organizations such as the CAW proved central sites for postwar debates about women's roles and contributions as citizens. Progressive and radical women activists took up these questions in part as a strategic move to give public voice to their political critiques of U.S. imperialism—which had entered a period of Cold War retrenchment buttressed by war efforts in Korea and a burgeoning military-industrial complex. This strategy gained particular momentum as leftist formations, including the CP, focused their resources on "the building of the people's anti-monopoly and peace coalition against American imperialism."[39] Black women played a key role in these organizing efforts, not only serving as leaders in women's organizations such as the CAW and AWP, but also pushing these organizations to embrace a politics sensitive to the ways race and economic opportunities shaped women's experiences differently.

The 1945 WIDF conference, in Paris, served as a spark for the formation of a number of progressive peace organizations. The WIDF represented a mixture of left-leaning and communist, working-class, and professional women from throughout Europe and the United States. This international organization viewed its mission as combining the fight for world peace and women's equality. The WIDF outlined these goals as it called for the "eradication of all remnants of Fascism . . . and the maintenance of world peace; the advance of women into full economic, political, and legal status; and the full protection of children."[40]

It was under this banner that the Congress of American Women was formed in 1946 as the U.S. branch of the WIDF. CAW leadership included women who had attended the WIDF conference, such as Thelma Dale Perkins, of the National Negro Congress, and Columbia professor Gene Weltfish, as well as those who supported the conference, including the journalist Susan B. Anthony II and Mary van Kleeck, from the Russell Sage Foundation.[41] It also received broad support from CP women such as Elizabeth Gurley Flynn, Eleanor Flexner, and Claudia Jones. The CAW put forth a progressive politics that embraced an essentialist image of women's "natural role" as mothers and wives at the same time that it fought for women's full rights and equality at home and in the workplace. The CAW also took up a broad range of community issues, including supporting local women's organizing and black civil rights struggles and resisting anticommunist assaults on progressive leadership.

In February 1947, months before Petry's and Murray's essays would appear in the *Negro Digest* and Betty Millard published her two-part series "Woman against Myth," Thelma Dale Perkins penned a speech for the International Council meeting of the WIDF titled "The Status of Negro Women." Having traveled to London and Paris two years earlier to participate in the Federation's founding convention, Dale Perkins joined the February Council meeting with the explicit goal of moving the organization and women's groups more generally to take up serious action in addressing the specific concerns of black women. Arguing that the "important fact of Negro women today is that there is a growing concern with their plight," Dale Perkins urged the WIDF to follow the lead of organizations such as the CAW and trade unions that had come to realize "that there can be no real equality for all women until Negro women are also give[n] equality."[42]

Although Dale Perkins clearly aimed her comments at women's organizations and specifically the majority-white members of the WIDF, she did not limit her critiques to interracial organizing. Delineating the ways black women in the United States faced "the double oppression of both racial and sex discrimination" including having suffered in slavery as "breeders and hard-laborers," she located the legacy of this dual oppression in black women's continued inequality.[43] In Dale Perkins's opinion, this dual oppression made it nearly impossible for black women "to attain a position of equality with white women or even with Negro men." Speaking directly to the gender relations within the black community, she contended that "even when, in the case of most Negro women, they have been the main supporters of the family the man still maintained a superior status to that of women." Challenging the growing emphasis on dismantling the public-private divide as the path to women's liberation, Dale Perkins reminded her audience that access and employment opportunities, while necessary, were not enough to ensure black women's full equality.[44]

By 1950, the CAW's work faced increased government surveillance, and the organization was labeled as a subversive group and its leadership "foreign agents." American Women for Peace emerged that same year as a successor to the CAW. Like the CAW, AWP counted among its leadership a number of African American women, including Thelma Dale Perkins and the labor activist Halois Moorhead, who served as national executive secretary. The AWP, however, embraced a less explicitly militant political mission and shied away from challenging anticommunist policies.[45] Putting forth a mother-centered vision of peace activism, AWP supported uniting women of all races, ethnic backgrounds, and classes in a struggle that represented their "natural responsibility" to preserve life. The organization's declaration stated that "because the privilege of giving birth is uniquely the labor of women, it becomes a natural responsibility of all women to preserve life, and especially to protect it from the dangers of useless and criminal warfare."[46]

Such essentialism, long a trope of women's peace activism, spoke to the renewed emphasis on the role of women as mothers and wives. It can also be read as an attempt to gain greater mass support and to insulate the group from anticommunist assaults by mobilizing mainstream discourses celebrating women's contributions as mothers. Despite these political constraints, the AWP drew together a broad range of women, forming chapters throughout the United States. It also often served as an umbrella organization, drawing in representatives from local women's organizations and labor unions.

Civil rights activist Bessie Mitchell (left) and poet Beulah Richardson (Beah Richards) in New York in 1951. (Photographs and Prints Division, Schomburg Center for Research in Black Culture, New York Public Library, Astor, Lenox, and Tilden Foundations)

As Dale Perkins's speech indicates, it was within these interracial homosocial groups that the boundaries of interracial solidarity were most forcefully tested. Black women often pushed white allies in these organizational spaces to recognize the battle against white supremacy as a women's issue and to acknowledge their own racial and economic privileges as white women. Beulah Richardson clearly articulated these concerns in her eleven-page poem "A Black Woman Speaks of White Womanhood, of White Supremacy, of Peace." The poem also captures how tensions around interracial solidarity had intensified by 1951.[47]

Richardson's piece details the ways in which white supremacy worked as a "metalanguage" to construct and maintain a destructive divide between women of different experiences. This divide, she contended, relied on a racialized notion of womanhood, which deemed white womanhood superior and normative, racially encoding all discussions of women's activism and women's issues. Richardson wrote, "I would that I could speak of white womanhood / as it will and should be / when it stands tall in full equality. / But then, womanhood will be womanhood / void of color and of class, / and all necessity for my speaking thus will be past. / Gladly past."[48] Yet, Richardson viewed these divides not as justification for separating white and black women's struggles but as a challenge to white women to also take up the fight against white supremacy and work for "peace in a world where there is equality."[49]

In examining historically specific constructions of white womanhood, Richardson underscored a gendered notion of white supremacy that has been detrimental to all women. Exposing a history of interdependence and oppression that bound black and white women together, Richardson argued that only through a critical analysis of and an attack on these inextricably connected forces of racism and sexism can a truly united struggle for women's equality develop. She wrote, "and what wrongs you murders me / and eventually marks your grave / so we share a mutual death at the hand of tyranny."[50] Thus, her words represented an incisive critique of white women's organizations that took up "women's issues" without explicitly connecting such struggles to a fight against white supremacy. In this regard, Richardson's arguments provided a direct challenge to Betty Millard's view of a universal "women's oppression."

For Richardson, the interdependence of women's lives developed within a long history of white supremacy and gender oppression rooted in the institution of slavery, which marked black and white womanhood differently. As black women toiled under the chattel slavery of a white patriarchy, white women bowed to this same white patriarchy by accepting a constructed ideal of (white) womanhood. From bearing children for the same white man to white women's vengeful dominance of black women slaves, black and white women shared a context of experiences and complicated relations of dependence and hate because of the institution of slavery. The poem reads in part:

> They brought me here in chains.
> They brought you here willing slaves to man.
> You, shiploads of women each filled with hope
> that she might win with ruby lip and saucy curl
> and bright and flashing eye
> him to wife who had the largest tender.
> Remember?
> And they sold you here even as they sold me.
>
> My sister, there is no room for mockery.
> If they counted my teeth / they did appraise your thigh
> and sold you to the highest bidder / the same as I.

... They trapped me with the chain and gun.
They trapped you with lying tongue. / For, 'less you see that fault—
that male villainy / that robbed you of name, voice and authority
that murderous greed that wasted you and me,
he, the white supremacist, fixed your minds with poisonous thought:
"white skin is supreme." / and therewith brought that monstrous
change / exiling you to things.[51]

It is this history, reproduced over and over again through various forms of interaction, that Richardson examined as she spoke of black womanhood, of white supremacy, and of white womanhood.

In her piece, Richardson did not accept ignorance as the root of white women's refusal to acknowledge the interdependence of black women's oppression and white women's "protection," instead outlining some of the benefits white women gained from white supremacy, the exploitation of black women, and the degradation of black womanhood. She highlighted the ways in which the survival of a particular construction of white womanhood relied on the domination of black women, questioning, "What is this superior thing / that in order to be sustained must needs feed upon my flesh?" and connected black women's working lives to white women's "dictated idleness." Richardson asserts, as several historians of African American women have argued, that black women's labor as slaves and, later, as domestic workers allowed many white women to pursue other interests, including political activism.[52] But, white women gained more than simply exploited labor from the oppression of black women. Richardson's writing illustrates how the construction of black women as different—racially inferior, hypersexual, and "unwomanly,"—helped to sustain an "idealized white womanhood." This construction provided white women with both real and imagined protection, as black women's sexual exploitation remained unremarkable and served as a measure of white women's superiority (Roi Ottley and Betty Millard had both implied as much). "And you did not fight," Richardson wrote of white women, "but set your minds fast on my slavery the better to endure your own . . . and thought somehow my wasted blood confirmed your superiority."[53]

To progressive women within the AWP, Richardson's analysis brought "new understanding of the significance of the fight for unity."[54] It remains unclear how deeply these insights influenced the AWP. Less than two years later, the organization collapsed. Nevertheless, a hint of the impact of this critique can be gleaned from the award given to Richardson at the Chicago Peace Congress and the publication of her poem as a pamphlet. The pamphlet displayed a photo of a black woman presenting a document "for peace" to a white woman. The cover is perhaps indicative of the AWP's organizational understanding of the "fight for unity" as an exchange in which black women passed on their knowledge of racism to white women. Richardson cautioned against such a strategy for building interracial solidarity, warning, "so be careful when you talk to me / remind me not of my slavery, I know it well / but rather tell me of your own."[55] In this concluding line of her poem, Richardson foreshadowed the continued difficulty black women would encounter in contesting white supremacy in majority-white women's organizations.

While the concerns and opinions expressed in Richardson's poem served as a direct address to white women activists, her insights also represented some of the major concerns black women radicals were grappling with at the time. Therefore, it is not surprising that Richardson's writing struck a deep cord with these women. The stir produced by Richardson's determination as a black woman to speak forcefully on questions of white supremacy and white womanhood gave voice to many of the political struggles African American women encountered as activists in racially integrated organizations. As detailed in succeeding chapters, her poem also reflected a political vision articulated in much of the radical organizing carried out by black women. Two months after the Chicago Peace Congress, Yvonne Gregory wrote an article on Richardson for *Freedom* newspaper. Praising her as a voice of "all Negro women in anger and tenderness," Gregory also organized an enthusiastic welcome and a special reading of Richardson's poem in New York City.[56]

Cultural Activism and Racialized Womanhood

Black women radicals also used their cultural talents to counter racist and sexist constructions of black womanhood. Informed by a historical tradition of cultural resistance that included the work of black leftists during the Popular Front era, these radicals used art to create realistic and complex representations of black womanhood. They fought to, as Alice Childress wrote, "move beyond the either/or of 'artistic' and 'politically' imposed limitation." [57] Such cultural politics appeared particularly relevant during the early Cold War years as popular culture and mass media emerged as powerful mediums for constructing dominant images of U.S. life and Cold War politics.[58] Claudia Jones described the ideological discourses carried in mass media as "cheap philosophy" that served as "the alpha and omega of bourgeois ideological attacks on women." Jones's statement not only acknowledged popular culture and media as crucial tools in building U.S. hegemony but also suggested the need for progressive forces to create politically relevant counterdiscourses.[59]

Black women writers on the left took up this charge to provide a different interpretation of black communities and especially black women's lives that would expose the myths of mainstream cultural images of blackness and the mistreatment such imagery justified. Alice Childress captured this orientation as she described her work as inspired by an investment in "portraying have-nots in a have society, those seldom singled out by mass media, except as source material for derogatory humor and/or condescending clinical, social analysis."[60] While later in life Childress often claimed to have developed these politics in isolation and described herself as "being somewhat alone in [her] ideas," in fact they were developed within a dynamic community of black radicals and the array of political campaigns they led.[61] For example, the CRC's ongoing battle against "legal lynching" inspired numerous poems and creative pieces, including Yvonne Gregory's searing poem "Long Distance to Life" and one of Lorraine Hansberry's first publications, a poem titled "Lynchsong," which was printed in *Masses and Mainstream*.[62]

In many ways, cultural work provided one of the most effective and publicly visible venues for women radicals as they sought to theorize black women's experiences and intervene in ongoing political debates within the U.S. left and the nation. This is clearly at play in some of Lorraine Hansberry's writings during the period that gained a public audience only after her death. In one such piece, Hansberry examined the ways dominant gender constructions defined black women as hypersexual, and the oppressive conditions black women endured everyday because of these constructions. Her writing described how black women's exclusion from the ideals of (white) womanhood marked them in white men's eyes as sexual property. "I can be coming from eight hours on an assembly line or fourteen hours in Mrs. Halsey's kitchen . . . and the white boys in the streets, they look at me and think of sex. They look at me and that's *all* they think. . . . Baby you could be Jesus in drag–but if you're brown they're sure you're selling!"[63]

In several vignettes, three black women of different ages and economic positions speak these same words, emphasizing how little protection social or economic status offered black women forced to confront white supremacists' notions of black womanhood. In Hansberry's brief piece, she revealed how the intersecting force of race and gender trumped all other factors and descriptors in dominant society's view of black women.

Alice Childress's first play, *Florence*, staged by the American Negro Theatre in 1949 and published in *Masses and Mainstream* the following year, provides a powerful example of such a cultural work that did gain a public audience. Childress, who by the 1960s would make a name for herself as a critically acclaimed actress and writer, started her career as a playwright and actress in 1941 with the ANT. Founded in Harlem's 135th Street branch of the New York Public Library in 1940, the ANT became an important training ground for Childress as well as many other black artists, including Ann Petry, Sidney Poitier, Harry Belafonte, and Ruby Dee. As a member of the ANT, Childress not only honed her crafts but also operated as an active member of the black left. Sidney Poitier credits Childress with encouraging him to "explore the history of black people" and as the person responsible for his "meeting and getting to know" Paul Robeson.[64] Throughout the 1950s, Childress stood as a key force in the community of activists who lent support to Paul Robeson during his battles against government-led anticommunist attacks; she worked as a staff writer for *Freedom* and helped to found the left-leaning Committee for the Negro in the Arts (CNA), which challenged Hollywood's dual blacklist for radical black artists.[65]

It was in this context of political and cultural exchange that Childress developed the play *Florence*. The literary critic Mary Helen Washington reveals that Childress wrote the play "to counter the sexism of the men of the Harlem Left, demonstrating that women's stories were at the heart of, not peripheral to, racial issues."[66] Yet Childress's play also illustrates the centrality of race in the struggle to win women's equality. In the play, Childress explores the role of white supremacy and gendered norms in shaping interracial interactions and black women's lives, while also suggesting some strategies of resistance. The play is set in a southern train station, and, in keeping with the idea of centering women's experience in the battle for black equality, the main characters are two black women and a white woman, with the only black male character filling a marginal role as the station porter. The play's dialogue centers on an African American mother's debate over whether to reclaim her daughter, Florence, from the harshness of New York City or to support her in following her dreams. Suggestive of Childress's own efforts to find success as a writer in New York City, the character Florence is a talented but struggling black actress seeking to challenge the accepted ideology that defined black women as employable only as domestic workers.[67] Childress details the struggle Florence's mother (Mama) endures in supporting Florence, and the limitations placed on black women by narrow conceptions of black womanhood, through Mama's conversations with her younger daughter, Marge, and her encounter with Mrs. Carter, a successful white actress also traveling to New York City.

Throughout the one-act drama, Florence remains unseen as the primary interactions takes place between Mama, Marge, and Mrs. Carter. The opening dialogue occurs between Mama and Marge as they arrive at the train station. Marge urges her mother to remain firm in convincing Florence to return home. Marge complains to Mama that Florence "got notions a Negro woman don't need." Marge views her sister's efforts to demand more as not only futile but a threat to the family. Marge has come to accept that for black people "there are things we can't do cause they ain't gonna let us," and she implores Mama to make Florence come home. Through this exchange, Childress marks Marge as a black woman who not only accepts but also enforces the limited options dictated by intersecting forces of white supremacy and male supremacy.

The majority of the play, however, centers on a conversation between Mama and Mrs. Carter in which they explore the ways that while seemingly supportive, white women still perpetuated white supremacy. Mrs. Carter presents herself as outside the strictures of southern Jim Crow racism, "trying to understand" black people's experiences. Declaring herself "not a Southerner really," Mrs. Carter insists that she not be addressed as "ma'am." But it's soon revealed that behind these minimal efforts at "trying to understand" resides a deep investment in white supremacy. This emerges when, in response to Mrs. Carter's declaration of her willingness to support Negroes, Florence's mother ask Mrs. Carter to help her daughter get a job in New York City. Reflecting her inability to view a black woman as her equal, Mrs. Carter responds that she can get Florence hired as a domestic worker for one of her of friends in the business. In this conversation, Childress highlights Mrs. Carter's inability or unwillingness to see Florence as a colleague or protégé. In so doing, Childress invokes the difficulty many white women had in acknowledging the privileges of white supremacy and the ways they benefited from the oppression of black women, particularly as exploited domestic labor.

In these moments, Childress's play addresses many of the same concerns about the limits of interracial solidarity and the stifling effect of dominant constructions of black womanhood that emerged in other black women's writings and political activism. Yet, Childress also points to black women's resistance to these dominant images and the forces of white supremacy. This resistance is reflected in the surprising force of Mama's growing anger at Mrs. Carter's racist and self-serving imaginings of African Americans. In the end, Mama decides to support Florence's dreams. Declaring that "she can be anything in the world she wants to be! That's her right. Marge can't make her turn back. Mrs. Carter can't make her turn back," in the closing moments of the play Mama decisively allies herself with Florence and turns her back on Mrs. Carter and even on Marge. Childress concludes the drama by depicting a moment not just of unity based on a shared identity but of hard-fought solidarity between two black women. She also asserts the centrality of black women's struggles in the fight for black equality. [68]

Claudia Jones, Feminist Politics, and the Metalanguage of Race

Questions regarding black women's subjectivity and exploitation, the possibilities of interracial alliances, and white women's complicity with white supremacy emerged as central themes in the activism and writings of CP theorist Claudia Jones. A member of the CP since the age of twenty, Jones emerged as a crucial voice on "the national question" and "the woman question" (as the party termed theories and debates that addressed black liberation and women's liberation, respectively) during the early Cold War.

Jones's critical writings reflected, in part, shifting party politics as the CP embraced an increasingly radical rhetoric that pushed the party further and further left, some argued too far left given the political landscape and conditions. This political shift emerged with William Z. Foster's rise to CP leadership following his vocal opposition to Earl Browder's bold step in dissolving the CP as a party and forming the Communist Political Association. At the helm of the CP from 1947 through 1959, Foster emphasized ridding the CP of right-leaning policies called Browderism and rooting the party more deeply in Marxist-Leninist theory and practice. This political shift included a renewed emphasis on black self-determination, "the national question," and "the woman question."[69] The new emphasis, which in practice often proved limited, did provide a key opening for African American and women party members to employ the charge of Browderism to challenge the white and male chauvinisms of members and to push for more organizing and theorizing around issues of white supremacy and women's oppression.[70]

Jones, a strong supporter of Foster, gained greater visibility during this period, in part by critiquing Browder's "false estimate of the relationship of forces in our nation and the world."[71] She wrote numerous articles concerning gender and race politics in the CP and the nation and fought to link party organizing strategies to women's equality and black liberation. Many of her writings appeared in the CP's theoretical journal, *Political Affairs*, including her most influential article, "An End to the Neglect of the Problems of the

Negro Woman!," a discussion article, "On the Right to Self-Determination for the Negro People in the Black Belt," and an assessment of women's organizing, "International Women's Day and the Struggle for Peace." In each of these articles, Jones highlighted the inextricable links that united the struggles of women, African Americans, and working people. Jones proclaimed that "the two main forces for democracy are the working class allied with Negro People" and argued that the party must understand "the importance of winning American women, especially working class and Negro communities, to militant resistance to Wall Street."[72] Jones's biographer, Carole Boyce Davies, details the groundbreaking impact of Jones's assessment of black women's "triply-oppressed status" and her "theorizing of the super-exploitation of the black woman," asserting that such insight assures Jones "a prominent place in transnational black feminist theoretic and practice." Boyce Davies traces the origins of Jones's theories to the "basic party position on capitalism" and "her personal experiences."[73] However, these theoretical ideas were also developed through debates within the CP over "the national question" and in response to white women progressives' theorizing of women's liberation. Moreover, Jones honed and tested these insights in conversation with a vibrant community of black women intellectuals, activists, and artists invested in building a more expansive radical politics.

In her writings, Jones outlined the variety of ways capitalism worked alongside women's oppression to fuel the exploitation of women as workers forced into a gendered and racialized labor market that denied them equal access to high-wage jobs. She also acknowledged the ways postwar conditions "penalize[d]" women from all strata of society, "especially the Negro women, the working women and the working class generally, but also women on the farms, in the offices and in the professions."[74] Jones especially emphasized the destructive impact of postwar constructions of womanhood that she termed the pro-fascist "kitchen, church, and children" ideology that put forth the false slogan "a women's place is in the home." She viewed these ideological slogans as "primarily designed to obscure the source of the many existing inequalities in the social position of women" and as disguised efforts to "undermine" the "many social and economic advances made by women during the anti-fascist war."[75] In her opinion, such reactionary constructions not only produced "limited opportunities for women in the professions" but also represented direct "attacks on woman's femininity, her womanliness, her pursuit of personal and family happiness." In these ways, Jones retained a Marxist politics that located the roots of women's oppression in the capitalist system, not in men. She also articulated the ways women's oppression operated outside the workplace. Jones pushed party members to integrate such politics into their everyday organizing and urged CP leadership to make a theoretical understanding of the woman question "a must for every Party member."[76]

Drawing on her experiences as a black woman in the United States, her Marxist-Leninist training, and her investment in transnational black liberation, Jones pushed even further. She refused to accept a narrow single-identity politics and used her position in the CP to defend these "protofeminist" politics that prefigured later black feminist positions. Jones argued that "only to the extent that we fight all chauvinist expressions and actions as regards the Negro people and fight for the full equality of the Negro people, can women as a whole advance their struggle."[77] Moreover, Jones often concentrated on the experiences of "triply-oppressed" black women workers to illustrate the interconnectedness of these struggles. She argued for the revolutionary and leadership potential of black women, not simply from an essentialist notion of identity but because their experiences forced to the forefront an intersectional analysis. In addition, Jones argued that black women represented a complex history within the United States as often the most marginalized sector of society as well as the most politically active force in emerging mass movements.

These politics were also expressed through Jones's activism within the CP. As discussed in chapter 1, Jones had been drawn to the CP through its work on the Scottsboro case of 1931. In her early years, she organized in Harlem through the Young Communist League, participated in the National Negro Congress, and worked for several communist newspapers. During the postwar period, Jones continued as a member of the Communist Party, working for the organizational paper the *Daily Worker* and as executive secretary of the party's National Negro Commission. In 1947, she would take on the role of executive secretary of the National Women's Commission and a year later joined the National Committee, the leadership body of the CP. Throughout these years, Jones remained active in women's and African American organizing, including advocating for black soldiers against Jim Crow treatment in the military, participating in the WIDF Peace Congress, in Paris, joining the CAW, and supporting civil rights activism around the Rosa Ingram case.[78] Such active engagement and support of black women's organizing brought Jones into contact with a range of political perspectives and helped to shape her feminist analysis by detailing the ways that a multitude of issues informed women's experiences.

Claudia Jones's theorizing and activism around "the woman question" and black liberation helped to make these central issues of debate within the CP during the 1950s. She also provided important support for black women within the CP's orbit. Indeed, Thelma Dale Perkins proudly recalled Jones as "tough" and unwilling to "take any stuff."[79] However, such political positioning and determination brought her into conflict with a number of white women communists who were also producing influential theoretical work and who were engaged in women's organizing. As highlighted in Kate Weigand's *Red Feminism*, many of the white women in this group found Jones's politics heavyhanded and at times viewed her as an unsupportive voice. They complained that Jones's constant urging that the party recruit black and working-class women proved counterproductive. In fact, Weigand reports that CP member Harriet Magil remembers Claudia Jones as being guilty of "the most awful reverse chauvinism."[80]

In "An End to the Neglect of the Problems of the Negro Woman!" Claudia Jones did contend that "the Negro question in the United States is *prior* to, and not equal to, the woman question."[81] She also proclaimed that, "for the progressive women's movement, the Negro women who combines in her status the worker, the Negro and the women is the vital link to this heightened political consciousness."[82] Jones's insistence, however, on emphasizing black liberation and black women's leadership within women's organizing reflected, in part, her response to white feminists in the party who verbally supported "Negro-white unity" but rarely theorized around or put into practice such politics. For example, as discussed earlier, Betty Millard's influential statement on women's liberation, "Women against the Myth," paid little heed to the ways race shaped women's experiences differently, invoking "the doubly-oppressed Negro women" only once in her two-part article.[83] Millard not only ignored the ways race marked a category of difference among U.S. women but also invoked Negro oppression and the struggles for black liberation in the most simplistic analogies to buttress her arguments. Such a perspective reinforced the centering of white women's experience as universal and ignored Jones's calls for theorizing around the points of interconnections between race and gender constructions. In addition, Jones believed many white women within the party often resisted recruiting black women into leadership by arguing that "they were too busy making ends meet" or by discounting newly recruited black women activists as "people who have to get their feet wet organizationally."[84] Therefore, part of Jones's theoretical insights reflected her response to the conflicts with and her criticisms of white chauvinism within the CP.

But Jones's insights also suggest an important theoretical reading of the ways race and white supremacy operated within the United States. Her emphasis on the Negro question as "*prior* to, and not equal to, the woman question" revealed her understanding of the ways race operated as the dominant discourse, what Higginbotham calls a "metalanguage," within the United States.[85] In a variety of her writings, Claudia Jones provided examples of her theoretical understanding of race as the central force in U.S. society, from her emphasis on "the Negro question in the United States as a *special* question, an issue whose solution requires *special* demands" to her assertion that Negro women represented a powerful activist base.[86] In her reading of postwar U.S. politics, Jones outlined a "special ideological offensive aimed at degrading Negro women" that works "as part and parcel of the general reactionary ideological offensive against women of 'kitchen, church, and children.'"[87]

Jones's political calculations also proved suggestive of the "metalanguage" framework as she highlighted the ways white supremacy informed a broad array of race and gender discourses. Jones outlined not only how race shaped black women's gendered experiences within U.S. society but also how it influenced gendered relations within black communities. Although Jones viewed white chauvinism as the primary contradiction and argued that the main fight for "both Negro men and women" was "against their common oppressors, the white ruling classes," she refused to allow this racial solidarity to make invisible black men's investments in male chauvinism. She remained critical of black male party members who condoned chauvinist practices. Jones maintained that "Negro men," presumably because of the ways racial and gender oppression overlapped, held a "special responsibility particularly in relation to rooting out attitudes of male superiority as regards women in general."[88]

Conclusion

Black women radicals employed their activism and writings in a variety of venues to engage postwar debates concerning women's roles as U.S. citizens. They articulated important alternative visions, which broadened conceptions of gender roles and feminist politics in the U.S. left. They also provided vital strategies of resistance to dominant definitions of black womanhood and the interconnected force of white supremacy and gender oppression. In doing so, they emerged as powerful advocates for organizing women across difference, theorizing around the intersections of race, gender, and economic status, and recognizing the limits of idealized patriarchal relationships in U.S. society. In the end, much of the political activism and analysis put forth by black women radicals met strong resistance, and their activities rarely gained full acceptance among progressive forces. Furthermore, their tendency at times to emphasize race over gender, coupled with the explosive debates that developed between black women radicals and white feminists, often softened and rendered less direct their critiques of male supremacy among black activists and black communities more generally. Nonetheless, their contributions set an important tone in women's organizing and feminist politics. This tenor not only pushed the left to redefine its political vision but also provided a vital roadmap for building a more inclusive women's movement. As discussed in the following chapters, this work also created space for a range of organizing campaigns led by black women in the CRC and other CP-affiliated organizations.

Reframing Civil Rights Activism during the Cold War

The Rosa Lee Ingram Case, 1948–1959

Tis the lawless laws of this land
that killed this man! . . .
It's jails packed full of innocent folks
with the real criminals judging in the court. . . .
But be calm my sons men and women will come.
Must come to defend a woman's right to her own body.
　　　—Beulah Richardson, *The Revolt of Rosa Ingram*, ca. 1953

Every Negro woman in the United States is on trial with Rosa
Ingram . . . Negro women have died too many deaths for their
right to life. They have suffered too long for their honor and a
chance to raise their children without shame. This struggle, we
won't give up.
　　　—Vivian Carter Mason, *Pittsburgh Courier*, 1948

In August 1951, Yvonne Gregory boarded a train in New York City
headed to Americus, Georgia, in the heart of the Jim Crow South. This young
black woman, a noted writer and staff member at Paul Robeson's *Freedom*
newspaper, was traveling to the home of Rosa Lee Ingram, who lived just
outside Americus. Mrs. Ingram stood at the center of one of the most significant civil rights cases of the decade.

In January 1948, Rosa Lee Ingram, a recently widowed sharecropper, and
two of her teenage sons were convicted of the November 1947 murder of
John Ethron Stratford and sentenced to death by electrocution. Stratford, a
white sharecropper who lived on a plot of land adjacent to that worked by
Rosa Lee Ingram, had died after a dispute with Mrs. Ingram turned violent

and Mrs. Ingram's sons came to her aid. Although the exact circumstances of the altercation remained contested, all parties agreed that Stratford had carried a gun into the dispute and struck Mrs. Ingram first.[1] The Ingrams' guilt was determined in a one-day trial in Ellaville, Georgia, the county seat, located nearly 140 miles south of Atlanta and 15 miles north of Americus.

The Ingram case initially garnered attention when a February 3, 1948, *Atlanta Daily World* article announced the conviction and sentencing of Mrs. Ingram and her two sons. The article detailed the plight of "the doomed" Rosa Lee Ingram and her sons, sixteen-year-old Wallace and fourteen-year-old Sammie Lee.[2] The *Daily World* article presumed that racial bias within the all-white-male jury, which "disregarded" evidence that Stratford had initiated the assault, had led it to return a guilty verdict with no recommendation of mercy.[3]

The publicity surrounding the case, including the harsh sentence and the Ingrams' imminent execution, which was set for February 27, provoked immediate protest from black communities throughout Georgia.[4] The outrage and organizing soon spread nationally as the *Pittsburgh Courier*, a black-owned newspaper with a nationwide circulation of close to 250,000, began to cover the story.[5] Such overwhelming grassroots support for this black woman's right to self-defense spurred into action the leading civil rights organizations of the period. The usually cautious National Association for the Advancement of Colored People (NAACP) Legal Defense and Education Fund added the case to its list of civil rights battles and, by March 1948, had taken over as sole legal counsel.[6] Seeking to bring a radical voice and analysis to calls for justice, the Civil Rights Congress (CRC), a Communist Party–affiliated legal defense organization, also voted to begin organizing around the case. The CRC had been founded in 1946, through a merger of several progressive organizations, including the National Negro Congress and the International Labor Defense, which had organized the 1930s Scottsboro campaign.[7]

In many ways, the activism in support of Rosa Lee Ingram exemplified the power of mass-based campaigns that advocated for black defendants convicted by a racially biased criminal justice system. In fact, the fight to end what activists provocatively referred to as "legal lynching" proved fundamental to African American civil rights activism and mass mobilizations during the 1940s and early 1950s.[8] Yet, as the historians Charles Martin and Gerald Horne have shown, the Ingram case displayed significant points of departure from most "legal lynching" cases.[9] As reflected in contemporaneous campaigns to free Odell Waller, Willie McGee, the Martinsville Seven, and the men of Groveland, Florida (as well as the earlier Scottsboro defendants), the most well-known "legal lynching" cases involved black men wrongly convicted and sentenced to die for alleged crimes against white victims, particularly for raping white women.[10] Rosa Lee Ingram turned this gendered paradigm on its head. The campaign focused on Ingram, a widowed black mother from the South, as the symbolic figure, even as her two sons also faced execution. In addition, as highlighted in the quotes that open this chapter, the case pushed front and center black women's experiences with sexualized racial violence and provided an implicit and at times explicit validation of a black defendant's use of deadly force in defending her own life. That this defendant was a black woman protecting herself from assault by a white man lent even greater moral and political force to the cause.

Given this context, Yvonne Gregory's trip to Georgia represented more than just a journalist's hunt for a high-profile story. A committed civil rights activist, she was a key member of the CRC and had worked as an organizer on numerous campaigns challenging the unjust treatment of African American men and women caught in a racist U.S. legal system. Her 1951 visit to the Ingrams' hometown, which she chronicled in the pages of *Masses and Mainstream*, coincided with a new wave of organizing efforts led by black women to free the Ingrams.[11]

In fact, the campaign to free the Ingram family proved a powerful touchstone for black communities and especially for black women activists. The NAACP discovered this in its own mobilizing, and the CRC noted as much in its internal discussions of the case, stating, "Negro women throughout the land stand ready to make Mrs. Ingram's freedom their own cause."[12] As reflected in Yvonne Gregory's travels, black women radicals affiliated with left-leaning organizations such as the CRC provided vibrant organizing and political leadership around the Ingram case. In particular, these activists sought to highlight black women's struggles with sexualized violence and economic exploitation and to engage in ongoing conversations over the meanings of black motherhood and womanhood within the United States. The Ingram case also provided a powerful challenge to long-established assumptions within African American communities about who the victims were, how leadership operated, and what counted as the central issues to be addressed through civil rights activism.[13] Such open discussion of black women's experiences and strategies of resistance reflected an important intervention in the debates over race and gender and over African American civil rights that would inform much of the postwar period.[14]

This chapter provides a detailed study of black women radicals' organizing in support of Rosa Lee Ingram. In writings, mass mobilizations, and organizing strategies, these women rejected a "politics of silence" to demand that black women's encounters with sexualized racism and violence be taken up as core civil rights issues, within both African American communities and in the context of broader government policies.[15] Moreover, in supporting Ingram's actions as self-defense, they advocated for self-protection as a right for all black women. This stance departed from more traditional civil rights calls that advocated the protection of "innocent" and "respectable" black women or framed the protection of black womanhood and black self-defense as the domain of black men.[16] The efforts of these women radicals to address such issues highlights rarely examined aspects of the Ingram case that push beyond understanding it primarily as a campaign to protect a black defendant's right to due process in the law—they reveal the ways many black women employed the case to reframe African American sexual politics and civil rights activism.[17] Such organizing speaks to black women radical's standing as significant strategic thinkers and activists during the early postwar period in defiance of a hardening Cold War anticommunism.

In addition, their efforts to articulate a politics of protection for black women, advocate for a woman's right to control her own body, and promote a broader vision of civil rights activism that explicitly engaged issues of gender, class, and sexual exploitation reflected an emerging feminist politics that offers new connections between civil rights activism and what is traditional called "second-wave" feminism.[18] Indeed, black women's political theorizing and activism around the Rosa Lee Ingram case challenges established narratives of post–World War II feminism that locates its roots primarily in white women's experiences within the civil rights activism of the 1960s and views the demands for greater attention to the intersections of race, gender, sexuality, and class as emerging in the late 1970s and 1980s.[19]

These women's political practices reflected the melding of multiple strategies and ideologies. They called for Negro-white unity, organized an all-black women's civil rights group, and demanded that sexuality and gender be addressed alongside issues of class and race, all in an effort to defend Rosa Lee Ingram and to make real their own visions of liberation. This expansive activism challenges the rigid divides drawn in much of the scholarship on African American radicalism between civil rights organizing and leftist strategies on one hand and integrationist and black nationalist ideologies on the other.[20] In these ways, the campaign to free the Ingram family allowed a community of black women radicals who had committed tremendous energy to civil rights organizing to claim a central role in constructing a broader civil rights politics. In so doing, they laid crucial groundwork for a range of civil rights, feminist, and black power politics that would emerge in later decades.

Leading from the Left

The Ingram case unfolded during the height of McCarthyism and government-led anticommunist attacks on most civil rights organizing. As outlined in chapter 1, for the Communist Party in particular, the postwar years marked a period of unexpected turmoil. By 1947, with the Truman Doctrine's announcement of a Cold War against communism and a growing national emphasis on cultural conformity, progressives were pressured to renounce all affiliations with the left.[21] Such pressure cast a shadow on a range of political work, including activism among black radicals.[22] However, the crisis within the Popular Front coalition did not mean complete defeat or erasure for the entire left. The language of equality and freedom, combined with emerging debates about race and gender, proved useful tools for creating fractures within a narrowing political and social landscape.[23]

The continued vitality of these militant voices reflected, in part, the double-edged sword of 1950s anticommunism. Governmental pressure and the stigma of being labeled "subversive" clearly made it more difficult to continue radical activism. However, those organizations that survived in the face of such pressure often became the only outlets for activists interested in mobilizing around issues such as the Ingram family's case. Therefore, although Atlanta-based members of the NAACP National Legal Committee served as the Ingrams' legal counsel and the national NAACP repeatedly rebuffed the CRC's offers of legal support; sustained national direct-action organizing fell almost exclusively to the CRC and other left-leaning organizations. Even in the midst of anticommunist attacks, a surprising number of African Americans supported these left-led campaign efforts. In fact, by 1951, as the NAACP's efforts ebbed, the Ingram family personally solicited the CRC to help keep the campaign alive. It was within this context of political limitations and opportunities that black women radicals emerged as powerful civil rights activists.

The CRC's National Committee to Free the Ingram Family (NCFIF) along with its more independent offshoot, the Women's Committee for Equal Justice (WCEJ), Paul Robeson's *Freedom* newspaper, and the black women's group Sojourners for Truth and Justice (STJ) each provided vital organizing spaces for an eclectic group of black women working on the Ingram case. Most of these women radicals initially became involved in the case through the Civil Rights Congress. In 1948, as the Ingram case made its way through the appeals courts, the CRC remained distant from the day-to-day legal efforts. CRC members committed much of their time to supporting the Ingram family, particularly Mrs. Ingram's nine youngest children (who were being cared for by her eldest daughter), joining protests, and monitoring the Ingrams' appeals process.[24]

Other women radicals also created women's organizations in support of the case. One of the earliest examples of these efforts was the United Women's Committee to Save the Ingram Family. The New York-based committee counted a number of leading black women activists among its membership, including the labor activist Vicki Garvin and the Harlem activist and CP member Audley "Queen Mother" Moore, who served as organizing secretary. The committee built its base among the "women of Harlem belonging to various organizations" and framed the case as "a flagrant violation of American Civil Rights" and "a shock to human decency." Although few records exist of the organization's work, United Women did distribute a flyer dated March 1948 that called for the Ingrams' "release from jail" and the dropping of "all charges against them" and asked that all property taken by their landlord be "restored to them [the Ingrams] in full." In campaigning for these demands, the committee also called on women to join a delegation to travel from New York to Washington, D.C., on March 18, 1948, to meet with President Truman and Attorney General Tom Clark.[25]

In March, as the United Women's delegation mobilized, the Ingrams' legal team filed a motion for a new trial, arguing that the evidence did not support the jury's verdict, that the defendants had been denied legal counsel, and that the Ingrams were coerced into making incriminating statements.[26] On April 5, 1948, less than a week after the hearing, Judge Harper denied the motion for a new trial but announced that, because of the circumstantial nature of the evidence in the case, he had exercised his judicial discretion to commute the sentences of all three defendants to life imprisonment, with the option for parole after seven years.[27] Supporters claimed a major victory, and the NAACP vowed to continue the legal fight by appealing to the Georgia Supreme Court.

The Ingrams had been convicted by an all-white jury selected through the systematic exclusion of African Americans from the jury pool, a practice deemed illegal in several federal court cases. However, their original court-appointed attorney, S. Hawkins Dykes, failed to challenge this illegal process during the initial trial, thus excluding it as an issue for appeal. Nonetheless, Austin T. Walden, of the NAACP, and his team of defense lawyers presented their case to the State Supreme Court, spotlighting issues similar to those raised in the motion for a new trial, particularly the coerced testimony, the lack of conclusive evidence, and the Ingrams' legal right of self-defense.[28]

On July 13, 1948, the Georgia Supreme Court decided against the Ingram family. The court conceded that it was "difficult from testimony alone to fully comprehend the nature of the State's case" and that the State's arguments "rested upon incriminatory statements made by all three of the defendants." But, it maintained that the jury had had enough evidence to suggest that the fight had occurred in two separate struggles, with Stratford being murdered during the second, and thus that there was enough evidence for the jury "to find there was a sufficient cooling time" between the two struggles "to attribute the slaying to deliberate revenge."[29] The NAACP lawyers immediately filed a motion for a rehearing for Rosa Lee Ingram, which the court also denied.[30] This marked the last of the Ingrams' legal options. After a detailed analysis, the NAACP's Legal Defense Fund determined that an appeal to the U.S. Supreme Court was futile, especially with the question of jury selection a dead issue. Instead, Walden, the lead attorney, embarked on behind-the-scenes negotiations to gain pardons or early parole for the Ingram family.[31]

With the victory of a commuted sentence still fresh and the legal campaign ending, CP member and future CRC executive director William Patterson saw an opportunity for the organization to become a central force in the campaign without coming into "violent conflict" with the NAACP.[32] Asserting "unconditional freedom" as "the basis for the only compromise," Patterson pushed the CRC to build a relationship with the Ingram family and to more "sharply" publicize the "moral issues" of the case to "blast White Middle Class [sic] America out of its complacency."[33] However, a more substantial mobilization around the Ingram case would require building a base among women, particularly black women.

Drawing from CRC staff and a range of women's organizations, Patterson sought to build a mass-based committee of women to work specifically on the Ingram case. This organizing strategy was a clear response to the power of black women's activism in support of the Ingram case and the CRC more generally. It also proved a key opening for black women radicals to serve as the visible leadership of and to set the agenda for a celebrated civil rights campaign. On March 21, 1949, the CRC formed the National Committee to Free the Ingram Family. Founded as a multiracial, women-led effort, the NCFIF drew leadership from a diverse group of black women, including

One of the numerous interracial delegations to travel to Georgia during the 1950s in support of the campaign to free Rose Lee Ingram. Photo by Norma Holt. (Photographs and Prints Division, Schomburg Center for Research in Black Culture, New York Public Library, Astor, Lenox, and Tilden Foundations)

Mary Church Terrell as chairman, Ada Jackson as national vice chairman, Theresa L. Robinson as national executive secretary, Halois Moorhead (later Robinson) as national treasurer, and Maude White Katz as national administrative secretary. These women spanned the spectrum of progressive politics and most operated well beyond the purview of the CP.[34] White Katz and Moorhead, who carried out much of the day-to-day work in the CRC's New York offices, were most closely tied to the CP.[35] The eighty-six-year-old Mary Church Terrell, a founding member and former president of the National Association of Colored Women, was a renowned and distinguished political figure in the black community. Living in D.C. at the time, she added a recognizable national face to the organization. Several other women in leadership also had strong ties to prominent black organizations. Theresa Robinson held the title of National Grand Directress in the Civil Liberties Committee of the Elks, a leading black fraternal organization, and Jackson was executive secretary of Church Women United and co-chair of the Congress of American Women's Anti-lynching Committee.[36] In addition, the official list of sponsors included Mrs. W. A. Scott, co-owner of the *Atlanta Daily World*, who served on several delegations to Georgia; Vivian Carter Mason, of the National Council of Negro Women, who attended the early court hearings in Ellaville; and Velma Hopkins, Viola Brown, and Moranda Smith, all union organizers with the Winston-Salem Tobacco Workers Union, who helped to sustain local work on the case in North Carolina.[37]

As its inaugural action, in April 1949, the National Committee sent an interracial delegation of women to Georgia. Led by Theresa Robinson, the delegation proved a very successful start for the Committee. The delegates visited the Ingram family home and met with Rosa Lee Ingram in Reidsville Prison; although they were not able to meet with Georgia's governor, Herman Talmadge, in person, they did leave a statement at his office. Austin T. Walden, of the NAACP, also met with the delegation and praised Mrs. Terrell's work on the campaign. This represented one of the few public pronouncements of support from the NAACP for a CRC-affiliated action and increased the Committee's political legitimacy among mainstream African American organizations.[38]

This initial event utilized some of the key strategies that would shape much of the Committee's work on the Ingram case. Women in the Georgia delegation emphasized their broad base of support (highlighting the participation of prominent women not affiliated with left-leaning organizations), spotlighted women's leadership, and repeatedly referenced Ingram as a mother and her treatment as an outrage to the honor of American womanhood. Such points would be reiterated in future events and literature. For example, in its "Statement of Purpose," the NCFIF explicitly addressed the murder of Stratford as the act of a woman "defending her honor against a brute."[39] The National Committee was one of the few organizations to publicize Rosa Lee Ingram's May 1949 interview with the *Pittsburgh Courier*, in which she addressed the sexual politics of the case. Its literature prominently featured Mrs. Ingram's own description of the incident as she asserted, "Me and my children was getting along all right until he started at me. He could not make me go his way and he was mad. . . . That is just what it is about—me not having him. I did not want him and I did not have him."[40] The issue of Stratford's sexual advances had not been raised during the trial and had been discussed only sparingly in the media, even as it was often an assumed fact by those outraged at the treatment of Rosa Lee Ingram.

While the National Committee's literature highlighted Stratford's murder as a defense of "Negro womanhood," many of its events centered on Ingram's more "respectable" role as a mother. In a Memorial Day action, the National Committed presented more than thirty thousand signatures to President Truman and Congress from "the American people, and particularly the mothers." The petition urged the release of Mrs. Ingram, the "widowed colored mother of twelve."[41] This petition drive also overlapped with a Mother's Day card-writing campaign that ended with close to ten thousand cards being sent to Washington. Over the next year, the Committee continued to bombard President Truman with petitions, presenting another twenty-five thousand signature in November and collecting almost one hundred thousand signatures in total by the end of the drive.[42]

The National Committee highlighted its defense of black womanhood and emphasized Rosa Lee Ingram's experiences as a mother as a way to frame a radical civil rights politics within more acceptable debates over motherhood and women's citizenship. Ruth Feldstein's work on constructions of motherhood and race details the centrality of debates about respectable womanhood and the role of mothers in the immediate postwar period, including in civil rights activism.[43] The National Committee's rhetoric revealed a strategic choice by black women radicals to engage dominant discourses around American womanhood and to redeploy them in the service of often demeaned and excluded black women. In one respect, this represented a savvy political move, because it allowed black women radicals to present an intersectional analysis that illustrated how racist and classist conceptions of American womanhood (assumed to be white and middle-class) excluded or pathologized nonwhite and working-class women.[44] Moreover, the strategy successfully brought attention to Mrs. Ingram's plight and especially helped to galvanize black communities invested in defending black womanhood. Yet, from another perspective, the persistent emphasis on womanhood and motherhood worked to reinforce limited gender roles for both black and white women and, in the context of radical organizing, relegated black women's leadership to the narrowly defined terrain of "women's issues."

In addition to undertaking mass-based organizing, the National Committee also appealed to the United Nations (UN) for intervention in the case. The National Committee recruited W. E. B. Du Bois to write a UN brief. It also sent delegations to the UN to garner support for its cause and encouraged a letter writing campaign to Warren K. Austin, the U.S. delegate to the United Nations, and to Eleanor Roosevelt, chairman of the Human

Rights Commission, requesting their support. On September 21, 1949, Mary Church Terrell presented the brief to Alva Myrdal, the Acting Assistant Secretary General of the Department of Social Affairs of the UN Secretariat, and, in March 1950, the UN Commission on Human Rights was sent a summary of the Ingram Petition. The campaign created an international stir as the NCFIF publicized the letters of support it had received from around the world and encountered hostile responses from the United States's UN representatives.[45]

Hoping to build on this momentum, in April 1950 the Committee began organizing a protest at the office of the U.S. delegation to the UN. Strategizing for the proposed protest, the NCFIF sought to make broad connections between the Ingram case and earlier struggles that linked African American and women's liberation. The women organizers proposed that protesters dress as Harriet Tubman, Susan B. Anthony, or Sojourner Truth and chant, "We fought for woman's suffrage and won! We fought for the abolition of slavery and won! We came back to free Mrs. Rosa Lee Ingram and her sons!"[46] Such language reflected the Committee's desire to link issues of African American civil rights, international human rights, and women's equality. In employing these strategies, the Committee hoped to push the Ingram case and African Americans' demands for an end to Jim Crow justice beyond a national context and to situate them within international Cold War debates concerning democracy and human rights.

By late 1950 and early 1951, the work of the National Committee to Free the Ingram Family began to ebb. Although the exact cause of this decline remains unclear, part of the slowdown appears related to growing demands within the CRC, which overburdened women involved in the Ingram campaign. Throughout 1951, the CRC intensified its work on Virginia's Martinsville Seven case and Mississippi's Willie McGee case. As court appeals failed and the execution dates neared for these defendants, the CRC sought to raise its level of organizing to save the men.[47] In addition, during the later months of 1951, the CRC published the celebrated book *We Charge Genocide: The Historic Petition to the United Nations for Relief from a Crime of the United States Government against the Negro People.* Edited by William Patterson, with the aid of a range of scholars and CRC activists, including Yvonne Gregory, the petition became a major organizing tool and garnered international attention.[48] The expenditure of energy demanded by such intense mobilizing and the eventual execution of the Martinsville Seven, in February 1951, and Willie McGee, in May 1951, seems to have left the work of the National Committee at a near standstill.[49]

The Sojourners for Truth and Justice

In August 1951, as the National Committee's work on the Ingram case tapered off, a number of left-leaning black women came together to organize a September protest casted as a Sojourn for Truth and Justice. The initiating committee for this event included key activists such as *California Eagle* newspaper editor and owner Charlotta Bass; recent New York transplant Beulah Richardson, who had gained national attention for her poem "A Black Woman Speaks"; Alice Childress, a writer and staff member of *Freedom* newspaper; Louise Thompson Patterson, a longtime CP member and a leader in the black left; Rosalie McGee, the wife of Willie McGee; and Shirley Graham Du Bois, a member of *Freedom*'s editorial board. These organizers sought to bring black women from across the country to Washington, D.C., to meet with members of the Justice Department and to demand a "redress of grievances."[50] Embracing the idea that "those who would be free must strike the first blow," the Sojourners' initiating committee urged black women to unite in "dedicating ourselves to fight unceasingly for the freedom of our people and the full dignity of Negro Womanhood."[51] The Sojourn, which lasted three days, attracted more than 130 "representative" black women from across the nation.[52] The protest specifically emphasized "the wives, mothers and victims of race hatred" and drew inspiration from Mrs. Ingram, whose "militancy had become the symbol of the Sojourn itself."[53]

The organizers made the focal point of the event women who had experienced firsthand the brutality of Jim Crow justice. Among these women were Josephine Grayson, wife of one of the recently executed Martinsville Seven men; Amy Mallard, from Georgia, whose husband had been shot for trying to vote; and Bessie Mitchell, sister of Collis English, one of the six black men arrested for and convicted of armed robbery after a brutal police sweep of the black neighborhood in Trenton, New Jersey.[54] Many of these women had been politicized through their own experiences and their work with the CRC. The protest also centered on the wives of black leaders facing anticommunist investigations, such as Eslande Robeson, the wife of Paul Robeson, and Dorothy Hunton, the wife of W. Alphaeus Hunton, as well as Graham Du Bois and Thompson Patterson, whose husbands, W. E. B. Du Bois and CRC head William Patterson, respectively, also faced harassment. Promoting the slogan "Negro Women dry your tears and speak your mind, we have a job to do," some sixty Sojourners staged a protest at the Justice Department, where they shared their stories of struggle and demanded "the locking up of some of these lynchers."[55] The three days of action also incorporated a press conference at the historic home of Frederick Douglass and a meeting at an area church. Although the event attracted little national coverage, it did garner notice from the FBI, which began a lengthy surveillance of the organization.

The D.C. protest helped to spotlight the indispensable work of black women radicals in linking women's organizing to civil rights activism and sparked the formation of the Sojourners for Truth and Justice (STJ), an all-black women's national civil rights organization.[56] An initial organizing meeting of the STJ in New York on November 10 attracted almost twenty women reflecting a range of progressive politics.[57] Attendees included Claudia Jones, the highest-ranking black woman in the CP, who had been prevented from attending the October Sojourn because of a pending charge under the Smith Act; Audley "Queen Mother" Moore, who had recently left the CP because of its inattention to the African American "national question" and black nationalism; and several women affiliated with local chapters of the NAACP.[58] In its recruitment literature, the new organization also welcomed black women from a range of political perspectives. The preamble to the organization's constitution declared as its goal "to unite all Negro women and extend our united hands to all freedom and peace loving men and women in our nation." In addition, its yearly membership card defined the Sojourners for Truth and Justice as "an independent non-affiliated Negro women's organization."[59] In spite of these efforts at building broad unity, the STJ's core support came from black women who had a history of working both on the Rosa Lee Ingram case and with CP-affiliated groups; they included Yvonne Gregory, Beulah Richardson, Halois Moorhead Robinson, and Bessie Mitchell. A 1952 roster of the National Organizing Committee listed Charlotta Bass as president, Dorothy Hunton as treasurer, and Louise Thompson Patterson as executive secretary.[60]

In its membership, vision, and activities, the STJ represented a significant formation in black women's civil rights organizing. The women of the STJ, perhaps galvanized by a growing sense of their own political power, departed from other left-leaning civil rights activism in explicitly defining their organization as one run exclusively by and for black women seeking to build "a grass roots movement of Negro women."[61] Moreover, the group's dedication to working for "the complete freedom of the Negro people of the United States and the full dignity of Negro womanhood" signified an important if subtle political shift. Unlike CRC committees such as the National Committee to Free the Ingram Family and the Women's Committee for Equal Justice, the Sojourners did not strive to frame themselves as speaking primarily to "women's issues."[62] Instead, the organization claimed to speak and work for the "fifteen million Negro citizens," a domain that in both mainstream and radical organizations had long been dominated by black men.[63] Although the Sojourners rarely addressed intraracial gender relationship or conflicts, their organizing vision clearly challenged a male-dominated leadership. In part, this shift was tied to a political moment in which many established black male leaders, and the left more broadly, were forced to find new leadership as they struggled to weather anticommunist attacks.[64] It also reflected openings created by an increasing emphasis on questions of American womanhood and racial democracy within the public arena.[65] Yet, as their work on the Rosa Lee Ingram case revealed, these women made a concerted effort to step into these openings and to articulate an alternative vision of civil rights politics drawn from their own theorizing of and the lived experiences as black women in the United States.

Creating such space proved at times a complicated and tension-filled process. The founding of the STJ as an all-black women's organization met real resistance from many quarters. During one of its organizing meetings, a heated political disagreement erupted between Charlotta Bass and Beulah Richardson. Bass's September 19, 1951 letter of apology to Richardson suggests that the conflict emerged because of Bass's resistance to framing the initial sojourn as exclusively a black women's protest. In the letter, Bass regretted that her remarks "were construed in such a manner as to place [her] out of step with the Committee's planning" and assured Richardson that "I deem it way past the hour when we should strike out boldly and bravely."[66]

Perhaps strategically attributing critiques only to white activists, Claudia Jones also recounted how some white progressives questioned "whether it is 'correct' for Negro women to form their own organizations or 'shouldn't white women progressives be an integral part of this movement?'" Yet, for Jones, a member of the CP's National Women's Commission and of its National Committee (the party's main leadership body) and a vocal advocate of black self-determination, such concerns were "tinged with white chauvinist arrogance."[67] However, as the Bass encounter suggests, it was not only white members who raised concerns. An editorial in *Freedom* newspaper raised similar questions as it focused on STJ's role as a women's organization. The editorial praised the Sojourners as "forerunners" but believed that the group faced "many problems of policy and tactics." Asserting that "our Sojourners must find a way to place their aspirations in the mainstream of the demands of the majority of Americans," the editorial went on to question how the group would unite "the Negro domestic worker . . . with her white sister in the labor movement for a common assault against the special exploitation of all working women."[68]

Such political questions had long plagued black organizations affiliated with Marxist organizations based in the United States. Yet, these concerns did not deter black women radicals from creating independent spaces that supported their political activism and visions. In the publication *Negro History Week*, CP member Claudia Jones sought to answer these questions. She asserted that "the relationship of white women and white progressives to these emerging [black women] movements . . . must be one of alliance and support."[69] In Jones's view, the Sojourners for Truth and Justice reflected black people's growing self-determination and an advancement for revolutionary politics overall. Some progressive white women did voice their support for such efforts. During the initial Sojourn, the activist and scholar Gene Weltfish wrote a letter, signed by a number of progressive white women, that praised the "courageous leadership" of "our Negro sisters" and acknowledged that "for far too long have we [white women] passively stood by while you have suffered untold dignities and violence." The group gave its "wholehearted support to the Sojourners."[70]

In the months following the September 1951 protest, the Sojourners for Truth and Justice developed a strong base in New York City and a national reach. It established local chapters in the broader New York area, California, Richmond (Virginia), Cleveland, and Chicago, as well as a youth division.[71] The STJ set the "freedom of Mrs. Ingram" as its inaugurating goal. During this campaign, the Sojourners hoped to lead five hundred women to Georgia and invited "our white sisters to work with us as associates" in the fight to free the Ingrams.[72] They also convened an Eastern Seaboard Conference, in March 1952. The conference highlighted the fight for the Ingrams' freedom, urging black women to come and "speak out on a plan of ACTION that will free Rosa Lee Ingram . . . that will win full dignity for Negro womanhood and peace and security for the Negro family."[73] The conference commenced with a summary of the Sojourners' work, followed by discussions of future activities, and ended with several resolutions, including one on Mrs. Ingram. The event drew more than one hundred black women, including representatives from South Carolina and North Carolina.[74] In April, the STJ sent two representatives to the Ingrams' parole hearing. Disappointed by the board's continued refusal to release the Ingrams and by the limited national attention paid to the group's actions, STJ President Charlotta Bass sent a letter to Walter White, the head of the NAACP, seeking to "join hands with the National Association in working toward the freedom of Mrs. Ingram." Ultimately, little came of this push for joint action, and the STJ, as an organization, began to wane in the final months of 1952.[75] The demise of the STJ reflected, in part, just how challenging its politics proved to both the organized left's and more mainstream group's conceptions of civil rights activism. However, the STJ's influence in solidifying the political power and vision of black women on the left would have a lasting impact as its members branched out into other organizing efforts, from Charlotta Bass's groundbreaking 1952 vice presidential campaign on the Progressive Party ticket to black women's continued leadership around the Rosa Lee Ingram case.

Women's Committee for Equal Justice

Just as the Sojourn for Truth and Justice was taking shape, the CRC and its community of women activists began reformulating their work on the Ingram case with the founding of the Women's Committee for Equal Justice (WCEJ). While the WCEJ embraced an interracial membership and framed its work as a "women's issue," it would cover some of the same terrain as the STJ, demanding justice for Rosa Lee Ingram and even drawing support from a number of women, such as Yvonne Gregory and Beulah Richardson, who were also active in the STJ.

The founding of the WCEJ was sparked by a written appeal received August 7, 1951, from Mrs. Ingram's daughter Geneva Rushin, along with legal authorization from Mrs. Ingram for the CRC to take charge of her case.[76] The trip by the thirty-two year-old Yvonne Gregory to Americus during the "August dog days" coincided with this renewed activity. As discussed earlier, Gregory had been a key activist in the CRC campaigns to end "legal lynching" and had also worked on the genocide petition. Following the executions of the Martinsville Seven, in February, she wrote a poem, "Long Distance to Life," for *Freedom* newspaper that contained a searing critique of the U.S. government. The poem bemoans President Truman's refusal to respond to ongoing pleas for intervention and reads his lack of response as a sign of the U.S. government's disregard for black life.

> This here [*sic*] the point my heart sticks on:
> *Our* government lynched the seven
> That GOVERNMENT want to LYNCH us all
> And send US ALL to 'heaven'
> I want my heaven here on earth
> My people want to live
> In this earned land that gave us birth
> We'll TAKE what *you* won't give.[77]

Gregory's poem captured both her feelings of frustration at not being able to prevent any of the Martinsville Seven executions and her determination to continue the fight to end "legal lynching." The frustration would mount as Gregory and the CRC proved unable to halt the execution of Willie McGee less than six months later.

Her passion for justice and her frustration at defeat fueled Gregory's reinvestment in the Ingram case. Her refusal to concede defeat in the fight to prevent "legal lynching" and the recent requests from the Ingram family led her to Americus. Gregory's account of the trip, "Mrs. Ingram's Kinfolk: Two Telephone Calls and a Trip to Georgia," which was carried in the November 1951 issue of *Masses and Mainstream*, revealed these feelings. In it, Gregory confessed, "I got mean that night thinking about . . .Willie McGee . . . and I thought very hard about Mrs. Rosa Lee Ingram." Drawing a clear connection between the treatment of these two black defendants, one executed for "raping" a white women and the other imprisoned for defending herself from assault by a white man, Gregory located the problem in "the precious law." She declared that "[t]he law had got Mrs. Ingram, all right. The same old law that killed Willie McGee."[78]

Gregory's travels also represented one of the many trips to the South made by black women active in the fight against "legal lynching." Indeed, these women drew upon the legacy of Ida B. Wells's turn-of-the-century antilynching campaign and one of the key tactics of the CRC as they traveled to the cities where incidents of racial violence and civil rights injustice occurred to meet with the defendants' families, research the incident, and write personal accounts of their travels.[79] In this vein, Gregory spent several days with Rosa Lee Ingram's family, bringing financial support from the CRC and building ties with Ingram's oldest daughter, Geneva Rushin, and the surrounding community.[80]

Gregory's trip and the CRC's experiences with the Martinsville Seven and the McGee case clearly informed the new Ingram campaign. An outline of a new organizing strategy proposed building the Ingram case as a "nationwide struggle for Negro Rights," comparable to the "historic battles to save the lives of Willie McGee or the Martinsville Seven." The outline went on to frame the work as an opportunity to expose "the government hypocrisy concerning equal rights for the Negro people," while building a "broad national committee of Negro and white women."[81]

The newly formed Women's Committee was national in reach and multiracial in membership. Calls for Negro-white unity notwithstanding, African American women wielded greater leadership power within the WCEJ, with Mary Church Terrell reviving her role as chairman and Yvonne Gregory serving as executive secretary. Furthermore, although the WCEJ still made use of CRC resources, it sought to separate its work from other CRC activities by defining the organization's "sole purpose" as "fighting for the complete, unconditional freedom of Mrs. Rosa Lee Ingram and her two sons."[82] Thus, along with the name change came a growing assertion of independence. This move, undoubtedly linked to efforts to protect the Ingram campaign from the anticommunist attacks launched at the CRC, also suggests that the women of the WCEJ laid an informal claim to leadership and power. This assertion of control would play out in the daily functioning of the organization as several women took William Patterson to task for his gender politics and Mary Church Terrell strongly denounced efforts to use her name in support of other CRC cases.[83]

Working to publicize their analysis and to strengthen the fight to win an early release for the Ingrams, the WCEJ expanded on some of the tactics originally used by the National Committee to Free the Ingram Family. The WCEJ organized several interracial delegations to visit Mrs. Ingram and to meet with state officials in Georgia. In 1952, the Women's Committee led a multiracial Christmas delegation of ten women that gained national news coverage when state troopers halted the group with a court order barring the women from visiting Mrs. Ingram in prison. The interracial delegation also "bumped into" the state's segregation practices as it sought a meeting with Governor Talmadge at his plantation home. The women did eventually meet with the governor, although he "refused to discuss clemency."[84] These direct-action protests and the pressuring of state officials would continue over the next several years as the WCEJ planned yearly prayer vigils, Mother's Day visits, and additional Christmas delegations.

Along with these mobilizations, the Women's Committee brought a new emphasis to some of the common talking points and themes in the Ingram campaign. It continued to proclaim the Ingram case a "woman's issue." For instance, WCEJ literature asserted that, "the dignity and honor of American women, black and white, rests on the winning of justice in such cases as the persecution of Mrs. Ingram."[85] Embracing a theme clearly supported by progressive forces and perhaps seeking to tap into a growing movement for women's equality, the Committee billed the Ingram case as an important struggle for both black and white women.

In its organizing, the WCEJ highlighted the power of black-white unity. However, its brand of interracial solidarity pushed beyond leftist-inspired calls to "unite and fight" to demand that white women actively participate in dismantling white supremacy. The WCEJ acknowledged the ways "Negro women" viewed their freedom as "bound to the freedom of Rosa Lee Ingram" and boldly asserted that "it is high time white women recognize that this holds just as true for them." Articulating a critique of narrow gender politics that also emerged in Richardson's poetry and Claudia Jones's theoretical essays, these women's insights foreshadowed many debates between black and white women in the 1970s. The Women's Committee urged white women to recognize that they "can *truly* protect their rights only when they join with their Negro sisters to protect the rights of *all* women."[86]

Furthermore, in emphasizing the "woman's issue," the WCEJ, more than its predecessor, framed Stratford's sexual advances as a central issue in the case. Organizational literature presented the Ingram case as reflective of the "brutal use of hapless Negro womanhood by white men" that stood as "a vicious hangover from slave days, which still terrorizes every Negro woman." Seeking to connect the Ingram case to the lived experiences of black women in the United States, the Women's Committee reminded supporters that Ingram was "in jail because she defended herself against attack by a white man" and that the number of other Negro women who "have been so attacked in our nation's history is a matter that defies statistics."[87] Such strategies resonated strongly with black women by highlighting their long history of violent sexual exploitation at the hands of white men. This history had been erased in the racial/sexual triangle created by lynching (and "legal lynching") myths that cast black men as rapists, white women as victims, and white men as protectors. Such troubling racial mythology had long mobilized the black community to protest, but, even as these myths were challenged, the sexual exploitation and rape of black women often was not emphasized.[88]

The Women's Committee's efforts to center Rosa Lee Ingram within the history of lynching and sexual violence were captured most poignantly in the poem "The Revolt of Rosa Ingram." The author, Beulah Richardson, had moved to New York from Los Angeles after the success of her poem "A Black Woman Speaks" and at the encouragement of Louise Thompson and William Patterson.[89] In New York, Richardson found a home among the community of black women radicals affiliated with the CRC and *Freedom* newspaper and became an active voice in the fight to end "legal lynching" and a founding member of the STJ.[90] As the STJ ceased operation, Richardson, like many of her fellow members, continued to support the Rosa Lee Ingram campaign through the Women's Committee. Richardson's poem provided a poignant and inspiring dramatization of the case, from Mrs. Ingram's perspective:

But lo, this day there came upon me a
beast walking, talking like a man, but
who can understand the words he speaks
or the gun he carries in his hand . . .
What is this that offers me the end of
a hard and bitter life by letting it
feed, a parasite upon my flesh?
What, oh God can it be that hunts love
with a gun . . . ?

Highlighting the case as an act of resistance to sexual assault, the poem goes
on to indict a Jim Crow legal system that condones racial violence and "legal
lynching," yet denies a black woman the right of self-defense:

Tis the lawless laws of this land
that killed this man. . . .
It's the policeman's billy.
The policeman's gun.
It's lynchers running loose
and nothing ever done.
It's jails packed full of innocent folks
with the real criminals judging in the courts.

Reflective of a feminist politics that would not gain mainstream acceptance
for decades, the final pages of the poem defend Mrs. Ingram's right to her own
body, asserting "these are the laws that killed this man / no wonder he could'nt
[sic] understand / my body belongs to me. / But be calm my sons / men and
women will come. / Must come / to defend a woman's right to her own body."[91]
The WCEJ included the poem in the informational material it sent out to local
chapters. This created quite a stir among women activists, eliciting numerous
requests for copies from local women activists working on the case.[92]

By 1953, Rosa Ingram and her sons had been imprisoned for five years.
Motivated by this, the WCEJ began a new wave of organizing to secure
an early release for the Ingrams. In December, the Women's Committee
arranged another Christmas delegation to Atlanta that coincided with a
holiday letter-writing campaign. The letter campaign elicited at least some
response from Governor Talmadge; on December 2, he replied to a Brooklyn woman's letter that urged the governor to grant clemency to the Ingram
family.[93] Later in the month, the delegation, led by Mary Church Terrell,

Members of the Ingram delegation outside Georgia's State Board of Pardons and Paroles, n.d. Photo by Norma Holt. (Photographs and Prints Division, Schomburg Center for Research in Black Culture, New York Public Library, Astor, Lenox, and Tilden Foundations)

arrived in Georgia. The protest included a rally and a prayer meeting in front of the Georgia State Capitol, a presentation of petitions and meeting with Governor Talmadge, and an afternoon conference on the case. Although the delegation mobilized enough political power to have its demands heard in person, throughout the brief meeting with the governor he maintained that jurisdiction rested with the State Board of Pardons and Paroles and that he had "no authority" in the case.[94]

Hoping to build on this work, the WCEJ planned a year of extensive campaigns for 1954. The year's activities started with a major meeting aimed at recruiting leading black leftists to the campaign. The invite list included the labor organizer Vicki Garvin, who hosted the event at her home, as well as Eslanda Robeson, Claudia Jones, Paul Robeson, and longtime CP-affiliated activists Harry Haywood, Dorothy Burnham, and Esther Cooper Jackson.[95] The new push also sought to reinvigorate local CRC chapters and familiar allies such as the labor organizer Viola Brown, who worked on the Ingram case through the People's Defense Committee in Winston-Salem.[96] In addition, Patterson reached out to the antiracist activist Anne Braden in the hope of building support for the campaign among white women and church activists in Louisville.[97]

The WCEJ also emphasized its broad base of support as it continued to send out postcards and petition urging Governor Talmadge and the Board of Pardons and Paroles to release the Ingram family. The postcards, several of which included drawings by the renowned black artist and longtime CRC supporter Charles White, as well as other campaign material contributed by Elizabeth Catlett, reflected the CRC's efforts to increase the campaign's mass appeal by publicizing the support of established black figures.[98] One petition presented as individually signed Mother's Day cards, with the Charles White drawing on the front, implored the governor to honor the day "in deed by granting this mother a taste of freedom."[99] Another Mother's Day letter sent to the parole board in 1954 carried the signature of a number of "prominent Americans," including W. E. B. Du Bois, the Chicago attorney Earl Dickerson, Professor Louise Pettibone Smith, and Alice Childress. The letter reminded the Board that "every hour that Mrs. Rosa Lee Ingram suffers imprisonment widens and deepens the stain of dishonor on America's democratic record" and that public voices, including those of "the vice president of the Georgia Bar Association, the Colored Elks and Walter White . . . have all bitterly excoriated this case as a shocking aberration of justice."[100] These appeals coincided with the arrival in Atlanta of another interracial Mother's Day delegation of fifty women, including Rosa Lee Ingram's mother, Amy Hunt, who personally appealed to Board members for her daughter's release. Although the Board refused to take any action and unanimously voted to not review the case again until August 1955, the WCEJ delegation did garner widespread publicity.[101]

Moreover, this demonstration of broad-based support sparked a new wave of interest in the WCEJ and in the Ingram campaign. The WCEJ attracted the attention of a surprising range of women's organizations; the Woman's Convention Auxiliary of the National Baptist Convention sent a letter proclaiming "one hundred per cent [*sic*] " support, and a request for fliers was received from a black woman in Oregon who had recently heard about the WCEJ and felt "that I must do something for Mrs. Ingram."[102] The renewed wave of petitions, delegation visits, and growing mass support also forced a response from the White House. In June 1954, Maxwell M. Rabb, the secretary to the cabinet and the point person for President Eisenhower's civil rights programs, wrote to Mary Church Terrell to acknowledge the president's receipt of her April letter concerning the Ingram case.[103] In his response, Rabb denied that he had any power to intervene and argued that the case involved issues "concerning state jurisdiction and where Federal intervention is not appropriate."[104] While such continued refusals to intervene proved disappointing, the WCEJ's success in engaging key government officials helped to keep attention on the case and demonstrated the power of the group's direct-action protests.

After working for almost two years to re-energize its base of support, the WCEJ suffered a major blow in July 1954 with the passing of Mary Church Terrell. She was a singular figure among black women activists, and her stature and her investment in the work had provided the WCEJ with access to a network of African American organizations. The lost of Terrell's national leadership also coincided with increased anticommunist attacks on the CRC, as the U.S. government declared it a subversive organization and sought to gain access to its membership list. Within this context, it appears that, from late 1954 on, the WCEJ functioned only sporadically as a national organization. As a result, work on the Ingram case shifted to more locally based groups.

In 1955 the New York-based Provisional Committee to Free the Ingrams, under the leadership of Maude White Katz, emerged as a central voice in continuing the Ingram campaign. Working with the Georgia Ingram Club, the Los Angeles Committee to Free the Ingrams, and the Philadelphia Women's Committee for Equal Justices, the Provisional Committee issued a leaflet on "what you and your organization can do." In it, the Committee called for letter writing campaigns and local educational efforts to raise awareness about the Ingrams' plight.[105] White Katz and the Provisional Committee also coordinated the annual Mother's Day protest in Atlanta and in July joined a delegation to Washington that included Amy Hunt (Rosa Lee Ingram's mother) and the Reverend William Philpott. The delegation presented the Ingrams' case to the White House, the Justice Department, and the offices of Georgia Senator Walter George.[106] In August, another delegation of local Ingram committees from across the country traveled to Atlanta, this time for the Ingrams' hearing before the parole board. Many involved with the case felt hopeful because the August hearing marked the Ingrams' first official year of eligibility. Yet such optimism proved greatly misplaced, as the meeting ended in a two-to-one vote against parole.[107]

Over the next few years, black women radicals continued to use direct-action protests and mass mobilizations in the fight to free the Ingram family. White Katz and the Provisional Committee sought to link the case to "the brutal lynching of 14-year old" Emmett Till and to mobilize "people of goodwill here [in the U.S.] and abroad."[108] In a September 1955 mailing that listed Mrs. Amy Hunt as "Honorary Chairman," the Provisional Committee outlined a plan of action that included organizing a delegation to petition the UN's Commissions on Human Rights and the Status of Women, a national conference and protest in D.C. on Human Rights Day, and a letter-writing campaign to every member of the U.S. Congress.[109] The Provisional Committee also hoped to use Rosa Lee Ingram's birthday as a key date in its mobilizing and support campaign. The following year, the Women's Committee for Equal Justice also took up the birthday theme by sponsoring "an evening in honor of the 49th Birthday of Mrs. Rosa Lee Ingram." The event, scheduled for October 5, included appearances by the poet Beulah Richardson, the songwriter Earl Robinson (who performed his "Ballad of America"), and Josephine Grayson, a widow of one of the Martinsville Seven "martyrs."[110] While these activities helped to sustain some support for the campaign to free the Ingram family, they continued to produce little movement on the part of the parole board or other government officials.

Freedom for the Ingram Family

Resisting protests from black women activists and despite years of negotiations with the NAACP, the Georgia Board of Pardons and Paroles continued to deny the Ingrams parole long after they had served the seven-year minimum, in 1955. The Board's refusal to free Rosa Lee Ingram and her two sons would outlast most of the national campaigns to gain their freedom. The growing government harassment and prosecution of the black left clearly played a role in slowing down the work of national organizations such as the STJ and the WCEJ. The STJ had come under constant FBI surveillance, as reflected in the group's 460-page FBI file. In addition, throughout the group's existence, a number of the women active in its leadership, including Claudia Jones, Charlotta Bass, and Louise Thompson Patterson, were dealing with their own or their husbands' legal and financial battles.[111] The Civil Rights Congress and, by association, the WCEJ suffered similar fates. Although it refused to be politically bowed by government harassment, by 1955 the CRC could no longer sustain the fight financially as mounting legal bills led the organization to close its doors.

Anticommunist attacks on black women's activism around the Ingram case did not come solely from the U.S. government. Before the 1957 parole hearing, the *Pittsburgh Courier* published an interview with Hugh Carney, chairman of the Board of Pardons and Paroles. Assuring *Courier* readers that freedom for the Ingrams was imminent if "nobody 'rocks the boat,'" Carney specifically noted that the actions of the delegation led by the Provisional Committee and the continued letter campaigns "did not help the situation." Presenting Carney as the lone vote in support of paroling the Ingrams in 1955, the paper urged its readers to refrain from all demonstrations and protests before the hearing.[112]

The article lent fuel to a common complaint launched by the NAACP, which framed the CP-affiliated CRC and its direct-action protests as hindering legal negotiations.[113] But the degree to which the more radical strategies and affiliations actually hindered the legal campaign or simply provided a convenient excuse to explain the continued denial of leniency remains open to debate.[114] In fact, considerable evidence suggests that the CRC's organizing strategies proved central to pushing the campaign forward, particularly since the initial success in preventing the Ingrams' execution coincided with a wave of mass protest. Nonetheless, the perspective detailed in the *Pittsburgh Courier* gained a great deal of traction, particularly in the midst of Cold War anticommunism.[115]

Over the next few years, the Ingram case operated on a quieter register. The argument that protests were detrimental to the Ingrams' case appears to have curtailed the organizing efforts of local Ingram committees, including the Provisional Committee.[116] Yet, even after relatively calm hearings in 1957 and 1958, the Board continued to reject the Ingrams' request for parole, leading the *Courier* to concede by 1958 that the "Ingram seem to be a victim of Georgia's 'system.'"[117] Indeed, many African Americans came to believe that the fact that the NAACP, the CRC, and black women's organizing had not proved successful in winning freedom for the Ingram family reflected "rank discrimination" and the unwillingness of the U.S. government to address the entrenchment of "legal lynching" within the criminal justice system.[118] As the work of the scholar Charles Martin attests, whether led by local movements, the NAACP, or CP-affiliated organizations, few southern criminal defense cases were able to chart a path to victory for black defendants when a white victim had suffered.[119]

Not until August 1959, after the appointment of new Board members and after the Ingrams had spent more than ten years in prison, were Rosa Lee Ingram and her two sons, Wallace and Sammie Lee, awarded parole. Proclaimed "model prisoners" by the warden, Wallace, Sammie Lee, and Rosa Lee were released into the care of C. R. Yates, an Atlanta-based pharmacist, and Warren Cochrane, executive secretary of the Butler Street YMCA. There was intense press coverage of their release as the black press, including *Jet*, and the *Pittsburgh Courier* ran special features charting the Ingrams' adjustment to life after prison.[120]

Conclusion

Although the activism of black women radicals who found common cause with Rosa Lee Ingram and campaigned diligently for her freedom came to a difficult end, the work of these women would provide important political lessons and strategies for emergent social movements. Their strategic insights and analysis could be read as setting the stage for public campaigns such as Mamie Bradley's speaking tour to gain justice for her murdered son, Emmett Till, and for guiding the work of women's committees as crucial organizing spaces in the Montgomery bus boycott, which began in 1955. Their work also contributed to an important shift in the tone of civil rights activism, which increasingly presented black women's experiences as integral to defining the struggle for black civil rights. The shift, however, did not necessarily translate into greater acceptance of black women's leadership. Nonetheless, as detailed in chapter 5, this activism did provide a useful guidepost for future black women leaders and organizations and would resonate in defense campaigns launched in support of black women defendants such as the "Free Angela Davis" campaign led by the CP in the early 1970s and the 1974 Joan Little campaign.

4

Race and Gender at Work

*From the Labor Journalism of Marvel
Cooke to Vicki Garvin and the National
Negro Labor Council, 1935–1956*

It is the burning desire of every Negro woman to be free, to
live and work in dignity, on equal terms with all other workers.
Negro women are eager to undertake a greater role to give sub-
stance to freedom and democracy, to help build an America of
peace and abundance.
                                              —Vicki Garvin, *Freedom*, 1950

Thunderous applause greeted Vicki Garvin as she rose to issue the
opening remarks at the National Negro Labor Council's (NNLC) founding
convention, on October 27, 1951, in Cincinnati. "We are making history here
today," Garvin proclaimed, as the first official speaker of the meeting that
brought together more than one thousand black and white labor activists.
Referencing the organizers' vision of merging the struggle for civil rights
and the fight for "better jobs in industry for Negro men and women," Garvin
went on to proudly declare the convention a "major development in the
struggle of the Negro people for freedom and equality." Garvin's hopeful outlook reflected her own investment in the NNLC. Introduced by the convention's chairman, Sam Parks, who celebrated her as the person "who has done
more, in my opinion, than any one individual in order to make this Convention possible," Garvin had been involved in the organization since its inception at the 1950 National Conference of Negro Labor Councils, in Chicago.[1]
She also served as the lead member of the convention's National Planning
Committee and would go on to provide central leadership for numerous
NNLC campaigns.

Garvin, however, was not alone in her optimism for the national organization, which established its main office in Detroit. In reporting on the conven-

tion for *Masses and Mainstream*, Yvonne Gregory wrote, "[I]f I had to choose one word to fix the mood of the meeting, the handclaps, the speeches, the listening, the doing, I would choose the word gleeful."[2] The enthusiasm with which many labor activists welcomed the founding of the NNLC suggests its unique position within a labor movement that increasingly marginalized left leadership during the 1950. The NNLC's unapologetic affiliation with CP members clearly limited its influence. But, for many left-leaning labor activists who were committed to building multiracial and mixed-gender fighting unions, the organization's commitment to racial and gender equality and to active grassroots organizing provided a much-needed and inspiring alternative.

This proved especially true for black women active in the U.S. labor movement. The NNLC maintained a keen emphasis on organizing black women workers and emerged as a crucial hub for black women labor activists. The NNLC's attention to women workers reflected in part a response to the shifting dynamics of the U.S. labor force. The 1940s and 1950s marked a key period in the rise of women to positions of leadership within labor unions, and there was an increasing emphasis among African American women on addressing the intersecting forces of race, gender, and economic discrimination. As one black woman declared from the floor of the NNLC convention, "Negro women are on the offensive . . . we're on that other seat on the Freedom Train driving when that other man goes to sleep."[3]

Taking on leadership roles and theorizing around the race and gender politics of labor, black women radicals helped to carve out spaces for continued resistance. They strove to sustain an alternative radical voice in a U.S. labor movement whose top leadership had, for the most part, conceded to Cold War conservatism.[4] Focusing on the labor journalism of Marvel Cooke, who detailed the plight of black women domestic workers as an investigative reporter for *The Daily Compass*, and the labor activism of Vicki Garvin, from her work with the UOPWA and her writings in *Freedom* to her leadership in the NNLC, this chapter documents the political and intellectual contributions of these women radicals to developing a more expansive labor politics.

The work of Cooke, Garvin, and the women in the NNLC reveals some of the insights black women brought to debates over labor organizing and workers' rights. They insisted that trade unions should view the political struggles for African American civil rights and women's equality as key labor issues. Their writing and organizing often focused on the urgent nature of the struggles of black women workers. Yet, they worked to expose the ways race, gender, and region shaped all workers' economic opportunities and working experiences in the United States. These women advanced a political vision that expanded on a strict economic analysis, which viewed workers' rights solely in terms of working conditions and pay. Their activism highlighted the ways in which multiple social forces beyond the shop floor intersected to shape workers' options, needs, and opportunities. In so doing, they underlined the need for a labor movement that could address these realities.

Trade unions had long proved a core source of support and a crucial base of power for the organized left, including the CP, which had invested heavily in the founding of the Congress of Industrial Organizations (CIO) during the 1930s. Indeed, Michael Denning argues that "the base of the Popular Front was the labor movement, the organization of millions of industrial workers into the new unions of the CIO."[5] For many black women radicals, including Garvin and Cooke as well as Maude White Katz and Thelma Dale Perkins, the union movement served as a central site of politicization and engagement. Thus, the postwar curtailment of workers' rights and attacks on labor-left alliances reflected a profound reshaping of the U.S. union movement and the organized left. Historians of McCarthyism and U.S. Cold War domestic politics have thoroughly documented the costs and the constraints endured by left-leaning labor activists and the unions in which they worked.[6] However, the fallout and turmoil produced by the decline of powerful left-led unions does not tell the entire story of U.S. labor in the late 1940s and 1950s. A number of studies have uncovered pockets of resistance and radical union organizing during this period, particularly among women and African American workers.[7]

The labor activism of Marvel Cooke, Vicki Garvin, and the women of the NNLC should also be read in the context of these overlooked politics of resistance and organizing within the labor movement. While their lives clearly reflect some of the costs of radical affiliations and resistance, they also reveal the often-obscured political opportunities and victories that were achieved by black women workers and the labor left as they continued to challenge Cold War rollbacks. In the face of intense anticommunist attacks, these black women (and other) radicals continued their political affiliation with the Communist Party creating strategies of survival and communities of support that allowed them to maintain a militant politics. The continued labor activism of these women, largely outside formal union structures, marked them as a distinct community of activists that can be added to those insightfully defined by Dorothy Sue Cobble as "the labor feminists of the post depression decades." For, as Cobble outlines, these black women radicals also "articulated a particular variant of feminism that put the needs of working-class women at its cores" and "championed the labor movement [albeit in a more

Leadership of the National Negro Labor Council at work in 1951, with Vicki Garvin at the typewriter, Ernest Thompson (standing leg on chair), and William Hood (to the left of Thompson). (Courtesy of Miranda Bergman)

expansive and community-based form] as the principle vehicle through which the lives of the majority of women could be bettered."[8] Moreover, they demanded that labor unions address the multiple forces, including race, region, and gender, that limited women's opportunities.

The Left and Cold War Labor Politics

As suggested earlier, the early Cold War period presented the U.S. labor movement with a new set of challenges, openings, and constraints. As war mobilization produced a profound shift in labor demographics, African Americans, women, and southern migrants all gained greater power and visibility among unionized workers in the United States, particularly within the CIO unions. As the war came to an end, however, these gains came under attack. Industry, government, and, to a certain extent, unions moved to reinstall prewar job structures that prioritized employment for working men.

Hard-won government programs such as the Fair Employment Practice Committee (FEPC) began to lose what little power they held, while the U.S. Employment Agency, which had earlier urged women to take war-industry jobs, now supported the removal of women from the workforce so that both the jobs and the women were available to returning soldiers.[9]

Although in the postwar years women and African Americans faced greater limitation in their job options, the transformations wrought by war migration and wartime openings in industry and unions were not so easily curtailed. For most women workers, removal from higher-paying industrial jobs did not mean a retreat from working, just a shift to lower-paying "women's work," including clerical and service jobs or (for many black women workers) a return to domestic service. Therefore, while the number of women working in "durable goods industries" dropped 50 percent after the war, the overall net decline in the number of women workers in the first postwar year was considerably less. In fact, as the historian Ruth Milkman points out, "by the early 1950s the number of gainfully employed women exceeded the highest wartime level, and as early as 1948 the labor force participation rate of married women was higher than at the peak of the war boom."[10] This narrative of tempered gains also held true for black workers. As a result of seniority and racial discrimination, African Americans' postwar unemployment rates increased twice as fast as those of white workers, yet greater numbers of black workers were able to shift from lower-paying agricultural jobs to industrial and service work.[11]

The continued employment of African Americans and women as unskilled and skilled industrial workers even after "reconversion" helped to reshape trade unions. While women's union membership dropped in the immediate postwar period, by 1956 the number of female union members had reached more than three million, surpassing women's membership during wartime.[12] Newly unionized workers struggled to sustain their wartime gains and demanded that they be included in union leadership. In addition, the very presence of a more diverse membership forced trade unions to address issues of race and gender that even the most progressive labor unions had often sidestepped.[13] By protesting against unequal pay and job segregation, demanding union accountability, and organizing resistance to Cold War anticommunism, many workers, particularly those in CIO unions, pushed labor leadership to address their concerns. Black women leftists provided key leadership and on-the-ground activism on several fronts, including endeavors to maintain wartime gains, such as the struggle to create a permanent FEPC; campaigns to organize nonunionized workers and establish unions in the South, such as the drive to organize tobacco workers in Winston-Salem; and efforts to end pervasive job segregation.[14] These campaigns met with only limited success, as workers often had to battle both their own unions and government labor policies that sought to limit workplace activism, in addition to management's demands.[15]

By 1950, the labor movement found itself on the losing end of the dismantled New Deal liberal-left coalition. Established trade unions came under continued assaults from both industry and the government, most notably through the 1947 Taft-Hartley Act. The act placed legal restrictions on union activity, including banning secondary boycotts, allowing states to limit union shops, and requiring union officials to sign a noncommunist affidavit in order to win hearings before the National Labor Relations Board (NLRB).[16] This last provision empowered a variety of anticommunist forces within labor and fueled a series of purges of CP-affiliated labor activists between 1949 and 1950 that decimated some of the most progressive unions.[17] Many of these purges helped produce a more conservative labor politics that included an explicit resistance to fighting racial and gender inequalities, the use of destructive membership raids of weaker locals, and increasing concessions to business and government interests.

Leftists within the labor movement found fewer and fewer options for negotiating the limited political landscape as the postwar period gave way to Cold War policies. While many labor historians have highlighted these shifts as a moment of profound decline from the heights of Popular Front unionism, in many ways these clashes simply brought to the fore longstanding struggles within the labor movement that could not be contained or patched over in this period of crisis. In addition, the explicit anticommunist turn forced many in the labor left to develop new strategies for survival and resistance. While such resistance did not profoundly alter the overall conservative trends within the union movement, it did challenge the status quo and provide some important victories for both working people and unions.

Many black labor radicals continued to invest in union organizing but also sought to create change and a new base of support by linking their work to community and civil rights organizations. Maida Springer, a leading AFL activist in the anticommunist-dominated International Ladies Garment Workers Union (ILGWU), noted this shift as a guest writer for the *Los Angeles Tribune*. In the 1946 article "The Trend in Negro Leadership," she praised the increase in voices "of men and women from the ranks of labor" in community and culture organizations, and its impact in broadening the scope of their programs:

Negro workers have also taken their union education to heart and branched out. . . . As a result practically every big-town branch of the NAACP and the Urban League today gives increasing attention to workers [*sic*] problems, while Negro ministers—long regarded as the bulwark of conservative leadership—no longer hesitate to address union meetings. I for one consider this whole development to be healthy in every way.[18]

Much as Vicki Garvin outlined in her opening remarks at the founding of the NNLC, the work of black women active in the CP orbit—from Marvel Cooke's series of investigative reports on black women working at the economic margins to the efforts of the women labor activists who joined Garvin at the NNLC—helped to build key community-labor links. In addition, these women worked to create space for activists who advocated for black women workers during a period of shrinking options for radical labor organizing. Such activism reveals the conscious attempts by many labor radicals to connect to an emerging civil rights movement, even as more mainstream union leadership resisted such direct ties. Black women's efforts to redefine labor politics in the early Cold War years represent some of the often-overlooked organizing accomplished by radical women within the postwar period. Moreover, their active resistance and the political restrictions they faced provide a new context for exploring what Robert Korstad and Nelson Lichtenstein have defined as a moment of "opportunities found and lost."[19]

Marvel Cooke's Labor Journalism and the Domestic Workers' "Slave Market"

As underscored by the effort to establish a permanent FEPC and to achieve the goals of the NNLC, black women's relegation to low-paying, unskilled labor emerged as a defining issue in the fight to improve the conditions of all black workers. No job came to symbolize the exploitation of black women workers more than that of domestic worker. Historically, domestic labor was marked as black women's work and often provided the only source of employment for black women regardless of their training, education, and skills.[20] Thus, the disproportionate number of black women working as low-paid domestics had long served as the most prominent example of the limitations black women faced within a race-and gender-segregated labor market and as a symbol of the importance of organizing the unorganized. As noted in chapter 1, the exploitation of domestic workers proved a common concern for many black women radicals and a key entry point for engaging questions of race, gender, and labor during the 1930s. A number of black women supported the efforts of the National Negro Congress and the Domestic Workers Union (DWU) to improve conditions and to challenge the exclusion of these workers from social security protection.[21]

Marvel Cooke was a key voice in popularizing these issues and an active supporter of labor organizing more broadly. In 1935 she co-authored, with the future civil rights activists Ella Baker, her first exposé about the situation of black women domestic workers, titled "The Bronx Slave Market."[22] The brief piece detailed the struggles of black women seeking informal employment as day laborers during the Great Depression. The article produced quite a stir within black communities in New York as it brought increased attention to the issue.[23] During this period, Cooke also worked with the American Newspaper Guild to help unionize the editorial staff of the black-owned *New York Amsterdam News*. Following a successful boycott, Cooke returned to the paper as a reporter and a newly minted member of the Communist Party.[24]

Making use of her new position and her political affiliations, Cooke continued to push the issue of black domestic workers and black women workers more generally. She returned to the topic of her 1935 investigative piece, writing numerous articles between 1937 and 1941 on the treatment of black domestics. Under headlines like "Modern Slaves," "Bronx 'Slave Mart' Flourishes," and "Slavery . . . 1939 Style," Cooke tracked the mistreatment of black women domestics. Highlighting their long hours, low pay, and experiences with often-abusive employers, Cooke sought to give voice to many of the women's personal stories, including the limited opportunities that led them to work as day laborers. Each of the articles also presented the work of the DWU as a key part of the solution, alongside calling for legislative intervention.[25]

Cooke's persistent attention to the problem forced a response from local government. Mayor Fiorello La Guardia formed a "Committee on Street Corner Markets" and, in 1941, announced the opening of two employment agencies to combat the use of street-corner markets in the Bronx.[26] Despite the impact of her investigative reports, Cooke remained frustrated and unsatisfied with the sensationalist focus of the *Amsterdam News*. In 1942, she moved on to the *People's Voice*, a progressive black newspaper founded by Adam Clayton Powell Jr., a member of the New York City Council and a future member of the U.S. House of Representatives. Hired as an assistant managing editor, Cooke spent much of her time handling administrative duties and authored only a few articles. As a result of her new position and expanding wartime labor opportunities for black women, between 1941 and 1950 Cooke did not revisit the issue of domestic workers or the "Bronx Slave Market."[27]

As World War II came to an end, the mistreatment of domestic workers again emerged as a focal point in public discourse concerning the exploitation of black women workers. This renewed interest resulted from the rollback of black women workers' wartime gains in industrial employment, which actually led to a greater number of black women working in domestic service than had done so in 1940.[28] Labor activists highlighted the plight of domestic workers to illustrate the impact of these rollbacks and to push for greater opportunities for black women outside domestic work. This served as a major theme in much of the writing and organizing of Vicki Garvin and other members of the NNLC, as they demanded an end to job segregation and fought for union representation. Demands for better jobs often produced only limited, if strategically significant, results. Therefore, many black women radicals attacked the exploitation of black domestics with a twofold strategy designed to create better employment opportunities for black women and to establish some rights and protections for the many women workers who still relied on domestic employment, especially as informal day laborers.

This twofold strategy received particular emphasis among black women radicals seeking to push the left to speak more directly to the concerns of black women workers. Claudia Jones's 1949 article "An End to Neglect of the Problems of the Negro Woman!" included a four-page section titled "The Domestic Worker." In this section, Jones argued that the exploitation of black women domestics reflected the "crassest manifestation of trade union neglect" and stood as a prime example of the failure of the labor left to really organize the unorganized. She presented black women domestics as a powerful example of workers facing oppression both as women and as black people and described them as a central constituency in progressive politics. Yet, Jones also viewed "the continued relegation of Negro women to domestic work" as helping to "intensify chauvinism directed against all Negro women." She declared that "the very economic relationship of Negro women to white women" perpetuates "madam-maid" relationships between white and black women and "feeds chauvinist attitudes."[29] Such framing spoke to the ways black women radicals sought to support the rights of domestic workers at the same time that they hoped to disrupt domestic labor's attendant racial and gendered coding.

Alice Childress's column "Conversations from Life," which ran in *Freedom* on a regular basis starting in 1951, took a slightly different approach. She presented a more spirited and valorizing portrayal of black women domestics. Focusing on the insights of a wise and humorous domestic named Marge,

Childress addressed the experiences and concerns of domestic workers. Her column not only revealed the ways in which white supremacy shaped black women's interactions with their white employers but also underscored the unique gender and class politics that defined domestics in the workplace. The columns proved so successful that they were picked up by the *Baltimore Afro-American* and in 1956 were published as a book, *Like One of the Family: Conversations from the Life of a Domestic.*[30]

When Cooke returned to journalism in 1950 as a reporter at *The Daily Compass,* she joined these black women radicals in again publicizing the plight of black domestic workers. *The Daily Compass,* a short-lived New York City paper with a leftward tilt and private funding began publication in May 1949. Ted O. Thackrey, a former editor of the *New York Post,* served as publisher and editor. The paper, which had an ambitious initial run of 150,000 and more than eighty-five employees, billed itself as "independent" and "liberal," "a radical newspaper" seeking to "take a stand on issues." For Cooke, the only black person and the only woman on staff, the position marked her first time working for a large daily newspaper and within the mainstream white press. Although the experience was at times challenging, Cooke also remembered it as "very exciting—the most exciting time I had as a journalist." In part, this excitement came from the opportunity to do lengthy articles and investigative reporting, what she defined as the "creative work" of journalism.[31]

Cooke's five-part series revisiting the "slave markets" published almost fifteen years after her first exposé on the subject represented the type of "creative work" she relished. Cooke's articles won strong support from the paper's editor, garnering front-page billing and coverage in the *Compass Sunday Magazine.* The investigative reports, built around Cooke's account of her experiences posing as a domestic worker for hire in the Bronx, relied on her years of writing on the topic. Although the front-page lead touted "a personal experience" and "I was a slave" served as the article's provocative first line, Cooke actually used the first article of the series to detail the history of the "slave markets" in New York. "Born in the last depression the Slave Markets are products of poverty and desperation," Cooke warned readers. She tied the decline of the "market" since 1941 to government interventions and the availability of factory jobs for unskilled and skilled labor. But Cooke maintained that "as Negro women are thrown out of work . . . the markets threaten to spread. . . . They grow as employment falls. Today they are growing."[32]

In Cooke's analysis, black women workers faced exploitation not because they were household workers but because they were "unprotected workers" who could be hired informally by the hour or day "at depressed wages." Thus, for Cooke, it was not the job itself that proved problematic but the fact that these black women were treated as a "commodity." Equating the humiliating experience of being selected from the scores of women waiting on a corner to be hired with being purchased at a slave market, Cooke described the "primitive" process as follows:

> The housewife goes to the spot where she knows women in search of domestic work congregate and looks over the prospects. She almost undresses them with her eyes as she measures their strength to judge how much work they can stand. If one of them pleases her, the housewife asks what her price is by the hour. Then she beats that price down as low as the worker will permit.

Cooke zeroed in on the sexualized undercurrent of the exchange as well as "the viciousness and indignity" that forced black women to barter their bodies on the streets, comparing the process to "selling . . . a cow or a horse in the public market."[33]

As Cooke experienced firsthand, the real economic exploitation of domestic workers occurred once they accepted a job. While the standard hourly rate for domestics stood at around one dollar an hour, Cooke discovered that in the market the going rate peaked at only seventy-five cents. Often employers (usually white housewives) would push workers to complete more work than agreed upon, charge for meals, or "criticize work as a build-up for not paying the worker the full amount of money."[34] The exposé also called attention to the ways that the employment of black women domestics as casual day labor allowed many white women who could not afford a full-time domestic to access domestic services and its attendant increase in social status, if only on a temporary basis. In addition, the labor of black women domestics, from the backbreaking tasks of washing windows and scrubbing floors to ironing, proved crucial in allowing white women to live up to the ideal image of women as skilled homemakers. The same access to the status and markers of womanhood did not exist for the black women who provided this largely hidden labor. These insights by Cooke reflected a common theme that emerged in the writings by black women on the left as they critiqued the ways white women participated in and benefited from black women's exploitation.

The indignity of the process for black women did not end with low wages or white women's racism. As Cooke also highlighted, such public exchanges of black women's bodies made them more vulnerable to "men on the prowl." In recounting her own experiences, Cooke writes, "Twice I was hired by the hour at less than the wage asked by the women of the market. Both times I went home mad. . . . Once I was approached by a predatory male—who made unseemly and unmistakable advances. And I was mad all over again." Although Cooke provided few specifics about these "unseemly" offers, she clearly rejected the stereotypical image of black women as sexual predators and invoked the long history of black women's vulnerability to white men's sexual exploitation.[35] Such references must have had particular resonance for those familiar with the issue of black women's sexual vulnerability and rights to self-protection that had been raised by the recently initiated campaign to free Rosa Lee Ingram. Cooke's encounters with "men on the prowl" led her to focus a subsequent investigative report on prostitution and the women's court. Unlike the series on domestic workers, these reports did not focus on black women's experiences, but the series did treat a similar theme: the exploitation of women who were reliant on informal employment markets, without any government resources or protection, in a postwar economy.[36]

Throughout the series, Cooke sought to convey the devastating impact of such exploitation on the women for whom the "slave market" was an "everyday experience." In part, she argued, the experiences marked these women in identifiable ways, ranging from the "dejected droop" of their shoulders and their "work worn hands" to their "look of bitter resentment" and the "paper bags" holding their work clothes. By employing less-than-flattering descriptions, Cooke sought to illustrate the harshness and injustice of their situation. Thus, most of her reports emphasized the destructive nature of domestic day labor and did little to valorize these women workers, even as she refused to lay blame with the women themselves and sought to publicize their personal struggles. As Cooke discovered, the majority of black women who worked within the unregulated world of casual labor and chose not to use free employment services did so to supplement their meager "relief checks" and avoid employment records. As one domestic explained to Cooke, "I'm on relief and if the relief folks ever find out I'm working another job, they'll take it off my check. Lord knows it's little enough now..."[37] Without any protection from a union or an employment agency, most of these women domestics had little recourse other than their own survival skills and determination.

For Marvel Cooke and others, the solution to improve the conditions of black women domestics resided in building organizations and altering legislation. In the final installment of her series, Cooke addressed "Some Ways to Kill the Slave Market." Similar to her other articles, Cooke celebrated the work of Local 149 of the Independent Domestic Workers' Union (formally part of the AFL). She highlighted the DWU's continued fight to change a policy holdover from the New Deal that excluded most household workers from the protection of minimum-wage and maximum-hour laws, as well as from the benefits of worker's compensation. Such government restrictions, as well as the specific circumstances and isolated working conditions of most black women domestics, presented real difficulties for those who were attempting to organize these women into traditional unions. Despite these barriers, Cooke argued that organizing women domestics and securing effective government regulations were the best and only definitive options for producing real change. In concluding the series, Cooke located the protection and "security" for domestic workers "in decent legislative safeguards, in employer education, and employee training, and above all in unionization." Cooke asserted that "these and these only will make Slave Markets disappear," as she dismissed government efforts to establish free hiring halls as not addressing the full scope of the problem.[38]

Unlike her earlier reporting for the *Crisis* and for the *Amsterdam News*, Marvel Cooke's coverage of the "slave market" for *The Daily Compass* brought the issue into the homes of many white progressives. The paper's editor, Ted Thackrey, hoped to elicit a response from the government by publishing an editorial personally addressed to New York City's mayor, William O'Dwyer, that called for "something a little more effective" for "these hardworking victims of a slackening economy."[39] The series did provoke some official response. The New York State Employment Service began to investigate "standards for protection of the workers." In addition, the Women's Committee of the American Labor Party and the recently revived Domestic Workers Union took up campaigns to outlaw "slave markets," secure a minimum wage for domestic workers, and raise job standards.[40] Cooke's series also resonated with a growing chorus of black women radicals pushing to reframe and expand labor activism. Her articles made it clear that improving these women's working conditions required understanding the ways their exploitation was fueled not only by low wages but also by race and gender discrimination, long-held stereotypes of black womanhood, the lack of government regulations, and the workers' own circumstances. Forced into informal employment, these women represented the need for a more expansive vision of labor activism and for more responsive union organizing.

Vicki Garvin's Trade Union Politics

As detailed in chapter 1, Vicki Garvin gained early experience with labor activism while growing up in Harlem during the 1930s. Garvin joined her first picket line during a Harlem-based protest aimed at gaining better employment for black workers in the community, and she worked summers in the garment industry to help fund her schooling at Hunter College. In 1936, as a new college graduate, Garvin traveled broadly in the political circles of New York. She found employment as a switchboard operator for the CP-affiliated American League for Peace and Democracy. She also became an active union member in the United Office and Professional Workers of America (UOPWA-CIO) and studied briefly at Columbia University.[41]

But Garvin's commitment to trade union work and radical activism would sharpen during her graduate studies at Smith College. As the only graduate student working toward a master's degree in economics, Garvin produced a thesis, "The American Federation of Labor and Social Security Legislation: Changing Policy toward Old Age Pensions and Unemployment Insurance, 1900–1932," that examined the tension that had emerged between the AFL's leadership and its members over the fight for "protective legislation." This early work provides some indications of Garvin's emerging trade union politics. In the thesis, she critiques the AFL leadership for focusing only "on the improvement of working conditions of the man on the job"—issues of wages and shorter hours—and for resisting the demands of its membership. She argues that the national union neglected broader work issues in order to secure its own power. For Garvin, the success in obtaining social security protection rested squarely with the work of local union members, particularly their willingness to champion the cause of a minority of workers and to make demands on the AFL's national leadership, as well as on the government.[42] Garvin's thesis foreshadowed her political alliances and positioning in postwar union fights that would pit the national union leadership against the political demands and desires of local union activists.

After receiving her M.A., in 1942, in the midst of World War II, the twenty-six-year-old Garvin found employment with the National War Labor Board (NWLB) as a wage rate analyst. A government wartime agency formed to regulate union-management relations and to set national wage policy, the NWLB proved an important learning opportunity for Garvin. As a staff member, she gained familiarity with the national labor scene and also became involved in labor activism, helping to organize an independent in-house union to represent the professional and clerical staff and serving as union president. The position even garnered Garvin some notoriety as a "Negro economist" when the *Amsterdam News* ran a story lauding the Region 2 office of the NWLB for its "integration of Negroes on the basis of merit and equality."[43] With the war's end and the dismantling of the NWLB, in 1946, Garvin moved on to full-time labor work as the national research director and co-chair of the FEPC within the CIO's United Office and Professional Workers of America Union.

In the left-leaning UOPWA, Garvin found a home for her wide-ranging politics. She also became immersed in the radical CP-supported labor movement. Garvin worked in the union to maintain some of the wartime gains won by African American and women employees. Serving as co-chair of the union's FEPC committee, she helped to obtain contract clauses that minimized seniority rules, which often left black and women workers "the last hired and first fired." With a strong CP influence among its staff and members, the UOPWA recruited a significant number of African American women for leadership positions and had notable success in negotiating with employers to hire black workers for white-collar jobs. The union's activities brought Garvin closer to CP activists as well as to the struggles of the working class. As Garvin recalled, the experience proved crucial in building her labor knowledge: "I went out on negotiations, strikes, the whole gambit as well as research so that only deepened my ties to working class people."[44] While a staff member at the UOPWA, Vicki Garvin also began to work closely with the National Negro Congress. She officially joined the Communist Party in early 1947.

During the early years of the Cold War, Garvin continued her work with a range of left communities, including as a member of the national staff of the UOPWA. As a sign of the shifting political landscape, the UOPWA faced increasing attacks from anticommunist forces both within and outside the CIO. By 1949, the CIO, under the leadership of Philip Murray, had adopted in its constitution an article that read in part, "No individual shall be eligible to serve either as an officer or as a member of the Executive Board who is a member of the Communist Party, any fascist organization, or other totalitarian movement."[45] This policy applied to leadership as well as to the affiliates and produced a series of hearings, which concluded with the expulsion of eleven CIO unions for communist activity, including Garvin's UOPWA.

Although national CP leadership advocated that union members comply with the CIO hearings, Vicki Garvin disagreed and refused to accept the purging of her union without a fight.[46] During the CIO's national convention, Garvin took the microphone to read from a six-page prepared speech.

Echoing themes she had written about as a student at Smith College, Garvin delivered an incisive critique of the CIO anti-organizing turn:

> In placing its reliance upon either the theory of mutual self-interest or the good will or the foresight of the Truman administration and industry to provide an economic climate in which workers can gain security, National CIO leadership has abandoned the only policy which can produce victories—namely that of independent activity engaged in by the rank and file trade union membership.

Garvin went on to decry the national CIO's support of raiding, its move away from a history of supporting the "militant struggle for the rights of Negro workers," and its failure to provide leadership in building a southern organizing drive. Garvin ended her speech with the query "Are these the CIO policies to which we must submit?"[47]

In the moment, Garvin's statement unnerved CIO leadership and elicited an immediate counterattack from a black supporter of Philip Murray. Although Garvin's fellow labor activists reassured her that even as a lone voice she "had made an impression in [her] duel with Murray" and praised her for her "extremely courageous leadership" during the convention, such resistance had little effect in stopping the CIO's anticommunist turn.[48] The purging of the UOPWA would, for the most part, mark the end of Garvin's official union work. In Garvin's view, the CP strategy of encouraging its CIO–based members to "find a home wherever you can" reflected another strategic misstep, as it allowed CIO unions to "absorb the membership" of communist-led affiliates and eventually get rid of their leadership.[49] Nevertheless, she accepted the strategy. In 1950, Garvin followed the UOPWA as it joined with the Food and Tobacco Workers and New York District 65–also expelled from the CIO—to form a new affiliate, the Distributing, Processing and Office Workers of America (DPOWA). She served as a vice president in the new union. A year later, in June 1951, Garvin was formally removed from her leadership post in the DPOWA.

Vicki Garvin, Freedom, and the NNLC

In the midst of this workplace turmoil, the focus of Garvin's labor activism began to shift. She joined the editorial board of Freedom newspaper and penned several articles on African American women workers for the paper. The pages of Freedom served as an important space for addressing the experiences of black women workers. From Garvin's articles and Alice Childress's fictionalized series about the life of a domestic worker to profiles of black women organizers like Octavia Hawkins and Viola Brown, *Freedom* gave attention to the work of "rank and file women leaders."[50] The very first issue of *Freedom* proclaimed this commitment in the headline of Garvin's full-page article, "Negro Women Workers: Union Leader Challenges Progressive America."

In the article, Vicki Garvin detailed the economic conditions of black women workers. Examining the combined impact of race and gender oppression that left them at the "very bottom of the nation's economic ladder," Garvin argued that "raising the level of women generally and Negro women in particular" served as an "acid test for democracy at this crucial point" in U.S. history. She went on to list the current failures in U.S. democracy as illustrated by the experiences of black women workers, who were "chained to menial service jobs" where, "in addition to low pay and deplorable working conditions, human dignity is least respected." Moreover, they were often excluded from leadership in and from the benefits of workplace unions. Speaking explicitly to the wage differential between white and black men and the ways it reshaped the patriarchal ideal that men should provide financial support for women, Garvin asserted that "getting a husband is not the answer for the Negro woman's search for security and release from backbreaking toil." She noted that three out of every five married black women worked as a "co-breadwinner," whereas only one out of every five married white women did so.[51]

Such insights foreshadowed how the issue of work would emerge in 1970s debates about the black family and women's liberation. But, unlike much of the discourse of the 1950s and the 1970s, Garvin did not see the solution to the problem as simply increasing marriage rates or raising black men's wages. Garvin and other black women radicals of the period upheld a politics of women's equality that sought to improve the lived experiences and opportunities of black working women and thus improve conditions for all workers. In the end, although she was in the process of being forced out of union work, Garvin still contended that unionization was the best solution to improve black women's work experiences. Echoing the challenge that Claudia Jones posed to the CP a year earlier, Garvin called on "progressive trade unions and women's organizations to spearhead" a program to address the particular barriers faced by black women workers and to promote "Negro women leadership at all levels of trade union activity."[52]

Beyond her participation in *Freedom*, Garvin also became a member of the Harlem Trade Union Council (HTUC). Founded in 1949, the Council included a number of Garvin's longtime allies, such as Ferdinand Smith, who was its executive secretary; Ewart Guinier, who served as chairman; and Pearl Laws, who served as treasurer. Each of these activists would play a role in building the NNLC. The idea for a national council convention emerged out of the "National Trade Union Conference for Negro Rights," held in Chicago in 1950 and sponsored by the Harlem Labor Council and the Chicago South Side Negro Labor Council. The conference brought together nine hundred trade unionists from most of the leading CIO unions and sparked a call for a meeting the following year to form a national labor organization for black workers.[53]

With the support of Paul Robeson and *Freedom's* editorial board, Garvin dedicated much of her time over the next year to organizing the NNLC convention. In the months leading up to the meeting, Garvin worked tirelessly to promote the message of the NNLC, penning several articles for *Freedom* that outlined the impetus behind the organization, and attempted to address possible criticism. Council organizers set an ambitious and radical agenda as they came together under what Coleman Young, a former leader in the CIO Council of Detroit, described as the "dual roles" of "bringing democracy to a trade-union movement . . . and using the trade-union base to move the trade-union movement and our white allies within it into the liberation struggle for black people."[54] Although the NNLC was framed as a primarily black-led organization, Garvin assured readers that "we will exclude no freedom fighter," and indeed the NNLC counted several white trade unionists among its leadership. Although it relied heavily on the skills and contacts of black trade union activists, Garvin presented the Council as "an independent movement of Negro workers fighting in all areas for equality" and drawn from "a wider variety of industries—organized and unorganized." Garvin concluded one article by declaring, "Our freedom is long overdue . . . the days of begging, compromise and patient waiting are drawing to an end."[55]

Yet, even as NNLC sought to build a broad base, it did not shy away from taking radical political positions, nor did it hesitate to include among its leadership activists with ties to the CP. Managing these politics proved a continuing struggle within the organization. Its emphasis on black identity could not have sat well with liberals or the CP leadership, two groups that shared an affinity for emphasizing the common economic bonds as the unifying factor among workers. Moreover, the NNLC's effort to recruit trade union activists led some union leaders to raise the cry of "dual membership," and its support for CP-affiliated activists proved a constant target for its enemies. Thus, from the organization's inception, the NNLC's radical politics, black nationalist leanings, and ties to the CP located it on the far left of the union spectrum.

Indeed, the historian Martha Biondi counts the NNLC as one of the "rare left wing groups that was founded during the height of the red scare."[56]

The NNLC, however, was not a solitary or isolated left organization.[57] The Council maintained strategic ties to black left organizations affiliated with Paul Robeson and the United Freedom Fund, which included the Council on African Affairs (CAA), the Committee for the Negro in the Arts (CNA), and *Freedom* newspaper.[58] The NNLC also championed a wide range of causes and tried to highlight important connections across organizing areas. In the call to the convention, the NNLC declared its commitment to "prevent the repetition of further legal lynchings of the Negro people, such as Willie McGee and the Martinsville 7, [and] the frame-ups [*sic*] of Rosa Lee Ingram," as well as its investment in the fight to end Jim Crow in the workplace. In addition, it served as another crucial space for black women seeking to sustain a more expansive politics. Such connections helped the NNLC to draw support, particularly on the local level, from a range of black activists, including those affiliated with such mainstream organizations as the NAACP.[59] Elaine Perry, a long-time activist with the United Electrical, Radio, and Machine Workers Association (UE), recalls being "very impressed" with the NNLC, despite the difficulties the organization faced because of "red baiting." It was one of the few organizations Perry participated in outside of her union work, and she remembers that its efforts "to better the living conditions and economic condition of the black people" had a lasting impact on her own political outlook as a black person.[60]

The strength of the NNLC's founding convention reflected its diverse appeal. The gathering attracted more than a thousand delegates, a third of them women, from both the AFL and the CIO in major cities throughout the nation, including Cleveland, Birmingham, San Francisco, Houston, and Denver.[61] The convention was a success despite the fact that, before the event, organizers faced pressure from "government agencies such as the F.B.I., the Cincinnati City Council which passed a resolution condemning our Convention and the Fire Department which harassed us." This led Vicki Garvin to declare the gathering of black and white workers "no small victory" as it demonstrated that "white workers will unite with us [black workers] under our leadership" and provided "concrete proof that despite pressure and hysteria Negro people will remain firm in their support of genuine struggles for progress."[62]

During its two-day program, the new membership of the NNLC adopted a national "Statement of Principles" and a "Program of Action." Members also passed a number of resolutions that outlined their organizing goals, including a resolution in support of "100,000 new jobs" for black workers, one calling for a Federal Fair Employment Practices Committee, and another calling for "Economic Equality for Negro women." As the convention came to a close, delegates elected national leadership that included William Hood as president, Coleman Young as executive secretary, Ernest Thompson from the independent UE as director of organizing, and Octavia Hawkins of the Chicago United Automobile Workers-CIO as treasurer. The NNLC also elected seven vice presidents-at-large, among them Vicki Garvin; Viola Brown, of the Food, Tobacco, and Allied Workers Union Local 22 (FTA-CIO) in Winston-Salem; and Maurice E. Travis, of the Independent Union of Mine, Mill, and Smelter Workers (IUMMSW).[63]

As noted earlier, the NNLC's effort to build a labor-community alliance elicited strong resistance from a range of anticommunist forces. The organization faced perhaps its strongest opposition from the anticommunist leadership within the AFL and the CIO and from black anticommunist leaders. Both national unions "publicly requested their respective members to shun the convention," while James Carey, the CIO's secretary-treasurer, dismissed it as "just another front for the Communist party."[64] Among African American activists, Lester Granger, of the National Urban League; A. Philip Randolph, of the Brotherhood of Sleeping Car Porters; and the New York–based labor organizer Frank Crosswaith reflected their affiliation with the Socialist Party and left-wing anticommunist politics by denouncing the NNLC for its ties to the Communist Party. Yet, on the whole, these black labor activists agreed with the NNLC's organizing goals, and by 1952 they felt the need to respond with a parallel, though explicitly anticommunist, organizing effort. With the backing of the AFL and the CIO, Randolph and Crosswaith joined "75 anti-Communist unions" to form the National Negro Labor Committee. The Committee clearly hoped to steal some of the spotlight from the National Negro Labor Council while articulating a more liberal politics. For example, the Committee's founding resolutions stood in sharp contrast to those of the NNLC, as they reaffirmed their "allegiance to democracy and liberty" and support for an "effective Federal anti-lynch law" that made no mention of "legal lynching."[65]

Black Women's Work and the NNLC

The NNLC's ability to build chapters despite continued anticommunist assaults and explicit efforts by the AFL and CIO leadership to undercut the organization reflected the strength of its political platform and activist base. The NNLC's goal of challenging job segregation and linking labor and civil rights politics clearly spoke to the needs and desires of black workers and the political aspirations of many in the labor left. For black women labor radicals, the NNLC proved a particularly attractive space to organize among allies. The NNLC proudly counted among its national and regional leadership some of the most active black women trade unionists. Included in this powerful group were Garvin; Viola Brown, who had been active in the FTA-CIO in Winston-Salem, North Carolina, whose left-leaning membership had also recently joined the DPOWA; and Pearl Laws, of New York's Fur Workers Union (FWU-CIO).[66]

Through the NNLC, these women found support for their efforts, both in their individual unions and in their broader organizing, to challenge gender and racial disparity among workers during the early Cold War years. Support for these politics were visible from the first day of NNLC's founding convention, which included a report by a black domestic, Helen Lunelly, on the need to organize domestic workers and a report from Pearl Laws on the Rosa Lee Ingram case and the recent Sojourn for Truth and Justice in Washington, D.C., which had been led by black women.[67] In turn, black women proved a key constituency in carrying out the NNLC's "Program of Action." They had been powerful voices at the founding convention as they spoke to a range of conditions faced by women workers and to the necessity of ending Jim Crow in the workplace. Having declared their commitment to take "the driver seat on the Freedom Train," these women, as exemplified by Vicki Garvin, led the charge in linking civil rights and labor rights in conjunction with addressing the effects of discrimination on all workers.

The NNLC's first national campaign focused on gaining more clerical and sales clerk positions for black women at Sears, Roebuck and Company stores. While the campaign relied on the organizing work of local councils, Garvin played a key role. The campaign made its first breakthrough in San Francisco in early 1952, as the local Negro Labor Council (NLC) forced Sears to alter its practice of limiting black women to menial jobs as janitors.[68] The San Francisco breakthrough occurred soon after Vicki Garvin completed an organizing visit to the West. In December 1951, Garvin had visited local Council chapters in Los Angeles and San Francisco, and most likely her work in the Bay area contributed to the success of the campaign.[69] Bill Chester, of the International Longshoremen's Union in California, noted as much. In a letter acknowledging Garvin's specific contributions in organizing, Chester wrote that "we were very glad to have had Vicki here . . . she did work among the women that no man could have done and she straightened out a lot of things in both San Francisco and LA." He went on to assure NNLC organizer Revels Cayton that "the Freedom Train is rolling here in the West Coast again—thanks to Vicki."[70]

The success of the campaign in San Francisco spurred other NLCs to pursue similar strategies with their local Sears, Roebuck stores. Several NLCs began negotiations with Sears, while others launched picket lines in major urban centers such as Cleveland, Philadelphia, Newark, and Detroit.[71] At its second annual convention, in November 1952, the NNLC passed a resolution urging "the continuation of the fight to crack Jim Crow in Sears Roebuck Stores," with a particular emphasis on ratcheting up the boycotts and picketing during the Christmas shopping season. By 1954, the NNLC could count its campaign against the color line at Sears as a clear victory. The company had opened up sales clerk positions to black women in all its stores—including the one in Chicago, home of the chain's national headquarters, which had been the last holdout.[72]

In March 1952, soon after returning from California, Garvin was appointed the new executive secretary of the New York Labor Council. She replaced the Jamaican-born black activist Ferdinand Smith, whom the U.S. government had recently deported because of his CP affiliations. Although Garvin felt that the new position posed some challenges for her as a black woman heading an organization in the male- and white-dominated world of New York labor leaders, it also reflected NNLC's continued support for black women leadership. With this organizational backing Garvin continued to push for organizing among women.[73] In one of her first public speeches as executive secretary, delivered at the New York Job Action Conference, Garvin noted that "some inroads" had been made "in the employment of Negro women in clerical, sales and other jobs," but she reminded her audience that such jobs remained "mainly unorganized and poorly paid." Reiterating the urgency of undertaking concrete job campaigns to better Negro women's employment opportunities, Garvin asserted that "our women have no choice but to fight" as she urged the audience to join the struggle: "We seek your full cooperation, viewing this problem not as a minor or subsidiary question but one of prime importance."[74]

Centering black working women became a common theme in the NNLC as women organizers sought to make the fight for women's equality an integral part of the NNLC's work. In early 1952, the NNLC sponsored a series of regional conferences entitled "Job Rights for Negro Women," in the hope of making such work a part of "local councils throughout the country."[75] At the November 1952 convention in Cleveland, the Ohio council passed a resolution calling for "an annual Negro Women's Day and Week" and also a "program for the full Rights of women in industry." *Freedom* newspaper celebrated black women's significant contributions at the convention. "Women

Unionists Prominent in NNLC Meet" proclaimed the centerpiece of the paper's two-page coverage of the convention. Highlighting the work of local women activists, including Julia White of Chicago, Molly Sims of Los Angeles, and Josephine Banks of Brooklyn, the article emphasized these women's community work as much as their ties to labor.[76]

Black women played a particularly key role in organizing in the South. Viola Brown, the southern region vice president, contributed an impassioned speech on the need to emphasize the plight of southern black women factory workers. Brown's speech set the tone for the convention's overall theme of organizing in the South. In his keynote address, President William Hood defined the South as the new battleground "in the fight for real equality."[77] The NNLC emphasis on organizing the South reflected the strategic importance these radicals placed on linking the fight for labor rights and civil rights to the black freedom struggle and black women workers' central role bridging these issues.

Following the convention, the Council's longstanding investments in southern-based labor organizing and building among black women workers came together in the 1953 campaign to end discriminatory hiring at the new General Electric (GE) production plant in Louisville, Kentucky. As GE planned to move its production to the South, the Louisville council worked in conjunction with local NAACP and Urban League chapters to provide technical training and to pressure the company to hire these newly trained black workers for skilled positions. General Electric, however, continued to refuse to hire black women workers except as "scrub women," even though half of its six thousand workers were white women. In ratcheting up the fight, the Louisville NLC produced provocative flyers that played on the gender politics of the day: "In advertisements across the land GE glorifies the American Woman—in her gleaming GE kitchen. . . . Nothing is too good for her—We guess this means Negro women too—unless she wants a JOB at GE in Louisville."[78] By both exposing the assumptions of whiteness embedded in debates about "the American woman" and challenging the hypocrisy of GE policies as the company ostensibly advertised goods to black women consumers but refused to hire them as workers, the NLC employed an incisive reading of gender and race to further its calls for black women's employment.

Still facing resistance from GE in 1954, the Louisville NLC joined forces with the NNLC in a national campaign to fight job discrimination at GE, Ford, and Westinghouse plants in Louisville. Under the call to "Let Freedom Crash the Gateway to the South," the National Council's efforts included filing a complaint against GE with the President's Committee on Government Contracts, with little result. By 1955, however, the national pressure produced a small concession as Ford and GE placed "a few Negro women" on the production line.[79]

Recalling the work of the NNLC, Vicki Garvin felt particularly proud of its organizing among black women. What made the NNLC commitment to women workers and women's equality unique is that it not only included specific campaigns to support black women workers but also infused such politics into almost every aspects of its organization. In its brochures, the NNLC paid special attention to addressing the particular struggles of black women. It also became a key part of the NNLC's continued fight to establish a second Fair Employment Practice Committee, following the FEPC's initial defeat in Congress in 1946. The NNLC's pamphlet "The Truth about the FEPC Fight" included a special section titled "The Economic Position of Negro Women." The section, most likely drafted by Vicki Garvin, drew on statistical evidence to highlight the "compounding of two kinds of discrimination against Negro workers who are women."[80] This politics also influenced the work of NNLC members in their own unions. Jack Burch and Ernest Thompson, both active in the UE-CIO, felt that the NNLC's emphasis on coalitions and women's rights helped them to build important ties between the UE's black caucus and its powerful women's caucus.[81]

Although the fight for equal rights for black women workers served as a cornerstone of the NNLC's work, the Council still had to negotiate issues of sexism and the politics of male dominance. Throughout the organization's five-year span, black men held all of the organization's top leadership positions. In fact, a photo of the national officers taken at the third annual convention, in Chicago, includes only four women among the twenty officers.[82] Thus, while Vicki Garvin argues that she "never felt inferior" to the male leadership and that the men "never tried to run roughshod over" her, she did have to fight against some sexist practices. Garvin laughingly remembers having to assert herself to have her voice heard on issues not related to women workers: "I wanted my say not in a pigeonholed way only on certain issues. . . . Train [Ernest Thompson] used to call me 'Bricktop,' he said I had a hard head. He said I wasn't malleable . . . you know I would stand up and fight for my position."[83]

Despite these limitations, the NNLC provided valuable skills and opportunities that allowed black women to develop as labor leaders. Women in New York's black left were greatly invested in the NNLC, especially as it furthered their broader effort to position black women as central voices in the U.S.

left. For example, the announcement of Vicki Garvin's appointment in 1952 as executive secretary of the New York NLC was celebrated as a significant achievement for all black women radicals. Garvin received public congratulations from a range of black women organizers. In its letter of congratulation the Progressive Party, which under the leadership of assistant manager Thelma Dale Perkins and manager C. B. Baldwin was organizing Charlotta Bass's campaign for the U.S. vice presidency, declared: "We believe it is highly significant that your organization which is very akin to ours in its fight for a more democratic America has recognized the importance of the leadership of Negro women." The Sojourners for Truth and Justice recognized Garvin for her "fearless leadership in the struggle for liberation" and stated that her accomplishments served as "a constant inspiration to all Negro Women to unite in the battle to which the Sojourners are dedicated."[84] The context and the content of the congratulatory notes served two important functions: first, to formally and publicly acknowledge the significant contribution of black women leaders, and, second, to tie Garvin's work to a range of other struggles led by black women radicals.

These exchanges suggest the ways in which black women radicals who worked in a number of organizations affiliated with the CP understood themselves as part of a community supporting black women's leadership on the road to building the larger black freedom struggle. These connections and support were based on real alliances that often pushed beyond the boundaries of party politics. Black women activists supported the NNLC, while many women in the NNLC were also active in other left-wing organizing efforts. Vicki Garvin worked with *Freedom* newspaper, while Velma Hopkins and Viola Brown helped to sustain work on the Rosa Lee Ingram case in Winston-Salem, and Pearl Laws worked with the American Women for Peace, supported the Progressive Party, and joined the Sojourners for Truth and Justice.[85] This overlapping organizing work tied the NNLC to a network of activists who championed the importance of strategic alliances among black women and understood the expansive labor activism of the NNLC as a crucial component of the black freedom struggle during the early Cold War years.

Neither in Decline nor Defeat: The Closing of the NNLC

From its inception, the NNLC had faced government harassment because of its radical politics and its affiliation with the CP. These attacks heated up in 1952. Vicki Garvin was called to testify at the Senate hearing investigating the DPOWA, while NNLC president William Hood's UAW Local 600 came under investigation by the House Committee on Un-American Activities (HUAC).[86] In a public hearing held in Detroit, Hood defiantly testified before the committee, denouncing claims that he was a member of the CP as "a damn lie."[87] Although the hearing proved no connections between Hood and the CP, it set the stage for continued government investigation. The NNLC initially escaped the attention of Attorney General Herbert Brownell Jr., who in 1953 requested that the Subversive Activities Control Board (SACB) begin proceedings to have twelve groups, including the Civil Rights Congress and the Council on African Affairs, registered as "Communist-front organizations."[88] Yet, in 1954, HUAC issued the pamphlet "The American Negro and the Communist Party," which denounced the NNLC as "deceitful." Pointing to the organization's charges of discrimination lodged against the UAW, the document argued that, through such actions, the NNLC had "encouraged disunity, rather than unity and thereby performed a distinct disservice to the cause of the Negro Worker."[89]

The NNLC proved resilient in the face of these continued anticommunist attacks. While the national convention in Chicago in December 1953 marked the last such national organizing meetings, work on the local and national levels continued. Many local NLC campaigns—from the "Let Freedom Crash the Gateway to the South Campaign" and the "Fight for Full Freedom" to organizing efforts to elect black candidates to local and state offices and the New York campaign to end bias in hotel hiring—continued with much success well into 1955. The "Gateway" campaign published several pamphlets in 1955, including "Give Us Our Daily Bread" and "GE Discriminates against Negro Women," and New Jersey Council members helped elect Irvin Turner, Newark's first black official, to the city council in 1954.[90] The NNLC also sounded a note of caution about the 1955 AFL-CIO merger conference. Garvin penned an article for *Freedom* in support of the merger but urged the new federation to "give leadership by example" and to incorporate into its constitution "a clear-cut clause on non-discrimination policy for all affiliates," while setting up "definitive guarantees" for enforcing these polices. The NNLC detailed its position in an open letter to the AFL-CIO and distributed one hundred thousand copies of the letter, many at the merger convention.[91] Perhaps as a final act of defiance and as a sign of its continued relevance, in 1956 the NNLC gave an award to Rosa Parks for her role in the Montgomery bus boycott. In a letter from the Montgomery Improvement Association, Parks thanked the NNLC for its work "to make the noble precepts of Democracy living facts lifted out of the dusty files of unimplemented and forgotten court decisions."[92] She also accepted an invitation from NNLC members active in UAW Local 600 to speak in Detroit.[93]

As one consequence of the Council's continued success, Attorney General Brownell finally requested, in September 1955, that SACB require the NNLC to register as a "Communist-front organization" and turn over a list of its officers and its financial details. NNLC leadership refused to comply but worried that it would not be able to continue to carry out its day-to-day work and "defend our leaders and members" before a SACB hearing. This forced the Council to make a "grave decision."[94] "In surveying the situation," NNLC leaders decided to "not dissipate the energies of our members attempting to raise tremendous sums of money required . . . and at the same time, jeopardizing their personal well-being when the freedom struggle is at its present height." Thus, during a final meeting of the NNLC leadership, in April 1956, the organization agreed to "immediately dissolve."[95]

While government interference was clearly an important factor in this decision, the closure was not simply a result of continued harassment. A mix of pressures and political strategy also influenced the NNLC leadership's decision to dissolve. The SACB hearing came at a moment of shifting circumstances, as an upswing in the black freedom struggle began to take hold throughout the nation. As suggested in the NNLC's statement, a number of members felt that the resources—both human and financial—that would be required to fight the government's charges could be better used to support this "higher phase" in the black freedom struggle. In addition, CP-affiliated members had to adjust to an emerging view among CP leadership that support should be withdrawn from members working in a number of black leftist groups, such as the NNLC and the CRC in favor of building ties with more mainstream organizations like the NAACP.[96] For Vicki Garvin and a number of other black communists, this decision reflected the growing "revisionism" in the party that (harkening back to rightward shifts of Browderism) sought to combat the damage of McCarthyism and a declining base by embracing more mainstream politics. Garvin viewed this path as a conscious "liquidation of the black question" that allowed some black organizations to "go by the wayside."[97] In this context, the NNLC's decision, in 1956, to close its doors during a rise in the fortunes of the black freedom struggle proved a contested and yet strategically informed choice that reflected the combined pressures of Cold War anticommunism and differing points of analysis.

These circumstances help to explain why the National Negro Labor Council and its members did not silently fade away and why the organization's ending does not fit the traditional narrative of Cold War decimation and defeat. The NNLC officially closed its doors after passing a "resolution on dissolution" at the April 29 gathering in Detroit. The NNLC marked the

Cover of "Brownell Adds to Our Country's Shame," a pamphlet issued by the Civil Liberties Committee of the National Negro Labor Council in 1956. (Ernest Thompson Papers, Special Collections and University Archives, Rutgers University Libraries)

end of its five-year run by issuing a pamphlet that defiantly celebrated its accomplishments and launched a stinging critique against HUAC, SACB, and Attorney General Brownell. Entitled "Brownell Adds to Our Country's Shame," the pamphlet includes stark and evocative cover art depicting a white man, labeled "Jim Crow Law," preparing to lynch a black woman, labeled "Civil Rights," as Attorney General Brownell covers an NNLC sign with black paint from a can labeled "smear." The image clearly invoked the long battle against "legal lynching" most clearly represented in the ongoing campaign to free Rosa Lee Ingram. Yet it also linked the work of the NNLC to the ongoing freedom struggle in a broader sense as the authors of the pamphlet decried the government's eagerness to prosecute their organization while remaining shamefully silent about the racial violence embraced by white citizen councils and about the government's own efforts to label all black freedom organizations as subversive.[98] The remainder of the sixteen-page pamphlet detailed the campaigns and successes of the NNLC. The pamphlet's closing paragraph proclaimed that the "The Fight for Freedom Goes On" and touted the ways in which the NNLC "played an important role in awakening the latent power of such forces and in demonstrating the methods by which victories can be won in such struggles."[99]

Perhaps as her own gesture of resistance to the decision to close shop, Garvin, a key figure in the NNLC leadership, did not attend the final meeting. She cast her vote in support of dissolution in a letter to Coleman Young, presumably to be read at the gathering. Garvin's letter requested that Young convey to NNLC members her "deep appreciation" for their contributions "in the unconquerable fight for Negro Rights, freedom and democracy." Ever defiant, Garvin closed her letter in an assured tone, asserting that "with full confidence that the 'Freedom Train' to which we added our share of fuel and drive will surely and shortly turn that bend, I remain Fraternally yours."[100] While the letter included Garvin's own parting shot at the U.S. government's attempts to silence black radicalism, it also revealed the strong bonds she had formed with NNLC members, as well as her continued investment in radical politics and organizing. For Garvin, the NNLC represented "the closest collective" she had ever experienced: "I never felt surrounded by better comrades in my life, where we would have really strong ideological fights, really sharp but we would leave as friends." [101] These bonds and hard-fought ideological investments would continue to shape Garvin's activism for the next thirty years.

Conclusion

As illustrated by Vicki Garvin's work with the NNLC and the writings of Marvel Cooke, the struggles of black women workers served as an important organizing issue for black women radicals during the early Cold War period. In large part, this labor activism emerged from these women's experiences, political investments, and training. Cooke's labor journalism represented both her talents as a journalist and activist and the broader investments of black women radicals in making visible the specific struggles of black women workers. Garvin's work with the NNLC revealed a similar investment, as it highlighted the ways black women radicals pivoted from local grassroots organizing to national leadership and maintained a strong commitment to building their vision on both levels. Such organizing revealed black women radicals' ability to address a substantial need within labor politics, as an increasing number of black women workers moved into the labor movement. These postwar shifts provided an important context for black women radicals to articulate a raced and gendered workers' politics.

Through such openings, black women radicals were able to assert leadership in the labor left and to push for a labor politics that moved beyond the workplace to address workers' concerns and needs within the context of their communities and their everyday lives. As demonstrated by Garvin's diverse organizing talents, more often than not, these women radicals articulated their views in a broad array of spaces, from trade unions and independent labor organizations to left-leaning newspapers. They also operated as leaders in organizations built on the margins of more established unions. Black women radicals used these diverse locations to advocate for labor radicalism, a more integrated union movement, and their own political vision. Their emergence as militant voices brought greater visibility to the issues and concerns of black women workers. This work pressured many labor activists and union leaders to take seriously the demands to organize the unorganized, address race and gender discrimination as workplace and economic issues, and expand labor politics beyond the bounds of the shop floor.

5

From *Freedom* to *Freedomways*

Black Women Radicals and the Black Freedom Movement in the 1960s and 1970s

> It is so strange to be going around doing "A Black Woman Speaks." I feel as if magically I've gone backwards but without the same joyousness we had when first we organized the Sojourners. That's really what is needed now. Some sense of oneness that of course we know is there. But experience weighs heavily on my attitude and remembrance of the viciousness of last time grounds me somehow. . . . I'm often down but never out.
> —Beulah Richardson, 1976

Vicki Garvin's conviction that the NNLC had lent "fuel and drive" to a new phase of the black freedom movement would be borne out in the ensuing decades. Garvin and the community of women that came together around *Freedom* and the NNLC witnessed the upsurge in black protest and radical resistance not from the sidelines but as key contributors to ongoing political struggles. In fact, many of the women who articulated a black feminist vision and helped to sustain a radical politics in a range of Communist Party–affiliated organizations during the height of the early Cold War would remain active well into the 1960s and 1970s. During these later years, they established new organizations, where they contributed their strategic insights and mentored a new generation of radical activists.

From the founding of the Negro Women's Action Committee (NWAC) and sustaining *Freedomways* as an outlet for black radical thought and culture to their participation in the "Free Angela Davis" campaign and their advocacy of transnational solidarity, these women continued to make use of their varied political skills and lessons learned during the heated days of the Cold War. Moreover, much of this new activism resonated with the political investments and strategies that had shaped their earlier decades of organizing. Such continuity reflected the influence and legacy of Popular Front black radicalism well beyond the 1940s. In carrying out their work, black women radicals made a concerted effort to highlight these connections and to leave a record of their own contributions to the black freedom struggle for a new generation of activists.

For most of these women radicals, the shift from Cold War activism to the social movements of the 1960s and 1970s also marked major changes in their work and personal lives. The demise of black left institutional spaces such as the CRC, *Freedom* newspaper, and the NNLC forced many of the women to find new venues for employment, as well as activism. By 1957, both Vicki Garvin, of the NNLC, and Thelma Dale (Perkins), who had been on staff with the Progressive Party and took over as managing editor of *Freedom* during its final year, were working at Barney Josephson's The Cookery for extra pay. While Dale married Larry Perkins later that year and could rely on her husband's income, the recently divorced Garvin felt increased "psychological, social, and financial insecurity as a single woman."[1] For Garvin, the frustration lay not only in her limited job options but also in her inability to find work that spoke to her political interests and her desire to avoid the boredom of a conventional nine-to-five job. She continued to seek employment in a variety of mainstream office jobs and even briefly returned to school to study marketing at New York University.[2]

After *The Daily Compass* folded, in 1952, Marvel Cooke also faced employment difficulties. She relied on her husband for financial support until she found suitable paid work. In 1953, Cooke accepted a position with the Council of Arts, Sciences, and Professions, a progressive organization for politically active artists and writers. However, the organization soon succumbed to the financial pressures created by the ongoing anticommunist attacks. By 1960, Cooke left progressive work altogether for a job as a medical writer and receptionist for Sam Rosen, a politically progressive doctor married to Helen Rosen and a close friend of Paul and Eslanda Robeson.[3] Yvonne Gregory would also struggle to find paid work within the left after 1956. By 1958, she had married her second husband, fellow activist Irwin Paderson, and was residing in Manhattan, working sporadically as a writer and proofreader largely outside the CP milieu.[4] As these women's experiences attest, Cold War anticommunist pressures caused financial hardships not only for black left organizations but also for many of the black women activists who relied on such organizations for their paid work. In the late 1950s, as left institutions and organizations closed and these activist women continued to face government harassment, they found few employment options that made use of their skills and education or fit with their political interests.

For a number of cultural artists, such as Lorraine Hansberry, Beulah Richardson (Beah Richards), and Alice Childress, the transition from black left organizations to more mainstream employment proved less turbulent. As they turned more fully to cultural work, many of these women found that the ties they had cultivated during the 1950s bore fruit in furthering their careers. Hansberry emerged as a prominent playwright and a national spokesperson for African American civil rights after her 1959 Broadway play, *A Raisin in the Sun*, garnered national acclaim for chronicling a black family's struggle with white supremacy. Alice Childress also found success in the late 1950s. In 1955, she earned an Obie award for the production of her play *Trouble in Mind*, which examined the stereotyping of black women actors. A year later, Independence Publishers issued *Like One of the Family: Conversations from a Domestic's Life*, a selection of Childress's "Conversations from Life" columns that had been originally published in *Freedom* newspaper. Throughout the 1970s, Childress continued to write plays and published several successful young adult novels. Beulah Richardson, taking the stage name Beah Richards, also gained steady employment in acting. After staring in Childress's off-Broadway production of *Trouble in Mind*, she served as an understudy to Claude McNeil in *A Raisin in the Sun* and toured with the show's national company. Richardson would go on to critical acclaim as a film actor in such productions as *The Miracle Worker* (1959) and *Guess Who's Coming to Dinner?* (1967).[5] Although each of these women undoubtedly faced career hurdles and encountered political constraints in their work, especially as they sought more mainstream exposure, in the 1960s and 1970s they all found some measure of success while still maintaining a political voice.

As these women radicals sought new employment paths and new sources of financial support, some also began to distance themselves from the CP. After 1957, a number of black women who had been active in the CP for most of their political lives moved away from the party. Vicki Garvin left the CP by 1958, troubled by what she viewed as its lack of support for black liberation struggles. According to historian Mark Solomon, Maude White Katz also "drifted away" from the party as she became increasingly frustrated by "the failure of some comrades to extend their political relations into personal friendships."[6] Moreover, black women such as Marvel Cooke, who remained connected to the CP well into the 1980s, became less active and distanced themselves from the intense political debates and internal conflicts that consumed the party during this period.[7] Cooke recalls being involved in few CP activities after 1955. She became reengaged with CP-affiliated activism only in the early 1970s through her work with the Angela Davis Legal Defense Fund and as a volunteer with the National Council for American-Soviet friendship and the *New World Review*.[8]

Regardless of their official relationship with the CP and the limited employment opportunities available to them, most of these women retained both their radical politics and their ties to the community of black leftists they had worked alongside since the 1930s. In fact, many remained connected and active in common organizations and campaigns. This organizing work often trumped political affiliations and even strong ideological differences over strategic shifts within the international communist movement. The sustainability of these collaborations highlight the way in which the political bonds between these women were not wholly defined by the CP or ideological lines but reflected a common commitment to building a black freedom movement and shared experiences as black women activists. Such political investments and bonds were key to the continued activism of these women as they joined a new generation of activists in a variety of social justice movements that emerged in the 1960s and 1970s.

The NWAC and the Emerging Civil Rights Struggle

One of the earliest efforts by this community of women radicals to engage the emerging social movements of the 1960s was the formation of the Negro Women's Action Committee (NWAC), which included Maude White Katz, Vicki Garvin, Louise Thompson Patterson, and Shirley Graham Du Bois. As one of its first actions, the NWAC "participate[d] as an organization in picket lines at Woolworth's."[9] These New York-based civil rights protests, organized by the Congress of Racial Equality (CORE), were in support of the wave of student sit-ins throughout the South that challenged the store's practice of "white only" lunch counters. The first picket lines went up on February 13, 1960, just weeks after a series of student-led sit-ins in the South, sparked by a February 1 protest in Greensboro, North Carolina, garnered national attention. Although it is unclear exactly which picket lines the NWAC participated in, the support protests went on for months and drew in many of their old allies. Representative Adam Clayton Powell Jr. joined the March 12 picket line in Harlem that included student activists from North Carolina A&T, in Greensboro, while most of the cast of Lorraine Hansberry's Broadway play *A Raisin in the Sun* joined a picket line in midtown Manhattan on June 15. The NWAC's participation in these protests reflected its members' commitment to "supporting our youth in whatever form and manner possible" and the belief that such acts of resistance would "gain momentum" throughout the country.[10]

The group also looked to engage transnational politics as it sought to cultivate ties "with the women of Africa by preparing for a representative to their 1960 conference in Accra." The ten-day Conference for Women of Africa and African Descent was scheduled to run from July 15 to July 25 in Ghana. An initial conference program outlined a series of discussions to address black women's experiences across a broad range of areas; forums were titled "Economic Rights," "Health Problems," "Women in Public Life," and "Educational Opportunities," and another focused on strategies for establishing "a Closer Link between the Women of Africa and African Descent."[11] NWAC members' interest in sending a delegate to the conference reflected their transnational political vision, as well as Ghana's stature as one of the first independent countries in sub-Saharan Africa and Kwame Nkrumah's longstanding connections with the U.S. black left. It also built upon these women's earlier initiatives and interactions with the continent. In 1958, Shirley Graham Du Bois and Eslanda Robeson had both traveled to Ghana to speak on behalf of their respective spouses, W. E. B. Du Bois and Paul Robeson, at the All African People's Conference, hosted by Nkrumah.[12] In addition, since 1958, Louise Thompson Patterson had been a member of the Afro-American Committee for Gifts to Ghana, which drew together a number of left-leaning writers, including Langston Hughes and Aaron Douglas, with the goal of sending a collection of works by leading black writers and artists to Ghana.[13] These earlier efforts clearly informed the NWAC's interest in the 1960 conference. Shirley Graham Du Bois led the effort to send a NWAC delegate and traveled to Ghana to attend the conference, although it is unclear whether she did so as the NWAC representative.[14]

The range of activities taken up by NWAC bespoke the increasing optimism and opportunities these women discovered as the 1950s came to an end and their political investments appeared to find new life in the radical activism expanding around them. White Katz and Garvin's "Statement of General Purpose" captured these feelings. They asserted that "as the cry for freedom rings the world our own hearts pound and our vision brightens." Revealing their ties to an earlier decade of activism, Garvin and White Katz invoked the longstanding slogan of the National Negro Congress as they proclaimed their effort to attract "all Negro women who want to strike a death blow to jim crow [sic]." More specifically, Garvin and White Katz believed that the NWAC could "make concrete gains now in the arena of 1) political representation . . . 2) community life—more improved and integrated schools, housing, medical facilities etc." Yet, they also took heed of the difficult lessons they had learned over the years, particularly the price of political isolation, as they asserted that "our call is for unity, not rivalry, action, not silence" and advocated "submerging inconsequential differences and pre-occupations." Seeking to rally the women of the NWAC to an organizational plan and structure in which they would build solidarity among black women at the "grass roots level," Garvin and White Katz concluded by reminding members that their success would be "a victory for a living, dynamic democracy for all Americans and for the freedom-seeking people of Africa."[15] There is little record of the NWAC after the summer of 1960. However, the political agenda represented in the NWAC's early actions and detailed in its "General Statement of Purpose" provides a clear outline of the types of activism that these black women would continue to undertake, both individually and collectively, in the ensuing decades.

From Freedom *Newspaper to* Freedomways *Journal*

As the NAWC came together in early 1960, another group of black radicals began to plan for a new publication aimed at providing a voice for the emerging political movements. *Freedomways* developed from an idea formulated by former *Freedom* editor Louis Burnham and by NNC activist Edward Strong in discussions with Esther Cooper Jackson. All three, along with their respective spouses, Dorothy Burnham, Augusta Strong, and James Jackson, had worked together in the Southern Negro Youth Congress (SNYC) during the late 1930s and been reunited in New York in the 1950s. In Cooper Jackson's opinion, the journal's origins rested in these bonds among "a group of friends." Yet, *Freedomways* would not come to fruition until after Burnham and Strong had died, leaving Esther Cooper Jackson to serve as a founding and managing editor.[16]

At its height the journal provided an important platform for activists engaged in the black freedom movement of the 1960s and 1970s and a base for an older generation of black leftists, particularly many women who had worked so tirelessly to maintain a left resistance during the early Cold War period. As the historian Ian Rocksborough-Smith demonstrates, *Freedomways* served "as a bridge between several generations of black radicals" and "communicated and linked the experiences" of Popular Front black radicals "with a younger generation of activists, organizers, and writers."[17]

From its early conception, *Freedomways* relied heavily on the community of New York black leftists that had coalesced around Paul Robeson's *Free-*

dom and the Freedom Associates during the height of McCarthyism. The first year's masthead listed Shirley Graham Du Bois as editor, W. Alphaeus Hunton as associate editor, and Esther Cooper Jackson as managing editor; both Graham Du Bois and Hunton were former members of *Freedom*'s editorial board. In addition, W. E. B. Du Bois, J. H. Odell, John Henrik Clark, Ruby Dee, Augusta Strong, and George Murphy Jr., who served as general manager of *Freedom* for most of its run, all served as editors or on the editorial advisory board. In building its foundation among this community, the journal also grounded itself in their particular brand of radical politics. This meant that the journal also espoused a clear black feminist politics that celebrated the political activism and cultural work of black women radicals.[18]

Such feminist politics reflected the experiences and vision of this older generation of women radicals. As they had for *Freedom*, these women served as staff, writers, and critical leaders for the journal and often highlighted the central contributions and analyses of black women. In addition to Cooper Jackson, Graham Du Bois, and Strong, who all held leadership positions, Maude White Katz, Louise Thompson Patterson, Alice Childress, and Beulah Richardson all contributed numerous articles, book reviews, and behind-the-scenes support to *Freedomways*. Even those women who were not directly involved in the journal's activities maintained ties with this community and regularly read the quarterly. Marvel Cooke, who briefly volunteered with *Freedomways*, remembered it as a journal that "I admired a lot" and that "approached the problems of black people all over the world in a manner that I felt was proper."[19] In many ways, the journal served as an important point of connection for this community of black women, allowing them to continue to articulate a radical politics that centered black women's experiences and also build ties with new organizing efforts.

Published four times a year from 1961 to 1985, *Freedomways* enjoyed greater longevity than its predecessor, *Freedom*, but continued the newspaper's emphasis on supporting black radical politics, providing access for up-and-coming black artists and writers, and seeking to "unite and mobilize" those actively fighting for black liberation. The journal included writings by many leading figures in the black freedom struggle in the North and South, such as Martin Luther King Jr., Angela Davis, Fred L. Shuttlesworth, Gloria Richardson, and numerous members of the Student Nonviolent Coordination Committee (SNCC), which published its anti-Vietnam statement in the journal. *Freedomways* also published an astounding array of black writers and artists, from James Baldwin, Alice Walker, and Gwendolyn Brooks to Audre Lorde, Tom Feelings, and Max Roach, as well as the perspectives of an impressive list of international activists and leaders, including Julius Nyerere, in Tanzania, and President Kwame Nkrumah of Ghana. Indeed, with a publication run of up to fifteen thousand copies per issue, the journal was accepted by a broad range of black political communities.

The inaugural issue of *Freedomways* reflected the Popular Front alliances its founding members had developed since the 1930s, as well as their efforts to build unity with an emerging generation of activists. This April issue included an essay by W. E. B. Du Bois, a key adviser to and supporter of the journal, and articles by its future associate editor John Henrik Clarke, who had been active in New York's black left since the 1930s, and by the artist Elizabeth Catlett Mora, who had served on staff at the NNC's *Congress View.* If these authors demonstrated the journal's connections to black Popular Front politics, the opening editorial sought to connect *Freedomways* to the emerging struggles to "do away with discrimination, segregation and to demand full citizenship" that had taken hold among African Americans. "We are born in a tremendous time of change," noted the editors as they presented the journal as "a vehicle of communication which will mirror developments in the diversified and many sided struggles of the Negro people" and as "a public forum for the review, examination, and debate of all problems confronting Negroes in the United States." In a tone similar to the one taken by NWAC, the editors also assured their readers that the journal had "no special interests to serve save those already clearly stated—no political, organizational or institutional ties."[20] Throughout the journal's run, *Freedomways* editors would seek, if not always successfully, to maintain this ambitious goal of addressing the many sides of the struggle for black liberation and of engaging a wide array of radical politics.[21]

From the journal's first year, its community of seasoned women radicals produced articles that documented black women's contributions to black liberation struggles and highlighted the importance of women's equality to the overall strength of the black freedom movement. Maude White Katz, who had a long history of radical activism since joining the Communist Party in the 1920s, served as a regular book reviewer for the journal and wrote several key articles for the journal. She published two significant essays focused on African American women's history in the journal's 1962 winter and summer issues. The first article, "She Who Would Be Free—Resistance," examined black women's experiences during slavery and their acts of resistance in the fight for freedom. The second article, "Negro Women and the Law," traced the impact of the legal structures of slavery on the current status of black women in the U.S. legal system. White Katz drew on her own history of activism as evidence to support her arguments. She presented the Rosa Lee Ingram case as one clear example of black women's continued mistreatment under the U.S. justice system. She also invoked the numerous cases of police violence and assaults on black women in New York City.[22] While both articles provided a historical context for understanding black women's contemporary experiences, White Katz also invoked the early postwar activism of women radicals to spotlight black women's contributions as fighters in the long struggle for black freedom. For example, a slightly revised version of Beulah Richardson's 1951 poem "A Black Woman Speaks" accompanied White Katz's article in the winter issue.

Black women radicals' allusions, in a number of *Freedomways* articles, to their years of groundbreaking activism coincided with more explicit efforts to connect their own history of resistance to the emerging political movements. These articles not only documented an important history of black radicalism but also provided critical examples for current struggles and organizing efforts. In the 1964 special issue on "the southern battle fronts," Augusta Strong's article, "Southern Youth's Proud Heritage," detailed the twelve years of political work carried out by the Southern Negro Youth Congress. Strong acknowledged the pressure of McCarthyism in hastening the closing of the SNYC, in 1949 but asserted that "what the movement began, the seed it planted did not fall on barren ground. What has happened since, in the last several years especially, is ample testimony."[23]

Three years later, Strong wrote a more comprehensive article, "Negro Women in Freedom's Battles," that recounted black women's activism since slavery. Although Strong referenced only Claudia Jones by name, the essay explicitly celebrated the work of Popular Front black women radicals as a political community "of courage and conviction" that formed "another chapter in the freedom struggle." Strong defined Jones and "others, like her," as a generation of radicals "who rose from the ranks during the hunger years of the 1930s" and "developed local and national leadership" in "the newly-born CIO, in Harlem and in the Black ghettos of big cities fighting racism, police brutality and racial oppression in all areas of life."[24] Maude White Katz's 1979 article "Learning from History—The Ingram Case of the 1940s" also spoke directly to the activism carried out by these women as she recounted the work of the "Ingram Committee" and reprinted the petition to the United Nations written by W. E. B. Du Bois on behalf of Rosa Lee Ingram.[25] Although framed by White Katz as the work of the 1940s, much of the campaign to free the Ingram family occurred in the 1950s. While both Strong's and White Katz's articles celebrated the radical past of the authors' and their black women allies, the essays also suggest that, even as these women underscored their leadership in the long black freedom struggle, they still felt some ambivalence about fully acknowledging their communist pasts in the pages of the journal.

The community of women radicals who had honed their politics in the 1930s and 1940s demonstrated little hesitation in engaging current political questions. Several women contributed important essays to *Freedomways* that addressed contemporary issues and organizing efforts. The winter 1966 issue reprinted the speeches given during a panel titled "Negro Women in American Literature" that was part of a three-day conference, "The Negro Writer's Vision of America," held at the New School for Social Research in New York City. The journal's reprints included the comments of the writers Sarah E. Wright, Paule Marshall, and Alice Childress and of the singer Abbey Lincoln. Reflecting a black feminist analysis developed through decades of cultural activism, Childress's presentation carried the most powerful critique of the depiction of black women in popular literature and media. Commenting during a year in which Assistant Secretary of Labor Daniel Moynihan issued the report *The Negro Family: The Case for National Action*, which defined black women as emasculating "matriarchs" of the black family, Childress challenged as "too easy" and "misleading" the growing assertion that the black woman's strength in surviving "has taken her femininity" and made her "the main culprit in any lack of expressed black manhood."[26] Drawing on her own investments in black women's history, she detailed the ways in which "the Negro woman has been *particularly* and deliberately oppressed, in slavery and up to and including the present moment." Childress argued that few works included this real history or other aspects of "the Negro woman's story." Urging black writers to engage the past, Childress concluded that "the Negro woman will attain her rightful place in American literature when those of us who care about truth, justice and a better life tell her story with full knowledge and appreciation of her constant, unrelenting struggle against racism and for human rights."[27]

These women's analyses also appeared in several special issues of *Freedomways*. For the summer 1964 special issue, "The People of the Caribbean Area," the editors solicited an article from Claudia Jones titled "The Caribbean Community in Britain." Jones, a Trinidadian immigrant who would take center stage in Strong's 1967 article, was one of the highest-ranking black women in the Communist Party USA and had been deported to England in 1955 under the anticommunist McCarran Act. Jones's article examined the history of black Caribbean life in Britain and reflected her developing activism and her leadership in the London community as editor of *The West Indian Gazette*.[28]

Beulah Richardson also penned several articles for the winter 1964 special issue on the "southern battlefronts." As she had for her assignments years earlier as a staff writer for *Freedom* reporting firsthand on events in the South such as the 1951 shooting of Walter Lee Irvin and Samuel Shepard in Groveland, Florida, Richardson traveled south to report on the ongoing political activism in Alabama, and in her home state of Mississippi.[29] Richardson's three-part article recounted her experiences in Greenwood, Vicksburg, and Birmingham in 1963 during a period of major community mobilizations led by SNCC and the NAACP. Richardson detailed her thoughts while "participating as an observer" in organizing meetings and during direct-action protests. She reported on the violence of "white supremacists," the continued harassment faced by protesters, and the humor and unity that drew young and old, men and women, to the movement.[30]

Echoing a political outlook shaped by her work on the CRC's *We Charge Genocide* publication, Richardson defined the struggle as a revolutionary "fight for human rights, not Negro rights or equal rights." Still, Richardson had arrived in the South "hopeful, anxious, eager but unconvinced" by nonviolent resistance. She left impressed by the "effect of non-violent struggle on it participants" and by the strength of the unity within these communities. Declaring these efforts the "beginning of a revolutionary struggle that will sweep the nation," she contrasted them with her visit to Vicksburg, Mississippi, the hometown she had left long ago, where "no collective activity in pursuit of freedom helps the people transcend the miseries of a bleak, hard life." Perhaps reflective of her own difficulties growing up, Richardson viewed activism in Vicksburg as stymied by unrelenting poverty and the "color cast . . . division among Negro citizens." She did, however, witness some stirrings of resistance, which led her to conclude that "one sweet day" Vicksburg would "join the fight for Human rights."[31]

In addition to contributing political and historical essays, these longtime activists proved valuable resources in other *Freedomways* efforts. Richardson, White Katz, Louise Thompson Patterson, and Augusta Strong all wrote numerous reviews, which helped the journal to maintain an impressive book review section that covered the latest publications on African and African American history, the black freedom struggle, and black culture. Prominent writers such as Alice Childress and Lorraine Hansberry contributed pieces to *Freedomways* retrospectives celebrating the political contributions of W.

E. B. Du Bois and of Paul and Eslanda Robeson.[32] Moreover, as suggested by the special issues on Caribbean communities and the reprints from the panel "Negro Women in American Literature," as well as the journal's editorials in support of the "Free Angela Davis" campaign and on the Joan Little case (two of the most celebrated criminal defense campaigns of the period, to which many of these women contributed their leadership and organizing skills), black women radicals provided important strategic insights about and ties to on-the-ground organizing.

Maude White Katz and the Fight to "End Racism in Education"

As the political landscape changed during the 1960s, the political activism of these seasoned black radicals also shifted. As illustrated by their work in *Freedomways* and with the NWAC, they remained committed to the radical views that they had forged in the Popular Front and during the early Cold War period. Nonetheless, as they engaged new venues and organizing campaigns, their politics also took on the emphasis and tone of the period. Maude White Katz, who had spent much of her early life as a member of the CP fighting white supremacy in the trade unions and advocating for interracial cooperation, emerged in 1966 at the age of fifty-eight as a vocal activist in New York City's struggles over public education. White Katz served as president of the Concerned League of Harlem (CHL); as a member of the Parent-Community Committee (PCC), a coalition of community-based organizations; and, most visibly, as chairman of the 1967 boycott of West Harlem's P.S. 125.

As "the parent of two daughters attending public schools in New York," White Katz, along with fellow CHL members, early in 1966 launched a campaign to open up exams for specialized high schools to more sixth-grade black and Puerto Rican students. Clearly foreshadowing White Katz's calls in her 1968 *Freedomways* article to challenge the racist "education hierarchy" that denied students of color the same "quality and quantity" of guidance as white students, the fight proved a limited success as the Board of Education increased the number of African American and Puerto Rican students selected for the Hunter College High School exam.[33] With the formation of the PCC, in November 1966, White Katz became a part of the broader fight for improving public education in New York City. By the following year, White Katz and the PCC were embroiled in a tense battle with the local school board over community input in the administration of the merging of P.S. 125 and P.S. 36, including the community's wish to have a voice in the hiring of a new principal. Drawing support from an array of community members, including black and white parents, church leaders, and faculty and students at nearby Columbia University, on March 13, 1967, the PCC launched a nine-day boycott of P.S. 125.

The boycott proved an overwhelming success as almost 1,500 of the 1,850 students stayed away, with more than 1,000 students attending the alternative neighborhood "Liberation School." The protest also won concessions from the Board of Education and garnered mainstream media coverage. A *New York Times* headline declared, "Boycott Keeps 1,450 Out of School in Harlem." Illustrating the diverse cross-section of activists involved, the *New York Times* article included interviews with Maude White Katz as the boycott chairman; Sidney Jones, a staff member from the Congress of Racial Equality, as the boycotters' spokesman; and Dr. Preston Wilcox, a professor at the Columbia School of Social Work and the principal of the "Liberation School." The student population of P.S. 125 was 17 percent white, 55 percent black, and 28 percent Puerto Rican. Supporters argued that this diversity was reflected in the boycott, which represented a "democratic, multi-class and multi-race community effort" in the midst of growing racial and economic polarization around public education.[34] In May 1967, the PCC hoped to build on this success by running a slate of officers for the Parents' Association with White Katz as its candidate for president. However, the May 2 Parents' Association election produced a highly contested and politicized vote. During the election meeting, numerous new white members unexpectedly emerged to nominate Manuel Romero, a black man, as an opposition candidate to White Katz. As a result, White Katz suffered a surprising defeat. The ensuing turmoil embroiled the PCC and the Parents' Association in an increasingly racially charged debate as several of White Katz supporter's circulated a petition that decried the vote as "rigged" and argued the election was "taken over by white parents" as a backlash against black parents' attempts to claim some power.[35] Such racially charged suspicions reflected the heated political climate of the period.

The work of the CHL and of the PCC emerged during a period of intense conflict in New York City public schools as a growing number of black and Puerto Rican parents began to challenge inequalities in the school system. The movement had been building since at least the 1950s. However, several key struggles had come to define this political fight as one that pitted black and brown parents against an intransigent Board of Education. These struggles included the 1958 "Harlem Nine" case, in which nine black parents refused to send their children to an inferior school in Harlem and were taken to court by the Board of Education, and the February 3, 1964, protest, led by the Reverend Milton Galamison and Bayard Rustin, in which more than 450,000 students boycotted New York City public schools, demanding an end to segregation. Both moments paled in comparison to the defining force of the highly publicized 1967–1968 Ocean Hill-Brownsville conflict over "community control" in Brooklyn, which seemingly placed African American and Puerto Rican parents in heated conflict with the Board of Education and the majority-white United Federation of Teachers. These protests exposed the ways segregation and racial inequalities operated with impunity within the city's education system. Emerging in the North during the growth of black power politics, these political struggles were entangled with debates about race, class, and culture, as well as with issues of segregation and racist practices.[36]

Thus, it was in this context that Maude White Katz found a space to articulate a politics that boldly challenged the ways "Southern prejudices" shaped New York City schools to produce what amounts to the "planned retardation of nonwhites, beginning in kindergarten."[37] White Katz outlined this analysis most explicitly in her contribution to the *Freedomways* 1968 special issue on the education crisis in New York City, titled "End Racism in Education: A Concerned Parent Speaks." White Katz was one of only two women to contribute to this issue, which included articles by leaders in the fight for equality in education, including the former president of Lincoln University, Horace Mann Bond; the Reverend Milton A. Galamison, president of the City-Wide Committee for Integrated Schools; and Columbia University professor Preston Wilcox. Speaking, however, as a black parent and black woman, White Katz contributed an article that marked a bold pronouncement on the issue and that would be reprinted in the groundbreaking 1970 anthology *The Black Woman*, edited by Toni Cade.[38]

The article defended the growing movement among parents of color for community control of schools and critiqued the longstanding discrimination faced by black students in the U.S. education system. Tracing the history of an education system created to "fulfill the needs of business and financial interests," to defend the "Establishment," and to regulate the competition for jobs and resources, White Katz presented a keen economic analysis. She also articulated aspects of the contemporary black power politics as she disparaged the "mere token" number of black teachers hired to teach a majority-black and -brown population and warned that "the union is at the service of the Establishment [*sic*] who does not want educated Black masses." In addition, White Katz leveled a stinging critique at "Black teachers" and "Black professionals" who "barter their heritage for a fee." She viewed the problems in northern urban education as rooted in the intersections of racial and economic inequalities and located the key to creating change in the leadership of the black parent "who has nothing to lose but her poverty." [39] Such political insights, while not reflective of a strict class analysis, did not stray far from the analysis White Katz had articulated in her sharp critiques of white supremacy as she fought to integrate the Needle Trade Unions in the 1930s and her support of Rosa Lee Ingram's right to self-defense in the 1950s. Indeed, Maude White Katz's politics revealed the ways many black women radicals continued to bridge the divides between integrationist ideals and black nationalist solidarities.

Forging Transnational Solidarity: Vicki Garvin's International Travels

As demonstrated by Louise Thompson Patterson's leadership in the Afro-American Committee for Gifts to Ghana and the NWAC's solidarity efforts, black women radicals who had faced Cold War harassment for their efforts to connect black liberation to a more expansive international politics found, in the 1970s, an encouraging environment in the renewed emphasis on transnational politics and Third World solidarity. The independence movements in Africa and Asia provided new opportunities for these women to engage their longstanding international politics. Shirley Graham Du Bois's and Eslanda Robeson's participation in the 1957 All African People's Conference reflected some of these new options as the African continent, and Ghana more specifically, emerged as the center of pan-African activism. The African continent had long been deemed the imagined and historical homeland of black people born in the United States, but, as the struggle for African independence gathered victories, these new nations became crucial touchstones for black liberation movements.[40] Between 1955 and 1966, hundreds of African Americans relocated to decolonizing nations throughout Africa, particularly those countries, such as Ghana, Kenya, and Tanzania, whose leaders held strong diasporic ties. A number of black radicals joined in the exodus, hoping to put into practice their political theories and commitments regarding transnational solidarity.[41]

In the midst of these vibrant international exchanges, Vicki Garvin embarked on her own transnational journey, traveling first to Nigeria, then to Ghana, and finally living for nearly six years in China. Vicki Garvin made her initial decision to leave the United States after her close friend Thelma

Dale Perkins approached her with an offer of employment in the newly independent African nation of Nigeria. The job, working for a Nigerian businessman, was set up through Dale Perkins's uncle Dr. Frederick Patterson, the former president of Fisk University. Although ideally looking to follow other activists who had relocated to Ghana, which had a growing black expatriate community, Garvin accepted the opportunity to live and work in Lagos, Nigeria. [42] It offered her "a breath of fresh air" both personally and politically, as well as an opportunity to actualize her commitment to pan-Africanism by "returning" to the African continent. [43]

Vicki Garvin arrived in Lagos in May 1961, less than one year after the nation gained formal independence from Britain. She hoped that living in a newly independent Nigeria would, in her words, "reinforce my resolve and confidence in our ultimate victory." Garvin's optimism for the trip was also fueled by the enthusiasm of her new employer, a well-established Nigerian businessman and parliamentary official named Chief Ayo Rosiji. In negotiating the work contract, Chief Rosiji assured Garvin that she "will be received here [in Nigeria] with open arms." Perhaps knowingly playing to her own desires for belonging or simply reflecting the enthusiasm of the period, he reminded Garvin that "you are coming here to your true home and to your own people." [44]

Garvin's desires for a rejuvenating homecoming were tempered by the political and gendered realities of daily life in Nigeria. Her brief journal entries, written sporadically during her initial month in the country, provide some insights into her struggles to adjust to the cultural and economic demands of life in Lagos. Garvin struggled to acclimate to disorganized work conditions as well as to the difficulties of being an "Amer[ican] woman living alone" and her consequent loneliness. She was also forced to negotiate the realities of neocolonialism as she noted "beggars, men with facial tribal marks, people lying and sleeping on streets (unemployed, homeless)" alongside "many modern bldings [sic] big Chase Man. Bank & other, Amer. [sic] oil companies, etc & remaining big British firms." Garvin's stay in Nigeria lasted two trying years. [45]

Years later, in writing about her time in the country, Garvin succinctly noted, "2 years in Nigeria neocolonialism-disillusionment." [46] This shorthand can be read as her critique of the simmering internal political divisions and concessions to Western Cold War interests that would soon send Nigeria into civil war. However, it also speaks to the limited community and political opportunities Garvin found in what she had imagined as her "homeland." Garvin noted this point in her diary. "It is interesting (and significant

I think)," she wrote, "that I (& possibly other American Negroes) who feel while in the U.S. a kinship with brother-sister Africans experience some preliminary difficulty in assimilating." During her time in Nigeria, Garvin had come to realize that, even with the "intellectual-political sympathy" between African American and African activists that she believed to be "theoretically true," there was still "nothing automatic" about building such diasporic solidarity.[47] Throughout her stay in the country, Garvin struggled to not "remain aloof" from local culture, yet ironically found her strongest community among a number of African American women working with the U.S. State Department. In 1963, faced with the country's unstable employment picture and growing political uncertainty, Garvin decided to head back to the United States after making a quick stopover in Accra, Ghana, to meet up with W. E. B. and Shirley Graham Du Bois, who had recently arrived in the city.

By this time, Ghana had emerged as the meeting site for black activists from throughout the Diaspora. Ghana's leader, Kwame Nkrumah, broadly defined pan-African politics as unity among continental Africans, as well as solidarity with the struggles against racial discrimination faced by Africans throughout the Diaspora.[48] In this vein, unlike the Nigerian government, Nkrumah claimed a position of "positive neutrality" in the Cold War and argued that Ghana faced "neither East nor West but forward."[49] The African nation's central positioning in the African Diaspora was amplified for communist-affiliated African Americans by the growing number of black left expatriates, including the husband-and-wife tandems of Julian Mayfield and Ana Livia Cordero, William Alphaeus Hunton and Dorothy Hunton, and Shirley Graham Du Bois and W. E. B. Du Bois, who settled in Accra as Nkrumah's invited guest.[50] Each of these activists maintained strong ties to New York's black left, including members of the *Freedomways* collective and Harlem's cultural left.

The possibility of reconnecting with allies from her New York community clearly fueled Garvin's attraction to Ghana, and she soon decided to stay on in Accra. Garvin settled into sharing a house with two other single African American women, Alice Windom and Maya (Angelou) Make. All three women could be counted among the group of African American expatriates with a history of association with the U.S. black left. These activists, generally in their thirties and forties, became known in Ghana as the "politicals" of the Afro-American set—or, as one expatriate described them, "professional protestors."[51] Disquieted by the domestic Cold War and cautious about the liberal tendencies within the growing civil rights movement, they refused to retreat and instead turned to newly independent African nations as vital sites for sustaining and internationalizing the black radical movement.[52] As a result of these circumstances, they felt a profound loyalty to Nkrumah's project of African socialism and cheered his sharp critiques of U.S. foreign policy. Moreover, in contributing their skills and talents to Ghanaian development, these African American radicals sought to do their part to "hasten socialism and African unity," often by publicizing their own critiques of U.S. domestic and foreign policies and challenging visiting American officials at every turn.[53]

In Africa, Garvin hoped "to be really useful, to represent the best of thinking Negro Americans." However, the gender and political dynamics of life in the new nation made it impossible for Garvin to find paid work that made use of her skills as a labor activist and organizer. Believing she "had no special skills to contribute to Ghana," Garvin could find employment only as an English teacher through the Foreign Language Institute.[54] Nonetheless, her claim to have "no special skills" rings false, given Garvin's past political and professional experiences and her activism in Ghana to strengthen the bonds of solidarity between nationalist struggles in Africa and black liberation organizing in the United States. One example of this activism was the August 1963 protest at the U.S. Embassy in Ghana. Building on her earlier support of student sit-ins, Garvin, alongside Alice Windom and W. Alphaeus Hunton, organized expatriates in Ghana to participate in a solidarity protest, picketing the embassy as the historic March on Washington occurred in the States. The demonstration criticized U.S. intervention in Vietnam and hostilities toward Cuba and included a declaration opposing racial discrimination that was addressed to President John F. Kennedy.[55] Such activism unnerved U.S. policymakers, who from the early years of decolonization had feared Africans' exposure to African Americans critical of U.S. racial policies.[56] The State Department placed these activities and activists under intense surveillance. However, this scrutiny did not prevent the protest from receiving extensive coverage in Ghana and in black radical publications in the United States.[57]

Garvin, drawing on her extensive connections in radical communities, also worked to politicize the visits of a growing number of black activists seeking to experience for themselves one of the first independent black nations in Africa. The local community of black radicals served as a welcome center of sorts for newly arriving African Americans, from CP members such as James Jackson to artists such as Camille Billup and the playwright William Branch. Malcolm X, who arrived in Ghana in May 1964, became the most celebrated of these African American visitors. Pulling together an ad hoc committee that included Garvin, Alice Windom, Maya Make, Julian

Mayfield, Ava Livia Cordero, and several others, the expatriates organized a "refugee night" for people to meet and talk with Malcolm X. Vicki Garvin recalls of Malcolm's visit that "Maya, Alice and I became his guardian three musketeers—mother hens who accompanied him to many affairs."[58]

Garvin, however, proved more than a "guardian." As the historians Gerald Horne and Kevin Gaines have noted, Malcolm X's visit to Ghana and his exchanges with black radicals broadened his ideas about coalitions and the importance of unity in the black liberation struggle.[59] Drawing on the contacts she had made through her work as an English teacher with staff at several foreign embassies, Garvin played an important role in facilitating Malcolm's introductions to a range of international revolutionaries. She arranged meetings for Malcolm X with officials at the Algerian and Cuban embassies and with the Chinese ambassador, Huang Hua. She also served as the interpreter during Malcolm's meeting with Algerian officials. For Malcolm, such conversations proved central to deepening his international perspective, and, for both Garvin and Malcolm X, these connections would influence their future transnational travels and alliances. Soon after these meetings, the Chinese ambassador, Hua, extended an invitation to Garvin to visit China, while Malcolm X's meeting with Algerian officials would soon lead him to visit that nation.[60] Such conversations also seemed to mark an important exchange between Malcolm X and Garvin as she took every opportunity to share her political wisdom and to learn from the powerful young leader. Garvin's admiration of Malcolm's ability to take in other people's insights may have reflected the nature of these exchanges, as she recalled that "he believed in listening to other people. He was not a know it all. I greatly appreciated that."[61]

Garvin's description of herself as one of the "guardian three musketeers" and "mother hens" when discussing her contributions to organizing Malcolm X's visit also suggests how African American women radicals negotiated the complicated politics of gender and nation in Ghana. [62] On one hand, such a statement can be read as downplaying her role by embracing a more acceptable gendered and apolitical construct to define her political work. A concession to a limiting gender politics, enmeshed in the activism of this community of expatriates, which reinforced male dominance and shaped many of the diasporic networks. The African American activist Sylvie Boone angrily addressed this politics, contending that in Ghana it was "fixed so that there is no meaningful way for an Afro woman to participate."[63] On the other hand, such framing could also define a real and important mentoring relationship with Malcolm X. In this context, Garvin's use of the term "mother hens" most likely reflected an effort to mark her role as a knowledgeable elder (a role long gendered male) within the black liberation movement. As a veteran activist who had survived the earlier onslaught of government harassment, Garvin embraced her role as a valuable resource to a younger generation. She openly shared her experiences and insights, mentoring younger activists just as she had been mentored, even as the shifting political landscape and gender politics complicated these intergenerational exchanges.

Kwame Nkrumah's efforts at building African socialism and pan-African unity in Ghana ended on February 24, 1966, as a military coup ousted him from power. Many African American radicals who had found hope in Nkrumah's political rule experienced the coup as an opportunity lost that forced them to question their own place in the struggle.[64] "Nothing seems possible to me," moaned Alice Windom following the coup, adding that "all the purpose has gone out of being in Africa now that it has turned into a bloody minstrel show, but I can't yet face going back to the States."[65] Still, many had seen the impending crisis developing as internal conflicts intensified in 1962 and Nkrumah increasingly feared assassination. Vicki Garvin joined those who read the writing on the wall and left Ghana before the coup occurred. But, like Windom, she could not bear to return home. As she chose to continue to live outside the United States, Garvin turned her hopes eastward. In 1964, she moved to China accepting an offer from the Chinese ambassador to work as an English-language teacher in Shanghai and later as a "polisher" in Beijing for the English-language translation of the *Peking Weekly Review*.[66]

Garvin would arrive in the People's Republic of China alone and not knowing the language, but she would not remain isolated for long. In traveling to China, Garvin joined with a number of African American radicals who sought to develop ties with the communist nation. Shirley Graham Du Bois would continue to build her connections to China, traveling there frequently, although she remained based on the African continent. In addition, Robert F. Williams, the black radical from North Carolina who was forced into exile for advocating armed self-defense, and his wife Mabel Williams also found a new home in China in 1965. Garvin, Graham Du Bois, and the Williamses had all been connected to New York's black left. Garvin had counted Graham Du Bois as a friend and ally since the early 1950s and it's more than likely that she had met Robert Williams almost a decade earlier when he contributed several articles to *Freedom* newspaper.[67] In China, Shirley Graham Du Bois and Robert Williams carried added clout as popular figures in the black freedom struggle, and the Chinese government welcomed them as key dignitaries. Garvin's reputation in China as a revolutionary and behind-the-scenes strategist did not garner her the same lavish treatment and accommodation afforded Graham Du Bois and Williams. However, all three activists contributed to solidifying China's standing as a committed supporter of black liberation as reflected in Mao Zedong's 1963 statement in support of the civil rights movement. In turn, China provided these black radicals with a base from which to continue to act on their international vision and communist politics, as well as a significant connection to the emerging U.S. black power movements that advocated Third World solidarity and a revolutionary nationalist vision inspired by the Chinese Revolution and the writings of Mao.[68]

While in Shanghai, Garvin honed her skills as a teacher working at the Shanghai Institute of Foreign Languages, teaching advanced classes in English and establishing her own course on African American history. By 1966, as the Chinese Cultural Revolution brought the closing of schools, Garvin found herself out of a job and one of the few foreigners still residing in Shanghai's Peace Hotel. After meeting and marrying Leibel Bergman, a fellow American living in Beijing, Garvin relocated to the bustling capital city to work for the *Peking Weekly Review*. It is here that Garvin built a lasting relationship with Robert and Mabel Williams and with Gerald (Gerry) Tannenbaum. In Beijing, they became "close friends and allies" as part of the small community of Americans who remained in China through the start of the Cultural Revolution. During these years, they "shared countless hours recounting the history of the revolutionary struggle" as together they watched, analyzed, and debated the social and political upheavals occurring in China and the United States in the late 1960s.[69]

In all, Garvin spent six years in the People's Republic. Garvin rarely spoke in detail about the turbulence she must have witnessed during her stay in China. Instead, she credited her time there with teaching her much about "the working of imperialism, neo-colonialism and socialism," and she remained a staunch supporter of the Chinese Communist Party (CCP) for the rest of her life, even returning to the country in the late 1970s.[70] Her support of China was strengthened, in part, by a number of lasting connections and friendships she developed while there, particularly with the Shanghai Institute and with several of her former students. In fact, one of Garvin's most powerful experiences in China was the invitation she received from her students to return to the Shanghai Institute of Foreign Language in 1968 to address a pre-rally meeting in celebration of Chairman Mao's second statement on the black liberation movement, "In Support of the Afro-American Struggle against Violent Repression," issued after the assassination of Martin

Luther King, Jr. Recounting the experience, Garvin remembers it as a "privilege" and a moment of overwhelming support that moved her to tears.[71] Such experiences led Garvin to continue to view China and the CCP as "a valuable resource for exploited and oppressed peoples everywhere who have so much in common."[72] Garvin's embrace of China reflected not only her continued investments in communism and black liberation but also a broad vision of transnational solidarity that led her to frame herself as "a pan-Africanist" and "a proletarian, working class, internationalist."[73]

Black Women's Liberation and the "Law, Again"

Upon returning to the United States, Garvin encountered a markedly changed country and political scene. Nonetheless, she must have found some of the political changes quite welcoming. With the emergence of a transnational black liberation movement, a growing feminist politics, and the New Left, Garvin's credentials as a longtime black radical and Third World internationalist resonated within the political milieu taking shape in the 1970s. In fact, the community of black women leftists who had defiantly sustained their radical politics during the early Cold War found the 1970s a surprisingly welcoming political environment. In particular, their radical vision, with its critique of white supremacy, gender inequalities, and U.S. imperialism, meshed well with the ideas emerging in black power politics, women's liberation, and the newly formed Marxist-Leninist and Maoist-based communist organizations.

Drawing on skills and strategies honed in their years of organizing with the Civil Rights Congress and their leadership in the campaign to free Rosa Lee Ingram, these women found common ground with new political communities and played key roles in two of the most celebrated legal defense campaigns to emerge in the United States in the 1970s, the campaign to free Angela Davis and the Joan Little case. The "Free Angela Davis" campaign centered on Davis, a young black woman activist and scholar, who was a member of the CP and its Los Angeles–based all-black collective, the Che-Lumumba Club. She was fighting the University of California Regents' efforts to remove her from her position as an assistant professor at the University of California-Los Angeles (UCLA), under a 1940s resolution prohibiting the employment of CP members. A supporter of the Black Panther Party, Davis also worked on a defense campaign for the Soledad Brothers, three black inmates at Soledad Prison who had been accused of murdering a white guard.

On August 7, 1970, in the midst of these political battles, Jonathan Jackson led a failed prison break at the Marin County courthouse. The deadly effort left Jackson, the brother of Soledad inmate George Jackson, as well as prisoners John McClain and William Christmas and Judge Harold Haley, dead. Linking Davis to the incident through her ties to George Jackson and the Soledad Brothers, investigators accused her of supplying the weapons for the attack. Facing charges of kidnapping, murder, and conspiracy, Davis immediately went into hiding. Davis was placed on the Federal Bureau of Investigation's Ten Most Wanted list and became the focus of an all-out police search until her arrest, in New York, in October 1970. [74]

Angela Davis's experiences, from her resistance to the anticommunist attacks aimed at her, to her commitment to fighting for black liberation from within the CP, must have felt quite familiar to many of the older black women radicals aware of her case. [75] As Davis went underground, many of these women, still affiliated with the CP, immediately mobilized support for her case and provided crucial organizational leadership. Forming the National United Committee to Free Angela Davis (NUCFAD), the CP led a highly successful national and international campaign to publicize the government's harsh treatment and faulty prosecution of Angela Davis. Louise Thompson Patterson and Esther Cooper Jackson both served on the New York Committee to Free Angela Davis, which Patterson chaired. Leading speaking tours, organizing fundraisers, and coordinating publicity efforts, under Thompson Patterson's direction the New York Committee worked diligently to mobilize party resources and to build broader coalitions based on her connections. [76] Many in New York's black left joined the campaign. *Freedomways* issued an editorial urging readers to support Angela Davis, and many of the journal's contributors lent their voices to the cause, including Nikki Giovanni, Ossie Davis, and James Baldwin, who penned a public statement in support of Davis that was published in the *New York Review of Books*. [77] Patterson also reached out to younger black women radicals, including Fran Beal and the members of the Third World Women's Alliance, which helped to organize an "Angela Davis Day" rally in New York's Central Park in September 1971. [78] As Davis's case moved toward trial, the CP formed the Angela Davis Legal Defense Fund. William Patterson personally asked Marvel Cooke to serve as national secretary alongside Ossie Davis as chairman. In charge of coordinating activities on both coasts and fundraising, Cooke helped to organize a major rally at Madison Square Garden. The fundraising event was scheduled for June 1972, but, after Davis's acquittal of all charges on June 4, the event became a victory celebration, with Angela Davis as the guest of honor.

"An Evening with Angela Davis," with Ossie Davis as the master of ceremonies and performances by Nina Simone, Carmen McCrae, and Chita Rivera, proved a great success, drawing more than fifteen thousand supporters and raising close to two hundred thousand dollars.[79] Such success in a campaign centered on a black woman radical must have been particularly inspiring for the black women who had worked so diligently in the CRC and in support of activists prosecuted under the Smith Act.

The public campaign in support of Angela Davis did not come without some backlash, but it did reflect a shifting tide in the political landscape and a growing suspicion of the U.S. criminal justice system. This change in public consciousness concerning the criminal justice system and the increased awareness of the specific struggles of black women in the United States would also shape the 1974–1975 Joan (pronounced Jo Ann) Little case. Little, a poor black woman imprisoned in North Carolina for robbery, became a celebrated figure in the black liberation and feminist movements when, in August 1974, she killed her white jailer, Clarence Alligood, in an act of self-defense in Beauford County, North Carolina, and then escaped. Although initial reports included none of these details, Alligood was discovered in Little's cell with his pants down, dead from numerous stab wounds made with an ice pick. After eluding an eight-day statewide search, Little turned herself in with the support of legal counsel. Joan Little contended that Alligood had instigated the incident by entering her cell and sexually assaulting her. This set the stage for what many viewed as an important legal and political test case for women's rights and black self-defense.[80]

The case drew together a broad range of activists, from feminist and black power advocates to local community groups, in a powerful "Free Joan Little" movement. It also attracted black women radicals such as Velma Hopkins, a longtime church activist who had entered radical politics through her work as a union organizer with the Food, Tobacco, and Allied Workers and the NNLC in the 1940s and 1950s.[81] Hopkins, alongside Viola Brown, had also served as a regional sponsor of the National Committee to Free the Ingram Family and been active in Winston-Salem's People's Defense Committee, which, in 1954, organized a delegation to protest Rosa Lee Ingram's conviction.[82] As a founding member of the Concerned Women for Fairness to Joan Little (later the Concerned Women for Justice), a statewide church-based civil rights organization, Hopkins drew on this past experience to provide key local leadership in the campaign to free Joan Little.[83]

The "Free Joan Little" movement also attracted a number of black women who had been active in the "Free Angela Davis" campaign, including CP member Charlene Mitchell, who served as head of the National Alliance against Racism and Political Oppression, and Angela Davis, who launched a powerful defense of Little in the article "Joanne Little—The Dialectics of Rape," published in *MS.* magazine in 1975 and who spoke often in support of Little.[84] Indeed, the "Free Joan Little" movement had an expansive reach, drawing in white and black feminists and civil rights activists, as well as black nationalist organizations such as the Black Women's United Front, and producing a wave of poetry, songs, and creative protests.[85]

The Little case emphasized black women's experiences of racialized sexual violence. The calls for supporting a woman's right to defend herself against such attacks struck a deep chord in black women activists seeking to make visible the intersecting forces of race, class, and gender, including members of the Third World Women's Alliance and the National Black Feminist Organization.[86] The "Free Joan Little" movement also shared common cause with the politics articulated by women radicals who had organized in defense of black womanhood during the 1950s and who had supported black women's longstanding struggles for control over their own bodies. In many ways, the Little case resembled the earlier Rosa Lee Ingram campaign; a broad spectrum of black women mobilized in support of Little, who, like Ingram, was a poor black southern woman facing murder charges and possible execution for having defended herself against the assault of a white man. In the context of the post-1960s civil rights movement and a burgeoning feminist politics, the case would test whether these claims held greater sway in the legal system and mainstream public opinion. *Freedomways* editors, perhaps looking back to the Ingram campaign, declared as much, asserting that, "as the court convenes on this issue, it is not Joanne Little who is on trial . . . it is the system of American justice, itself." Defining the "political issue" as one based on the race and gender of Joan Little and Clarence Alligood, the editors warned that "the conviction of Joanne Little would be a victory for racism and male supremacy."[87] On August 15, 1975, an interracial jury rendered its verdict. Joan Little, with the aid of a politically attuned and locally based legal team and an international public campaign, was acquitted of all charges.[88]

This successful organizing in support of Angela Davis and Joan Little, two young black women seeking to defend themselves within the U.S. criminal justice system, represented only one aspect of the common ground and political openings these veteran women activists found in the radical movements of the 1970s. Another notable connection emerged as a new generation of activists, influenced by an increasingly brutal U.S. war in Vietnam, the examples of indigenous socialist revolutions in China, Cuba, and African nations such as Tanzania, and the political vision of an older generation of black radicals, turned more fully toward challenging U.S. imperialism and advocating transnational solidarity.[89]

International Solidarity and the Old Left

In the radicalized political environment of the 1970s, challenges to U.S. imperialism often coincided with an explicit support of international communist and revolutionary movements. Many women radicals viewed such renewed interests in international solidarity as a way to reconnect with and help expand U.S.-based transnational peace and socialist solidarity organizing. Veteran black women radicals engaged these efforts through several left-leaning organizations, including the National Council of American-Soviet Friendship (NCASF), the longstanding journal the *New World Review*, and the U.S.-China Peoples Friendship Association (USCPFA) and its journal, *New China*.

The NCASF, under the leadership of the Reverend Richard Morford, who served as executive director from 1946 to 1981, worked to strengthen bonds between the people of the United States and those of the Soviet Union through educational programs and cultural exchanges and a particular investment in organizing U.S. "goodwill delegations" to the Soviet Union. The *New World Review*, founded in 1951 as the successor journal to *Soviet Russia Today*, allied closely with the NCASF to promote U.S.-Soviet solidarity, as they shared adjacent offices on Fifth Avenue in Manhattan. The journal, however, also viewed its mission as promoting solidarity with socialist nations by advocating in the United States for a "closer understanding and friendship with the U.S.S.R. and other socialist countries."[90] Founded in 1974, the U.S.-China Association, under the acronym USCPFA, embraced a similar solidarity effort as it sought to "build active and lasting friendship based on mutual understanding between the people of the United States and the people of China."[91] The USCPFA not only took up educational programs and solidarity trips but also provided firsthand accounts of Chinese life and political analysis through its magazine, *New China*.

Although the USCPFA garnered greater support among younger radicals than the NCASF, both these organizations and their journals relied on members of the "Old Left" to sustain their work in the 1970s. For example, *New China* counted among its contributors left-leaning activists such as Helen

Rosen, a longtime friend of the Robesons, and the scholar William Hinton, while the *New World Review* counted the black leftist and longtime journalist George Murphy Jr. as a member of its board of directors and the peace activist Elizabeth Moos as a regular contributor. Both Murphy and Moos also served as board members of the Council of American-Soviet Friendship, and Moos also contributed articles to *New China*. Both organizations specifically drew support from veteran black women radicals. Several black women who had worked closely with the *New World Review* and its editor, Jessica Smith, during the 1950s, including the civil rights activists Halois Moorhead, Eslanda Robeson, Shirley Graham Du Bois, and Vicki Garvin, returned to this type of solidarity work in the 1970s.[92]

In part, these connections were based on longstanding friendship and a history of exchange with the Soviet Union that for many dated back to the 1930s. Yet, a number of these women also continued to view the Soviet Union, despite the exposure, in 1956, of Stalin's brutality and the country's growing lack of credibility among the New Left, as a powerful model of revolutionary change and as an important alternative to U.S. dominance. The Soviet Union's support of the Cuban Revolution, along with Cuban and Soviet financial support for anticolonial revolutionary struggles in Vietnam and Angola (which the Chinese Communist Party did not support), lent powerful evidence to this claim.[93]

Some other black women were drawn to solidarity work with the *New World Review* and the NCASF through their desire to travel to the Soviet Union to view socialism in action. Alice Childress became involved with the NCASF and contributed to the journal through her travels to the Soviet Union as part of a NCASF "black delegation" that visited in August of 1971. The black leftist and journalist George Murphy Jr., a leader of both the *New World Review* and the NCSAF, had organized the delegation and personally recruited Alice Childress. Murphy also arranged for Childress to be interviewed about her experiences and for an article based on her interview to be published in the *New World Review*.[94] In the published article, Childress spoke of wanting to visit the Soviet Union out of a lifelong interest in and curiosity about the country and her desire to "see it for myself and make my own judgment." Reflecting her own longstanding political concerns, she addressed the treatment of women and Afro-Soviets in the country and celebrated her ability to "learn a great deal" about "how socialism works in the USSR," an experience she longed to share with "my people, African Americans." Although Childress proclaimed her desire to "to return again" to the Soviet Union, this never materialized. She had few interactions with Soviet solidarity organizing efforts after the trip, even though she remained interested in witnessing socialism at work and would later travel to China.[95]

Two years later, Thelma Dale Perkins made her first trip to the Soviet Union as part of an "Afro-American delegation" again organized by George Murphy Jr. Following the trip, Dale Perkins penned a piece for the *New World Review* in which she recounted her experience and impressions. Titled "A Letter to Paul Robeson on Our Visit to Mt. Robeson," the article was written as a letter to Paul Robeson in honor of his upcoming seventy-fifth birthday.[96] The letter addressed a set of concerns similar to those discussed in Childress's interview; Dale Perkins detailed her interactions with Afro-Soviets and her insights into the role of women in Soviet politics and industry. Yet, the article also noted the high esteem in which the Soviet people held black radicals such as Paul Robeson and Angela Davis.

Dale Perkins had worked with both the *New World Review* and the NCASF long before her travels to the Soviet Union. In 1971, she helped to plan a bon voyage party for Alice Childress and other members of that year's black delegation.[97] She also continued to work with these organizations after her own trip abroad. In 1974, Dale Perkins served as co-chairperson and key organizer of the *New World Review*'s April luncheon "in honor of the United Nations ambassadors of the socialist world." Held at the Waldorf Astoria Hotel, the "historic event" drew UN representatives from the Soviet Union, Cuba, and numerous Eastern European socialist countries; it also included presentations by Henry Winston, national chairman of the CP, and the recently acquitted Angela Davis. For the *New World Review*, the event represented one of their most successful efforts, as editor Jessica Smith proclaimed the gathering a "glowing affirmation of the increasing strength and unity of the socialist world" and "an international demonstration of the meaning of détente, of the retreat of imperialism before the advances of the world's socialist, peace and liberation forces."[98]

Other black women radicals joined the organizing efforts of the NCASF and the *New World Review* as a way to reengage with left politics. Marvel Cooke began working with both organizations after the Angela Davis campaign came to an end. For Cooke, the work proved an important form of radical activism that allowed her to remain connected to old allies while also engaging with a new generation of radical politics. Already acquainted with Jessica Smith and friendly with several people who worked with the NCASF, Cooke became involved in both organizations because of these relationships and "because they did greet me with open arms" and "there was plenty I could do there." She was also a strong supporter of the Council's exchange

Vicki Garvin (left) and Thelma Dale Perkins at a gathering for Louise Thompson Patterson in New York in 1987. (Louise Thompson Patterson Collection, Manuscript, Archives and Rare Book Library, Emory University)

programs and its continued ties to peace activism. Cooke worked on events organized by the *New World Review* and the Council and led their fundraising committee. She continued this work well into the 1980s, even taking on the position of national vice chairman.[99] Both Marvel Cooke and Thelma Dale Perkins remember fondly their work in building U.S.-Soviet solidarity during the 1970s and the diligent leadership of Jessica Smith. In part, their positive experiences reflected their support for the political work, but it also must have been exciting to reconnect with longtime allies, while actively engaging with a new period of radical internationalism.

While the majority of these black women who reconnected with socialist solidarity organizing did so through work with the Soviet Union, other women, such as Vicki Garvin and Shirley Graham Du Bois, who had lived in China for some years and who advocated a more explicitly nationalist politics, lent their support to the USCPFA. As Garvin readjusted to political life in the States, she sought to reestablish her political activism by working with the U.S.-China Friendship Network. Garvin gave numerous talks at schools and churches about her experiences in China, promoted the Network's activities, and called for greater support for China and the Chinese Communist

Party.[100] As the scholar Max Elbaum attests, the Network had widespread support, particularly among younger radicals. In 1973, more than twenty U.S. cities held celebrations in honor of the anniversary of the Chinese Revolution, and, by 1974, more than thirty-five local U.S.-China Friendship Network Committees existed throughout the country.[101]

Also in 1974, the Network expanded into the U.S.-China Peoples Friendship Association and began publication of a quarterly journal, *New China,* to publicize its solidarity efforts and to present informed accounts of life in China. Vicki Garvin joined the editorial board of the magazine, working alongside a fellow expatriate, Gerald Tannenbaum, and a number of younger activists and scholars. Garvin also reached out to black activists with whom she had worked in supporting Paul Robeson and *Freedom* newspaper. Garvin recruited Alice Childress to contribute an article on Paul Robeson for the June 1976 issue of *New China* to commemorate his recent passing and his lifelong support for the People's Republic of China. Childress had traveled to China in April 1973 as part of a tour organized by the *Guardian.* Although she left little record of her experiences and her reactions to the country, her willingness to contribute to *New China* suggests some continued affinity.[102] In the same issue, Helen Rosen published an interview with Harry Belafonte in which he discussed his longstanding interest in China and his continued desire to visit the country, as well as his recent performance at a *New China* fundraiser.[103] Garvin was not alone among the seasoned activists who had longstanding ties to a CP-affiliated black left but were increasingly drawn to the Chinese Revolution and the theoretical insights of Chairman Mao. In addition to Childress and Belafonte, Shirley Graham Du Bois was a very active member in the USCPFA and its New York chapter. Graham Du Bois was particularly engaged in the organization's effort to address the role of women in China, speaking at the USCPFA's 1975 "International Women's Day" program on "Women in China."[104]

Conclusion

The organizing and feminist visions that emerged from the campaigns in support of Angela Davis and Joan Little, as well as the international solidarity efforts with China, the Soviet Union, Ghana, and other decolonizing nations, were clearly reminiscent of the earlier politics that had shaped the campaign to free Rosa Lee Ingram, international women's peace activism, and Popular Front anticolonial struggles. These connections did not escape the notice of the black women who had been involved in such activism during the 1940s and 1950s and were still active well into the 1970s. "I feel as if magically I've gone backwards," wrote Beulah Richardson to Louise Thompson Patterson in late 1976. Richardson's comments referred most directly to the surprising revival of her poem, "A Black Woman Speaks," as a stage performance. Undoubtedly, this air of familiarity also spoke to the sense of political continuity she felt with organizing around the Angela Davis and Joan Little cases, as well as the broader political affinity with women's liberation, the emerging left, and the black power movement.

Nevertheless, for Richardson, the moment felt incomplete. Whether it was the "weight" of experience or her "remembrance of the viciousness of the last time," she found that this period of revival lacked "the same joyousness we had when first we organized the Sojourners . . . some sense of oneness that of course we know is there." Such a statement might at first glance appear counterintuitive, particularly given the framing of the 1950s as a nadir in radical activism. But, on closer analysis, Richardson's words speak to the importance of the pockets of resistance black women radicals created and sustained during this earlier period, as well as the ways anticommunist attacks at times led to greater unity among those who continued to be active.[105] These bonds and political solidarity outlived all of the CP-affiliated organizations that brought this community of black women radicals together and proved an enduring force in their lives and activism as they remained politically engaged and personally connected well after the 1970s.

Conclusion

Centering Black Women on the Left

As I began working on this project, I called Vicki Garvin for the first of several telephone interviews. After I described my interests in writing about the black left during the Cold War, Garvin, assuming that I wanted to hear about her ties to and the contributions of well-known black radical men, immediately began to recount her memories of working with "tremendous" leading men, such as Paul Robeson and Malcolm X, and her analysis of their work. She was quite surprised and a bit taken aback when I clarified that I was interested in discussing her own activism during the 1940s and 1950s.[1] From this first conversation and through numerous other interviews and research, I began to see a pattern in which the voices and memories of lesser-known black women radicals were called upon to recount the history of and to fill in the gaps in our knowledge of the lives of more celebrated leaders. Through oral histories, lectures, and essays, black women such as Garvin, Esther Cooper Jackson, Marvel Cooke, and Thelma Dale Perkins have emerged as important chroniclers of black radicalism, recounting their experiences as witnesses to key historical events and as colleagues and friends of leading figures, from Robeson and Malcolm X to W. E. B. Du Bois and Claudia Jones.

This use of black women's testimonies to help document the history of postwar black radicalism has shaped how scholars have come to understand this period of radical resistance, as well as these women's contributions. On one hand, as suggested by Garvin's response, many historical studies have relied on black women's memories and even mentioned their names, but rarely have they included any rich details about their activism, political thought, or roles as local and national leaders. Indeed, these women's longevity as radical activists has often been obscured by a top-down view of U.S. and black radicalism, as well as by the silencing force of Cold War anticommunism. Such invisibility has been compounded by black women's own understanding of their work as a necessary (not extraordinary) part of a larger collective effort. For example, when asked about her ability to continue as an activist amid the onslaught of Cold War anticommunism, Dale Perkins replied simply that "you had to stand up and do something" and asked incredulously, "What were we to do—give up?"[2]

On the other hand, women radicals have been able to provide their own interpretation of key leaders and of the impact of Cold War anticommunism. From Garvin's emphasis on Malcolm X's strength as a thoughtful leader and Dale Perkins's assertions about Claudia Jones's fierce support of black women's activism to their universal praise for Paul Robeson and his importance as a principled activist and mentor, these women offered recollections that challenged many popular images of both these historical figures and the period. They depict a movement dedicated to bettering people's lives, built through political exchange and day-to-day organizing, and not beholden to any one ideology or political party. In part, Dale Perkins's resistance to viewing her own activism as extraordinary reflects this view of radical politics as a collective process. In these ways, black women leftists used their position as eyewitnesses to document history while also conveying their own sense of how this historical period should be understood.

In *Radicalism at the Crossroads*, I have sought to insert both the analysis of black women radicals and their collective experiences into the history of postwar radicalism by centering their insights and documenting their contributions to sustaining a black left politics well into the 1970s. In so doing, this book builds upon an expanding new field of scholarship that examines the political leadership of black women radicals from the 1930 to the 1950s, even as it extends this research into the 1960s and 1970s. Emphasizing black women's voices by drawing on their writings, oral interviews, and the archival records of their organizing provides a more detailed view of these women's theorizing and activism. Investigating such activism introduces an alternative perspective on many key aspects of U.S. radicalism and postwar politics and de-centers dominant narratives that privilege the decimation of the U.S. left and the experiences of well-known leaders in the black left and in the CP.

In part, I have aimed to reveal, as the book's opening chapter discusses, the influences of the Great Depression and Popular Front politics on black women's work as intellectuals and organizers who helped to build the black freedom struggle for more than a half-century. Their political development was profoundly shaped by this period of economic crisis and radical resistance, as well as by their experiences of migration, education, and urban life.

Most of these women traveled extensively, either with their families or alone, and experienced 1930s black urban life, whether in Washington, D.C., Birmingham, Chicago, or New York City. In these urban spaces, they met other like-minded radicals, became involved in a range of organizing efforts, and witnessed, as Thelma Dale Perkins did through her work with the American Youth Congress, "that it's possible to change conditions." Working in the labor movement, in civil rights campaigns such as that which surrounded the Scottsboro Boys case, and a range of left-leaning artistic groups, these black women honed their skills as strategists and organizers. Esther Cooper Jackson underscored the significance of this period for her own political development as she recalled joining the CP and embracing a life of activism: "I felt the sense that I'm making a gigantic change in my life. A committed change in my life . . . I wanted to commit to changing things for the poor people in this country. . . . and it was a serious step."[3]

As chapters 2, 3, and 4 demonstrate, the commitments and politics forged in the 1930s continued to inform black women's activism and analyses, as well as their lives, in the ensuing decades. By the start of World War II, they began to solidify as a community and claimed a greater voice in left politics, particularly as the wartime mobilization provided opportunities for them to move into leadership positions in organizations such as the National Negro Congress. This convergence would continue as the postwar period evolved into a Cold War. Despite these shifts black women continued their activism and theorizing during the 1950s, evidenced by their work on the Rosa Lee Ingram case, their leadership in the National Negro Labor Council, and their writings in defense of black womanhood.

Black women radicals' political communities and activism emerged within the fissures created by a shifting postwar politics and the increasing heat of Cold War anticommunism. These openings allowed black women to claim significant organizing space as a shrinking left sought to adjust to the changing landscape. "A lot was happening . . . between 1950 and 1955," declared Esther Cooper Jackson, recalling the activism she participated in while facing increased government harassment.[4] Indeed, the political work taken up by these women radicals, which centered issues of African American women's civil rights and self-defense in the Ingram case, expanded the politics of the labor movement, and articulated the need for an intersectional analysis that addressed the diversity of women's gendered experiences; reflected core organizing platforms and points of debate from the Popular Front era. This activism during the 1950s provides a view of the ways these key political debates were hashed out and reframed in a Cold War context.

Through this work, women radicals emerged as unique organizers in the CP-affiliated left and as powerful strategists in sustaining black radicalism during the late 1940s and 1950s. As race and gender emerged as crucial discourses within postwar U.S. politics and as the left faced a narrowing political landscape, black women stepped up to articulate their own political vision. In debates within the CP over the theorizing of "the woman question" and "the national question" and over shifting strategies for building a viable movement and sustaining the fight for "real liberation," black women radicals responded by theorizing around the intersections of race, gender, and class. Such theorizing highlighted black women as an untapped revolutionary force, and presented a more cogent response to the specificity of black people's and women's experiences.

Moreover, their ability to negotiate the institutional constraints and ideological sectarianism of left party politics proved valuable tools in sustaining their activism. Black women drew on and blended multiple strategies and ideological tendencies, from black self-determination and a feminist politics to Marxist-Leninism and an internationalist vision for creating change. Thus, this group of women radicals not only organized to reframe dominant conceptions of racial justice and social equality but also created political spaces open to more eclectic ideas and theorizing. It was precisely this dynamism that allowed these black women to navigate the political openings and closings of the early Cold War years and to remain active for decades after.

The wealth of black women's organizing and theorizing carried out during the height of McCarthyism presents a more nuanced story of the impact of anticommunist attacks on the black left. These women generated a sustained resistance to anticommunism and, as Cooper Jackson asserts, their activity contradicts the dominant perceptions "that nothing was happening." Indeed, black women's radicalism attests to the range of activities and vibrancy of the period. Dale Perkins fondly recalls that "those were some great days at *Freedom*," while Vicki Garvin assessed her work in the NNLC as the "very highpoint of my development" and "the closest collective I think I have ever experienced."[5] Both women made these comments even though each faced very real repercussion for remaining allied with the left.

When met with increased government pressure, these women found support and power among their longstanding community of black radicals. Their lives specifically make more visible both their activism and the communities that supported the work of these "long-distance runners." Their experiences encourage us to view black radicals not simply as singular figures but as dedicated individuals shaped by rich historical moments and vibrant activist communities.

These women's political commitment outlasted the confines of the early Cold War landscape. Continuing to push a radical political vision as expressed through their support of African American civil rights, Third World solidarity, women's liberation, and economic justice, black women radicals operated from an ideological core that proved flexible enough to remain relevant in a changing world. Thus, exploring their activism also provides key insights into how issues such as challenging the mistreatment of black defendants, defining the links between economic justice and labor, and calls for intersectional analysis (which define much of their activism during the 1950s) would resonate with and be reimaged in the social movements of the 1960s and 1970s.

The articles written by black women radicals during the 1960s and 1970s, such as Maude White Katz's "Learning from History" and Augusta Strong's "Negro Women in Freedom's Battles" in *Freedomways*, Thelma Dale Perkins's "Letter to Paul Robeson" in *New World Review*, and Vicki Garvin's "China and Black Americans" in *New China*, reflected their continued political relevance in and affinity for the social justice movements emerging around them. Yet, the articles and the journals in which they appeared also clearly document the women's political ties to an earlier generation of black leftists. In part, these articles and the continued activism of women such as Dale Perkins, Garvin, and White Katz provide powerful evidence that "what the [1930s] movement began, the seed it planted did not fall on barren ground."[6] Their lifetime of activism reveals some of the vital strains of continuity that persisted during almost a half-century of black radical politics. Moreover, these women's ability to remain engaged and to maintain longstanding Popular Front–era affiliations marks them as significant, if not singular, figures worthy of a more prominent place in history.

Notes

INTRODUCTION

1. *Proceedings of the Founding Convention of the National Negro Labor Council* 73, 1951, box 1, folder 1, Ernest Thompson Papers, Special Collections, Rutgers University Archives, New Brunswick, NJ (hereafter ETP).

2. *Freedom*, 1950–1956, microfilm, Tamiment Library and Robert F. Wagner Labor Archives, New York University (hereafter Tamiment). For a history of the newspaper, see Lawrence Lamphere, "Paul Robeson, *Freedom* Newspaper and the Black Press," Ph.D. diss., Boston College, 2003.

3. Vicki Garvin, "Labor Council Links Fight of Negro People and Labor," 5–6; Alice Childress, "Conversations from Life," 2; and Lorraine Hansberry, "Women Voice Demands in Capital Sojourn," "They Dried Their Tears and Spoke Their Minds," and "Women Demand Justice Done," 6; all in *Freedom*, October 1951, microfilm, Tamiment.

4. I use the term "early Cold War" to refer to the roughly decade-long period from the announcement of the Truman Doctrine of containment in 1947 to the series of U.S. Supreme Court decision in 1957 that ruled the Smith Act illegal. During this period, which marked the initial wave of domestic Cold War anticommunism in the United States and which is often referred to as the second "red scare" or the McCarthy era, the U.S. government embraced a policy of intense harassment and surveillance of the Communist Party and its supporters.

5. "To Picket Woolworth Again," *New York Amsterdam News*, February 20, 1960, 34; "'I'd Do It All Over Again' He Says," *New York Amsterdam News*, March 19, 1960, 4; "Bias Foes Picket Woolworth Here," *New York Times*, June 16, 1960, 25. Vicki Garvin and Maude Katz, "Statement of General Purpose," n.d. (proposal for meeting on May 15, 1960), box 14, folder 9, Louise Thompson Patterson Papers, Special Collections, Robert W. Woodruff Library, Emory University (hereafter LTP); Shirley Graham Du Bois to Dear Members, March 30, 1960, box 14, folder 13, LTP.

6. Thelma Dale Perkins used this term to describe the politics African Americans supportive of the CP embraced and contended, "There was a difference between being a left-winger and being a card carrying member of the Communist Party." Thelma Dale Perkins, interview with author, October 3, 2007, Chapel Hill, NC.

7. I use "CP-affiliated," "radical," and "leftist" interchangeably since there was great political overlap and cross-fertilization. Moreover, most anticommunist politics and policies targeted a broad range of left-leaning activists and African Americans fighting racism and colonial policies.

For more on the STJ, see Erik McDuffie, "A 'New Freedom Movement of Negro Women': Sojourning for Truth, Justice, and Human Rights during the Early Cold War," *Radical History Review* 101 (Spring 2008): 96–97; and Jacqueline Castledine, "'In a Solid Bond of Unity': Anticolonial Feminism in the Cold War Era," *Journal of Women's History* 20, no. 4 (Winter 2008): 57–81.

8. *Congress View*, September 1945, Tamiment; and *Congress Vue*, April 1943, 3, part 3, reel 2, National Negro Congress Papers, microfilm, Posey Library, Harvard University (hereafter NNC Papers). *Congress Vue* was renamed *Congress View* in 1945; it also included Elizabeth Catlett as a staff artist and Marvel Cooke as a contributing writer.

9. See Nikhil Pal Singh, "Culture/Wars: Recoding Empire in the Age of Democracy," *American Quarterly* 50, no. 3 (1998): 471.

10. In 1948, Bethune withdrew from her work with Paul Robeson and the CAA (see Martin Bauml Duberman, *Paul Robeson* [New York: Knopf, 1989], 333 and 344), while in the 1950s Ella Baker cooperated with the NAACP's purging of suspected communists from its membership. She would later regret this position; see Barbara Ransby, *Ella Baker and the Black Freedom Movement: A Radical Democratic Vision* (Chapel Hill: University of North Carolina Press, 2003), 161, 234–235.

11. Dale Perkins interview with author.

12. Joy James, *Transcending the Talented Tenth: Black Leaders and American Intellectuals* (New York: Routledge, 1997); 59.

13. Joy James, *Shadowboxing: Representations of Black Feminist Politics* (New York: Saint Martin's Press, 1999), 41.

14. Elaine Tyler May, *Homeward Bound: American Families in the Cold War Era* (New York: Basic Books, 1988); Carol Anderson, *Eyes Off the Prize: The United Nations and the African American Struggle for Human Rights, 1944–1955* (New York: Cambridge University Press, 2003).

15. *Proceedings of the Founding Convention*, 79.

16. Ruth Feldstein, "'I Don't Trust You Anymore': Nina Simone, Culture and Black Activism in the 1960s," *Journal of American History* 91, no. 4 (March 2005): 1349–1379, and Rhonda Y. Williams, "Black Women, Urban Politics, and Engendering Black Power," in *Black Power Movement: Rethinking the Civil Rights and Black Power Era*, ed. Peniel E. Joseph (New York: Routledge, 2006), 79–103, both highlight this blending of ideologies in black women's activism during the 1960s.

17. Belinda Robnett, *How Long? How Long? African American Women in the Struggle for Civil Rights* (New York: Oxford University Press, 2000), presents the idea of black women in the Civil Rights Movement as bridge leaders, and there has been a dominant emphasis in the literature on black women as local organizers and grassroots activists.

18. See Esther Cooper Jackson and Constance Pohl, eds., *Freedomways Reader: Prophets in Their Own Country* (Boulder: Westview, 2001).

19. A prominent example that reflects both trends can be found in May, *Homeward Bound*. See also Rod Bush, *We Are Not What We Seem: Black Nationalism and Class Struggle in the American Century* (New York: New York University Press, 1999), which makes little mention of postwar radicalism, and Anderson, *Eyes Off the Prize*. Mary Helen Washington addresses this erasure in "Alice Childress, Lorraine Hansberry and Claudia Jones: Black Women Write the Popular Front," in *Left of the Color Line: Race, Radicalism and Twentieth-Century Literature in the United States*, ed. Bill V. Mullen and James Smethurst (Chapel Hill: University of North Carolina Press, 2003), 183–204.

20. Some early examples of this groundbreaking work are Gerald Horne, *Black and Red: W. E. B. Du Bois and Afro-American Response to the Cold War, 1944–1963* (Albany: State University of New York Press, 1986); Gerald Horne, *Communist Front? The Civil Rights Congress, 1946–1956* (Rutherford, NJ: Fairleigh Dickinson University Press, 1988); and Joanne Meyerowitz, ed., *Not June Cleaver: Women and Gender in Postwar America, 1945–1960* (Philadelphia: Temple University Press, 1994).

21. Martha Biondi, *To Stand and Fight: The Struggle for Civil Rights in Postwar New York* (Cambridge, MA: Harvard University Press, 2003), 6.

22. Penny M. Von Eschen, *Race against Empire: Black Americans and Anticolonialism, 1937–1957* (Ithaca: Cornell University Press, 1996), 5.

23. Daniel Horowitz, *Betty Friedan and the Making of "The Feminine Mystique": The American Left, the Cold War, and Modern Feminism* (Amherst: University of Massachusetts Press, 1998); Timothy Tyson, *Radio Free Dixie: Robert F. Williams and the Roots of Black Power* (Chapel Hill: University of North Carolina Press, 1999); Kate Weigand, *Red Feminism: American Communism and the Making of Women's Liberation* (Baltimore: Johns Hopkins University Press, 2001); Angela Dillard, *Faith in the City: Preaching Radical Social Change in Detroit* (Ann Arbor: University of Michigan Press, 2007); Nikhil Pal Singh, *Black Is a Country: Race and the Unfinished Struggle for Democracy* (Cambridge, MA: Harvard University Press, 2005); Biondi, *To Stand and Fight*; Michael Denning, *The Cultural Front: The Laboring of American Culture in the Twentieth Century* (New York: Verso, 1998); Jeanne Theoharis and Komozi Woodard, eds., *Freedom North: Black Freedom Struggles outside the South, 1940–1980* (New York: Palgrave Macmillan,

2003); James Smethurst, *The Black Arts Movement: Literary Nationalism in the 1960s and 1970s* (Chapel Hill: University of North Carolina Press, 2005); Gerald Horne, *Black Liberation/Red Scare: Ben Davis and the Communist Party* (Cranbury, NJ: Associated University Presses, 1994); Horne, *Black and Red*; and Jacqueline Dowd Hall, "The Long Civil Rights Movement," *Journal of American History* 91, no. 4 (March 2005): 1233–1254.

24. Singh, *Black Is a Country*, 52–53.

25. See Singh, *Black Is a Country*; Penial E. Joseph, *Waiting 'Til the Midnight Hour: A Narrative History of Black Power in America* (New York: Henry Holt, 2006); and Von Eschen, *Race against Empire*. Studies focused on majority-white women's activism include Weigand, *Red Feminism*; Ruth Rosen, *The World Split Open: How the Modern Women's Movement Changed America* (New York: Penguin, 2000), esp. chap. 1; and Susan Lynn, *Progressive Women in Conservative Times: Racial Justice, Peace and Feminism, 1845–1960s* (New Brunswick, NJ: Rutgers University Press, 1992).

26. Biondi, *To Stand and Fight*, 277. For examples, see Horowitz, *Betty Friedan*, and Singh, *Black Is a Country*.

27. Alice Childress and her family endured government surveillance for almost seven years, from 1951 to 1958. See FBI File, box 1, folder 8, Alice Childress Papers, Manuscript, Archives and Rare Books Division, Schomburg Center for Research in Black Culture, New York Public Library (hereafter ACP). "Statement of Miss Thelma Dale," *U.S. Congress Senate Committee Hearing, 74th Congress*, vol. 519 (1936), 223–225; "Testimony of Mrs. Marvel J. Cooke," September 1, 1953, *U.S. Congress Senate Committee Hearings, Communist Influence among Army Civilian Workers Investigation, 83rd Congress* (Washington, DC: Government Printing Office, 1953), 4–8; and "Testimony of Vicki Garvin,"

February 15, 1952, *Hearing before the Sub-committee to Investigate the Administration of the Internal Security Act*, 82nd Congress (Washington, DC: Government Printing Office, 1952), 204–211.

28. "Testimony of Dorothy K. Funn," *Hearings before the Committee on Un-American Activities House of Representatives, 83rd Congress* (Washington, DC: Government Printing Office, 1953), 1195–1229. Dorothy Funn was a key activist in the NNC.

29. Beulah Richardson, "The Revolt of Rosa Ingram," n.d. (1954?), part II, reel 15, frames 322–332, Civil Rights Congress Papers, microfilm, SC-Micro R6616, Manuscript, Archives and Rare Books Division, Schomburg Center for Research in Black Culture, New York Public Library (hereafter CRC Papers).

30. Much of the literature on African Americans and the U.S. left, especially the communist left, highlights the conflicts between Marxist doctrine and black equality and black nationalist politics. See Wilson Record, *The Negro and the Communist Party* (Chapel Hill: University of North Carolina Press, 1951); Harold Cruse, *Crisis of the Negro Intellectual: A Historical Analysis of the Failure of Black Leadership* (New York: Morrow, 1967); Bush, *We Are Not What We Seem*; and Earl Ofari Hutchinson, *Blacks and Reds: Race and Class in Conflict, 1919–1990* (East Lansing: Michigan State University Press, 1995). These women's politics, however, reveal a more complicated relationship to CP doctrine and black nationalist politics.

31. Von Eschen, *Race against Empire*; Robert Rodgers Korstad, *Civil Rights Unionism: Tobacco Workers and the Struggle for Democracy in the Mid-Twentieth-Century South* (Chapel Hill: University of North Carolina Press, 2003); and Anderson, *Eyes Off the Prize*, esp. 5–7. Here Anderson asserts that the black left was "destroyed by its own strategic blunders and the McCar-

thy witch hunts," leaving "no countervailing force, no matter how small."

32. In its broadest framing, this includes Ransby, *Ella Baker*; Alexis Deveaux, *Warrior Poet: A Biography of Audre Lorde* (New York: W. W. Norton, 2004); Chana Kai Lee, *For Freedom's Sake: The Life and Times of Fannie Lou Hamer* (Champaign: University of Illinois Press, 2000); Christina Greene, *Our Separate Ways: Women and the Black Freedom Movement in Durham, North Carolina* (Chapel Hill: University of North Carolina Press, 2005); Vicki Crawford, Jacqueline Anne Rouse, and Barbara Woods, eds., *Women in the Civil Rights Movement: Trailblazers and Torchbearers, 1945–1964* (Bloomington: Indiana University Press, 1993); Rhonda Y. Williams, *The Politics of Public Housing: Black Women's Struggles against Urban Inequalities* (Oxford: Oxford University Press, 2005); Annelise Orlack, *Storming Caesar's Palace: How Black Mothers Fought Their Own War on Poverty* (New York: Beacon Press, 2006); and Bettye Collier Thomson and V. P. Franklin, eds., *Sisters in the Struggle: African-American Women in the Civil Rights-Black Power Movements* (New York: New York University Press, 2001).

33. Although my research focuses on black women, other "racialized" women are also erased from traditional historical studies of the American left. These women's experiences are crucial if historians are to broaden our understanding of race beyond a black/white paradigm and build an analysis that does not view race, gender, class, sexuality, nationality, and so forth as distinct, static, and discontinuous subject positions.

34. Erik McDuffie, "'No Amount of Change Will Do': Esther Cooper Jackson and Black Left Feminism," in *"Want to Start a Revolution?" Radical Women in the Black Freedom Struggle*, ed. Dayo F. Gore, Jeanne Theoharis, and Komozi Woodard

(New York: New York University Press, 2009); Rebeccah Welch, "Spokesman of the Oppressed? Lorraine Hansberry at Work: The Challenge of Radical Politics in the Postwar Era," *Souls* 9, no. 4 (2008): 302–319; Carole Boyce Davies, *Left of Karl Marx: The Political Life of Black Communist Claudia Jones* (Durham, NC: Duke University Press, 2007). See also Regina Freer, "L.A. Race Woman: Charlotta Bass and the Complexities of Black Political Development in Los Angeles," *American Quarterly* 56, no. 3 (September 2004): 607–632; Gerald Horne, *Race Woman: The Many Lives of Shirley Graham Du Bois* (New York: New York University Press, 2000); Margaret B. Wilkerson, "Excavating Our History: The Importance of Biographies of Women of Color," *Black American Literature Forum* 24, no. 1 (Spring 1990): 81–83; Rebecca Hill, "Fosterites and Feminists, or 1950s Ultra-leftists and the Invention of AmeriKKKa," *New Left Review* 228 (March-April 1998): 67–90.

35. Horne, *Race Woman*, presents an illuminating and rich biography of Shirley Graham Du Bois, but provides few details of Graham Du Bois's activism in the U.S. during the 1950s, focusing instead on her international travels before moving on to her later work in Ghana and China. Erik McDuffie, in "New Freedom Movement of Negro Women," convincingly outlines the destructive force of government surveillance and Cold War anticommunism, but in focusing on the demise of the STJ the article obscures the ways black women radicals (individually and collectively) negotiated and survived such assaults and continued their activism in other spaces.

36. Three articles that reflect this are Washington, "Alice Childress, Lorraine Hansberry and Claudia Jones"; McDuffie, "New Freedom Movement of Negro Women"; and Dayo F. Gore, "'The Law. The Precious Law': Black Women Radicals and the Fight to End Legal Lynching," in *Crime and Punishment: Perspectives from the Humanities* 37 (2005): 53–83 (special issue of *Studies in Law, Politics and Society*, edited by Austin Sarat). See also Castledine, "In a Solid Bond of Unity."

37. Washington, "Alice Childress, Lorraine Hansberry and Claudia Jones," 199.

38. James, *Shadowboxing*, 44.

CHAPTER 1

1. "Biography Resume," box 1, Biography folder, Vicki Garvin Papers, Manuscripts, Archives and Rare Books Division, Schomburg Center for Research in Black Culture, New York Public Library (hereafter VGP).

2. Marvel Cooke, interview with Kathleen Currie, October 4, 1989, Session 1, Women in Journalism Oral History Project, Washington Press Club Foundation, 1–5; Marvel Cooke, interview with Kathleen Currie, October 30, 1989, Session 3, Women in Journalism Oral History Project, Washington Press Club Foundation, 51; Mark Naison, *Communists in Harlem during the Depression* (New York: Grove Press, 1983),152–153; Rodger Streitmatter, *Raising Their Voice: African American Women Journalists Who Changed History* (Louisville: University Press of Kentucky, 1994).

3. Carole Boyce Davies, *Left of Karl Marx: The Political Life of Black Communist Claudia Jones* (Durham, NC: Duke University Press, 2007), 18 and 32–44. Davies discusses the role of Claudia Jones in addressing these limitation but acknowledges that she "was not a lone singular figure or unusual" in articulating such politics.

4. Carol Marks, *Farewell, We're Good and Gone: The Great Black Migration* (Bloomington: Indiana University Press, 1989); Joe William Monroe Trotter Jr., ed., *The Great Migration in Historical Perspective: New Dimensions of Race, Class, and Gender* (Bloomington: Indiana University Press, 1991).

5. Sheila Gregory Thomas, telephone interview with Author, September 14, 2007, and June Cross, *Secret Daughter* (New York: Viking, 2006).

6. Claudia Jones, "Dear Comrade Foster: The Following Is the Autobiographical (Personal, Political, Medical) History That I Promised . . . Comradely Claudia Jones (December 6, 1955)," *American Communist History* 4 (2005): 85–93; Davies, *Left of Karl Marx;* "Alice Childress to Mr. Flanders, "December 31, 1974, box 1, folder 8, Alice Childress Papers, MG 649, Manuscripts, Archives and Rare Books Division, Schomburg Center for Research in Black Culture, New York Public Library (hereafter cited as ACP); La Vinia Delois Jennings, *Alice Childress* (New York: Twayne, 1995); Mark Solomon, *The Cry Was Unity: Communists and African Americans, 1917–1936* (Jackson: University of Mississippi Press, 1998): 106–107; Maude White Katz, interview with Ruth Prago, December 18, 1981, and Louise Thompson Patterson, interview with Ruth Prago, November 16, 1981, both in Radical Oral History Project, Tamiment Library and Robert F. Wagner Labor Archives, New York University (hereafter cited as Tamiment); Mark Solomon, "Rediscovering a Lost Legacy: Black Women Radicals Maude White and Louise Thompson Patterson," *Abafazi* (Fall-Winter 1995): 6–13.

7. Solomon, *The Cry Was Unity,* 106–107; Maude White Katz, interview with Ruth Prago, December 18, 1981; Jacqueline Jones, *Labor of Love Labor of Sorrow: Black Women, Work and Family, from Slavery to the Present* (New York: Vintage Books, 1985), 160–172.

8. Ella Baker and Marvel Cooke, "The Bronx Slave Market," *Crisis* (November 1935): 330–331. Vicki Garvin, interview with Lincoln Bergman, tape 1, Oak Park, IL, circa 1980, Freedom Archives Collection, San Francisco, CA.

9. Davies, *Left of Karl Marx;* Jones, "Dear Comrade Foster; Cooke, interview with Kathleen Currie, October 30, 1989, Session 3, 71.

10. Solomon, *The Cry Was Unity,* 148.

11. Cheryl Lynn Greenberg, *"Or Does It Explode": Black Harlem in the Great Depression* (Oxford: Oxford University Press, 1991); Robin D. G. Kelley, *Hammer and Hoe: Alabama Communists during the Great Depression* (Chapel Hill: University of North Carolina Press, 1990); Harvey Sitkoff, *A New Deal for Blacks: The Emergence of Civil Rights as a National Issue in the Depression Era* (London: Oxford University Press, 1978).

12. This moment of radical growth helped to bring to a close a decade of turmoil as U.S.-based communist and socialist organizations experienced a wave of contentious splits and significant realignments during the 1920s. The fracturing of the communist movement reflected real ideological differences and power struggles that would have a lasting impact on left organizations. In particular, it proved a double-edged sword for the Communist Party USA. While the expulsions helped to eliminate internal divisions and to build greater unity around a plan of action within the CP, the splits produced lasting political conflicts and an increasing anti-Communist Party sentiment among an already small and isolated U.S. left. These activists on the left crtiques of the Communist Party's political line were distinct from broader anticommunist politics. Robert J. Alexander, *The Right Opposition: Lovestoneites and the International Communist Opposition of the 1930s* (Westport, CT: Greenwood Press, 1981); Constance Ashton Myers, *The Prophets Army: Trotskyist in America 1928–1941* (Westport, CT: Greenwood Press, 1977); "Lovestonites," in *Encyclopedia of the American Left,* ed. Mari Jo Buhle, Paul Buhle, and Dan Georgakas (Champaign: University of Illinois Press, 1992), 435–437.

13. Kelley, *Hammer and Hoe*; Naison, *Communists in Harlem*.

14. Jones, "Dear Comrade Foster"; Buzz Johnson, *"I Think of My Mother": Notes on the Life and Times of Claudia Jones* (London: Karia Press, 1985), 7; Marika Sherwood, *Claudia Jones: A Life in Exile* (London: Lawrence and Wishart, 1999); Robin D. G. Kelley, "Jones, Claudia," in *Black Women in America: An Historical Encyclopedia*, vol. 1, eds. Darlene Clark Hine, Elsa Barkley Brown, and Rosalyn Terborg-Penn (Bloomington: Indiana University Press, 1994), 647.

15. Vicki Garvin, interview with Lincoln Bergman, tape 1.

16. "Toussaint L'Ouverture," *Wistarion: Hunter College of the City of New York*, vol. 34, 1936, p. 171, Hunter College Archives and "Biography Resume," box 1, Biography folder, VGP.

17. Miranda Bergman, telephone interview with author, June 28, 2007; Black Workers for Justice, "Celebration Women History Month with Vicki Garvin," in author's possession; "The Young People's Forum," *ABC Advance,* March 10, 1929; Wil Haygood, *King of the Cats: The Life and Times Of Adam Clayton Powell Jr.* (Boston: Houghton Mifflin, 1993).

18. Dorothy Douglas taught at Smith throughout the 1940s. Daniel Horowitz argues that she was an important influence on the political development of Betty Friedan, who attended Smith as an undergrad and who graduated the same year as Garvin; see Daniel Horowitz, *Betty Friedan and the Making of "The Feminine Mystique": The American Left, the Cold War, and Modern Feminism* (Amherst: University of Massachusetts Press, 1998), 50–55. Vicki Garvin, interview with Lincoln Bergman, tape 1; Victoria Holmes Best, "The American Federation of Labor and Social Security Legislation: Changing Policy toward Old Age Pensions and Unemployment Insurance, 1900–1932," M.A. thesis, Smith College, June 1942. "Best" was the name Garvin used after her marriage; although she rarely discussed this husband, it appears they remained married throughout her years at Smith.

19. Vicki Garvin, interview with Lincoln Bergman, tape 2, Oak Park, IL, circa 1980, Freedom Archives Collection, San Francisco, CA; "V. Best Represents Smith at Negro Youth Congress," *Smith College Weekly* (n.d.), and "V. Best Will Be Interviewed about Anti-Strike Legislation," *Smith College Weekly* (n.d.), box 1, newspaper articles, VGP.

20. Cooke, interview with Kathleen Currie, October 4, 1989, Session 1, 1.

21. Ibid., 17; Naison, *Communists in Harlem*, 70–76, 122.

22. Cooke, interview with Kathleen Currie, October 30, 1989, Session 3, 51; Naison, *Communists in Harlem*, 152–153; Baker and Cooke, "The Bronx Slave Market."

23. Thelma Dale Perkins, interview with author, October 4, 2007, Chapel Hill, North Carolina; Penny M. Von Eschen, *Race against Empire: Black Americans and Anticolonialism, 1937–1957* (Ithaca: Cornell University Press, 1996); and Doxey A. Willkerson, "William Alphaeus Hunton: A Life That Made a Difference," *Freedomways* 10 (Winter 1970), 254–258

24. Sheila Gregory Thomas, telephone interview with author; Yvonne Gregory, Federal Bureau of Investigation File, U.S. Government, FOIPA, in author's possession. See also June Cross, *Secret Daughter: A Mixed-Raced Daughter and the Mother Who Gave Her Away* (New York: Viking, 2006).

25. Audley Moore, interview with Cheryl Gilkes, in *Black Women's Oral History Project from Schlesinger Library on the History of Women in America*, vol. 8, ed. Ruth Edmonds Hill (Westport, CT: Meckler, 1991), 135.

26. Vicki Garvin, interview with Lincoln Bergman, tape 3, Oak Park, IL, circa 1980, Freedom Archives Collection, San Francisco, CA.

27. Maude White Katz, interview with Ruth Prago, December 18, 1981, Oral History of the American Left, 1976–1984, Tamiment; Mark Solomon, "Rediscovering a Lost Legacy: Black Women Radicals Maude White and Louise Thompson Patterson," *Abafazi* (Fall-Winter) 1995, 7; Harry Haywood, *Black Bolshevik: Autobiography of an Afro-American Communist* (Chicago: Liberator Press, 1978), 216 and 281.

28. In 1930, only 21.2 percent of Manhattan's black population had been born in the borough, while 49 percent had been born in southern states, with Virginia, the Carolinas, and Georgia contributing the largest number. See Naison, *Communists in Harlem*.

29. Louise Thompson Patterson, interview with Ruth Prago, tape 2, November 16, 1982, Oral Interviews of the American Left, Tamiment. For a more detailed discussion of these experiences, see Claire Nee Nelson, "Louise Thompson Patterson and the Southern Roots of the Popular Front," in *Women Shaping the South: Creating and Confronting Change*, ed. Angela Boswell and Judith N. McArthur (Columbia: University of Missouri Press, 2006), 204–228.

30. Margaret B. Wilkerson, "Excavating Our History: The Importance of Biographies of Women of Color," *Black American Literature Forum* 24 (Spring 1990): 81–83; Nelson, "Louise Thompson Patterson and the Southern Roots of the Popular Front."

31. Thelma Dale Perkins, telephone interview with author, September 12, 2007. Judith E. Smith, *Visions of Belonging: Family Stories, Popular Culture and Postwar Democracy, 1940–1960* (New York: Columbia University Press, 2004).

32. The Southern Negro Youth Congress (SNYC) was founded in 1936 by leading CP activists Louis Burnham and James Jackson.

33. NNC, "National Executive Committee Meeting," microfilm, July 11, 1943, part 1, frame 188, reel 23, NNC Papers. "Statement of Miss Thelma Dale," *U.S. Congress Senates Committee Hearing, 74th Congress*, vol. 519 (1936), 223–225. She possibly lost her job for refusing to sign a loyalty oath.

34. For more on the NNC and it relationship to the SNYC, see Erik Gellman, "Death Blow to Jim Crow: The National Negro Congress 1936–1947," Ph.D. diss., Northwestern University, 2006.

35. Dale Perkins, interview with author, October 4, 2007; Communist Political Subversion, part 2, Appendix to *Hearings, Committee on Un-American Activities, House of Representatives, 84th Congress, Second Session*, 7250; "Wilbert to Thelma," February 7, 1943, part 2, reel 1, NNC Papers.

36. Kelley, *Hammer and Hoe*, 204–205; Augusta Strong, "Southern Youth's Proud Heritage," *Freedomways* 1 (Summer 1964): 35–51; Esther Cooper Jackson interview with author, May 20, 2002, Brooklyn, NY; "An Interview with Esther Jackson," *Abafazi* 9 (Fall-Winter 1998): 2–8; Erik McDuffie, "'[N]o Small Amount of Change Could Do': Esther Cooper Jackson and the Making of a Black Left Feminist," in *"Want to Start a Revolution?": Women in the Black Freedom Struggle*, ed. Dayo Gore, Jeanne Theoharis, and Komozi Woodard (New York: New York University Press, 2009).

37. Naison, *Communists in Harlem*, 25; Weigand, *Red Feminism*.

38. For a range of estimates regarding membership, see Weigand, *Red Feminism*, 25; Fraser M. Ottanelli, *The Communist Party of the United States: From the Depression to World War II* (New Brunswick, NJ: Rutgers University Press, 1991), 42–45; and Harvey Klehr, *Heyday of American Communism: The Depression Decade* (New York: Basic Books, 1984), 324.

39. Naison, *Communists in Harlem*, xix.

40. Solomon, *The Cry Was Unity*, 3–22; Cedric J. Robinson, *Black Marxism: The Making of the Black Radical Tradition* (Chapel Hill: University of North Carolina Press, 1983), 213–228; and Minkah Makalani "For the Liberation of Black People Everywhere: The African Blood Brotherhood, Black Radicalism, and Pan-African Liberation in the Negro Movement," Ph.D. diss., University of Illinois at Urbana-Champaign, 2004.

41. Debates over how policy came into being and its meanings for African Americans can be found in Solomon, *The Cry Was Unity*; Naison, *Communists in Harlem*, 18–20; Klehr, *Heyday of American Communism*, ch. 17; and Gerald Horne, "The Red and the Black: The Communist Party and African Americans in Historical Perspective," in *New Studies in the Politics and Culture of U.S. Communism*, ed. Michael E. Brown et al. (New York: Monthly Review Press, 1993), 199–239. For a discussion of the African Blood Brotherhood, see Rod Bush, *We Are Not What We Seem: Black Nationalism and Class Struggle in the American Century* (New York: New York University Press, 1999), 100–112.

42. Solomon, *The Cry Was Unity*, 305–307; Naison, *Communists in Harlem*,177–188; Gellman, "'Death Blow to Jim Crow.'"

43. Solomon, *The Cry Was Unity*, 305; Cooper Jackson, interview with author.

44. "Domestics Plan to Form Union," *New York Amsterdam News*, October 17, 1936, 12.

45. Moore (Queen Mother Moore), interview with Gilkes, 132; Naison, *Communists in Harlem*, 136. James Goodman, *Stories of Scottsboro* (New York: Vintage Books, 1994), provides a more in-depth look at the incident.

46. Marvel Cooke, interview with Kathleen Currie, October 31, 1989, Session 4; Naison, *Communists in Harlem*, 176.

47. Robin D. G. Kelley, "Africa's Sons with Banners Red; African-American Communists and the Politics of Culture, 1919–1934," in *Imagining Home: Class, Culture and Nationalism in the African Diaspora*, ed. Sidney J. Lemelle and Robin D. G. Kelley (London: Verso, 1994), 46.

48. Kelley, *Hammer and Hoe*, 92–116; Naison, *Communists in Harlem*, 72, points to such flexibility in the Harlem CP during the early 1930s, yet argues this was denounced by CP leadership. For example, George Padmore was expelled from the Negro Workers Congress in 1934 for "advocating the necessity for the unity of all Negroes on a racial bias." Not until 1935, with the implementation of Popular Front did building broad alliances and flexible membership become official party policy as the CP formed "united fronts" with black churches, the NAACP, and the Socialist Party. See Earl Ofari Hutchinson, *Blacks and Reds: Race and Class in Conflict, 1919–1990* (East Lansing: Michigan State University Press, 1995), 147.

49. James Smethurst, *The New Red Negro: The Literary Left and African American Poetry, 1930–1946* (London: Oxford University Press, 1999); Bill Mullen, *Popular Fronts: Chicago and American Cultural Politics, 1935–1946* (Champaign: University of Illinois Press, 1999); William J. Maxwell, *New Negro, Old Left: African-American Writing and Communism between the Wars* (New York: Columbia University Press, 1999):

50. "Domestic Union Has Huge Benefit Here," *New York Amsterdam News*, December 7, 1940, 10.

51. Solomon, *The Cry Was Unity*, 174; Maxwell, *New Negro, Old Left*. 6; Naison, *Communists in Harlem*, 73.

52. George Washington Carver School brochure, part 2, reel 8, NNC Papers.

53. Today the library is home to the renowned Schomburg Center for Research in Black Culture. David Levering Lewis, *When Harlem Was in Vogue* (New York: Knopf, 1981), and Smith, *Visions of Belonging*, 295–297.

54. Jennings, *Alice*; Sidney Poitier, *This Life* (New York: Knopf, 1980); Washington, "Alice Childress, Lorraine Hansberry and Claudia Jones," 186–187.

55. The CP perceived Negro liberation or "the national question" and "the woman question" in very different lights. For, although racism and sexism prevailed in the organization, "the national question" was taken up much more in theoretical debates and political practice, despite the fact that by 1940 women made up more than one-third of the Communist Party membership. For an overview, see Gerald Horne, *Black and Red: W. E. B. Du Bois and the Afro-American Response to the Cold War, 1944–1963* (Albany: State University of New York Press, 1996). Horne, "The Red and the Black: The Communist Party and African Americans in Historical Perspective"; Weigand, *Red Feminism*; and Elsa Dixler, "The Women Question: Women and American Communist Party 1929–1942," Ph.D. diss., Yale University, 1974.

56. Jones, "Dear Comrade Foster."

57. Barney Josephson, the founder of Café Society, imagined the Café as a U.S. version of Europe's political cabarets and relied on CP supporters. His brother was a lawyer affiliated with the party, and the song "Strange Fruit" had been written under the pseudonym Lewis Allen by Abel Meeropole, a Communist Party member and a school teacher in New York. See Michael Denning, *The Cultural Front: The Laboring of American Culture in the Twentieth Century* (New York: Verso, 1996): 323–326.

58. Dale Perkins, interview with author, October 4, 2007.

59. Moore, interview with Gilkes, 132–135; Pauli Murray, *Song in a Weary Throat: An American Pilgrimage* (New York: Harper and Row, 1987), 103. Also, the initial formulation of the thesis received little support from black Communists apart from Harry Haywood, often for reasons similar to those cited by Murray.

60. Kelley, "Africa's Sons with Banners Red," 43–44; Maxwell, *New Negro, Old Left*, 130. For a discussion of masculinist discourse among leftists, see Elizabeth Faue, *Community of Suffering and Struggle: Women, Men and the Labor Movement in Minnesota, 1915–1945* (Chapel Hill: University of North Carolina Press, 1991).

61. Maxwell, *New Negro, Old Left*, 147–149. For a discussion of triangulation within the context of lynching, see Sandra Gunning, *Race, Rape and Lynching: The Red Record of American Literature, 1890–1912* (New York: Oxford University Press, 1996).

62. Maude White, "Against White Chauvinism in the Philadelphia Needle Trades," *Daily Worker*, January 28, 1931, 36; Solomon, *The Cry Was Unity*, 138–145; Haywood, *Black Bolshevik*, 384.

63. Louise Thompson, "Negro Women in Our Party," *Party Organizer*, no. 8 (August 1937): 26.

64. Interracial dating between black men and white women was a common, if at times exaggerated, occurrence, yet such racial intermingling between black women and white men occurred much less frequently. See Claudia Jones, "An End to the Neglect of the Problems of the Negro Woman!," *Political Affairs* (June 1949): 5–67.

65. Party members within the Harlem section of the Communist Party have recounted black women's strong reaction to such interracial liaisons; they even called on the party to regulate black-white interracial marriages. Naison, *Communists in Harlem*, 136–137.

66. Thompson, "Negro Women in Our Party," 27.

67. Vicki Garvin, "Personal History—Marriage," VGP; Jones, "Dear Comrade Foster;" Haywood, *Black Bolshevik.*

68. Marvel Cooke, "Mrs. Paul Robeson, Manager and Mate," *New York Amsterdam News*, October 5, 1935, 9; Bill Chase, "All Ears," *New York Amsterdam News*, August 1, 1942, 8.

69. Cooke, interview with Kathleen Currie, October 6, 1989, Session 2, Women in Journalism Oral History Project, Washington Press Club Foundation, 17–18.

70. Chase, "All Ears"; Thelma Dale Perkins, interview with author, October 3, 2007, Chapel Hill, NC.

71. Victoria Best to Friends, part II, reel 12, NNC Papers; Dale Perkins, interview with author; and "Thelma Dale Assumes Post of General Manager of *Freedom*," *Freedom* March 1955, 7.

72. Dale Perkins interview with author, October 3, 2007. Dale's marriage to Perkins reflected the social interactions of people involved in New York's black left, as Larry Perkins was the ex-husband of fellow *Freedom* staff writer Yvonne Gregory.

73. See Maurice Isserman, Which *Side Were You On? The American Communist Party during the Second World War* (Middletown, CT: Wesleyan University Press, 1982); Denning, *Cultural Front.*

74. Many progressive men demonstrated their support of the war effort by enlisting or willingly accepting the draft. Dorothy Healey and Maurice Isserman, *Dorothy Healey Remembers: A Life in the American Communist Party* (New York: Oxford University Press, 1990); Cooper Jackson, interview with author; and Von Eschen, *Race against Empire.*

75. Joanne Meyerowitz, ed., *Not June Cleaver: Women and Gender in Postwar America, 1945–1960* (Philadelphia: Temple University Press, 1994); Gerald Horne, *Black and Red.*

76. Strong, "Southern Youth's Proud Heritage;" Ossie Davis and Ruby Dee, *With Ossie and Ruby: In This Life Together* (New York: Morrow, 1998), 119,145. Horne, *Black and Red.*

77. Perhaps the most dramatic manifestation of this vision came when Earl Browder, head of the CP, despite resistance led by William Z. Foster, formally dissolved the Communist Party in 1944, reformulating it as a political pressure group under the name the Communist Political Association (CPA). Ottanelli, *The Communist Party of the United States,* 209.

78. Healey and Isserman, *Dorothy Healey Remembers,* 92; Kelley, *Hammer and Hoe,* 119–137; "Popular Front," entry in entry in *Encyclopedia of the American Left,* ed. Mari Jo Buhle, Paul Buhle, and Dan Georgakas (Champaign: University of Illinois Press, 1992), 594.

79. Browder based his analysis on the 1943 Teheran Declaration, signed by Churchill, Roosevelt, and Stalin, in which the signatories pledged to collaborate in an effort to defeat Germany and to make a postwar effort to ensure continued peace. See Earl Browder, "Teheran and America," in *Communism in America: A History in Documents,* ed. Albert Friend (New York: Columbia University Press, 1997), 330–334.

80. The implications of these concessions became clear in the postwar period as organizations like the Communist Party and the Congress of Industrial Organizations held only weak links to the emerging movements around the politics and meanings of race and gender. For a discussion of these concessions in the CIO-PAC and the CIO's Operation Dixie, see George Lipsitz, *Rainbow at Midnight: Labor and Culture in the 1940's* (Champaign: University of Illinois Press, 1994), and also Michael Honey, *Southern Labor and Black Civil Rights: Organizing Memphis Workers* (Champaign: University of Illinois Press, 1993).

81. Edward P. Johanningsmeier, *Forging American Communism: The Life of William Z. Foster* (Princeton: Princeton University Press, 1994), 297–313.

82. See Nikhil Pal Singh, "Culture/ Wars: Recoding Empire in the Age of Democracy," *American Quarterly* 50, no. 3 (1998): 471. For the March on Washington movement see Jervis Anderson, *A. Philip Randolph: A Biographical Portrait* (New York: Harcourt Brace Jovanovich, 1973).

83. Claudia Jones, "End Jim Crow," radical pamphlet collection, Tamiment. "William to Thelma Dale," February 7, 1943, part II, reel 1, NNC Papers.

84. Garvin, interview with Lincoln Bergman, tape 3.

85. Vicki Best and Ewart Guiner to Dear Friend, August 2, 1946, part II, reel 1, and Vicki Best to Dear, September 11, 1946, part II, reel 24, NNC Papers. The letterhead includes a list of the Manhattan Council's leadership, as well as the UPOWA union bug.

86. See Yvonne Gregory, "Negro Women and the War" *Congress Vue*; Marvel Cooke, "Aubrey Pankey," *Congress Vue*, (October 1943), 6; Mary McLeod Bethune, "Job Security and Negro Women," *Congress Vue* (May 1944), 8; and *Congress View* (September 1945), Tamiment.

87. "Non-Partisan Women to Hold Meet," *New York Amsterdam News*, September 30, 1944, A10.

88. Von Eschen, *Race against Empire*, 19.

89. For a discussion of Cold War rhetoric and the "containment" of white middle-class women, see Elaine Tyler May, *Homeward Bound: American Families in the Cold War Era* (New York: Basic Books, 1988). An alternative perspective can be found in Meyerowitz, *Not June Cleaver*. For an examination of shifts in racial discourse, see Von Eschen, *Race against Empire*, 153–158. Singh, "Culture/Wars," 471–522, discusses the role of corporate funding and academic studies in this process, especially Gunnar Myrdal's *American Dilemma*.

90. Brenda Gayle Plummer, *Rising Wind: Black Americans and U.S. Foreign Affairs, 1935–1960* (Chapel Hill: University of North Carolina Press, 1996).

91. The criticism of Browder came from an article critiquing his policies written by French Communist leader Jacques Duclos and reprinted in the United States in the *Daily Worker*. U.S.-based opponents of Browder, such as Foster, had long opposed Browder's political vision and built on this critique and the growing wave of anticommunism to further discredit Browder's analysis and leadership of the Party. See Johanningsmeier, *Forging American Communism*, 293–313; Ottanelli, *The Communist Party of the United States*, 210–212.

92. Isserman, *Which Side Were You On?*, 464–467. Denning outlines some of the forces at work in the defeat of Wallace and the decline of the Popular Front in the postwar period, although he attributes their failures to an inability to respond to major shift in U.S. society including an inability to connect with southern working-class culture. Denning, *Cultural Front*, 29–38.

93. The cause of the demise of the Communist Party USA and the attendant Popular Front coalition has been much debated. Harvey Klehr, in an extremely critical analysis, has dated the CP collapse to 1939 and the Nazi-Soviet Pact, while others have pointed to the defeat of Henry Wallace, in 1948, as the last gasp of Popular Front radicalism amid increasingly hostile anticommunist attacks. Most historians agree that, for the most part, the CP entered massive decline in 1956 after Khrushchev's revelations and his denunciation of Stalin's brutality.

94. Horne, *Black and Red*; Weigand, *Red Feminism*.

95. It is notable that Vicki Garvin joined the party in 1947, a year after Browder's expulsion and in the midst of the Cold War. See author's interview with Esther Cooper Jackson, Vicki Garvin, interview with Lincoln Bergman, tape 2, and Ruth Pago, interview with Louise Thompson Patterson; Martin Bauml Duberman, *Paul Robeson* (New York: Knopf, 1988).

96. Rebecca Hill, "Fosterites and Feminists, or 1950s Ultra-Leftists and the Invention of AmeriKKKa," *New Left Review* 228 (March-April 1998): 67–90; Gerald Zahavi, "Passionate Commitments: Race, Sex and Communism at Schenectady General Electric, 1932–1954," *Journal of American History* (September 1996): 514–48. While Hill's article focuses on black women's activism, Zahavi's article notes the shift to race and gender in his study of CP organizing in Schenectady, New York, although he argues that the emphasis on rooting out white supremacy marked a major strategic misstep for the CP.

97. Thelma Dale, "Why I Raised the Woman Questions," 1943, part II, reel 34, NNC Papers; Martha Biondi, *To Stand and Fight: The Struggle for Civil Rights in Postwar New York City* (Cambridge, MA: Harvard University Press, 2003), 221.

98. See Thelma Dale, "Reconversion and the Negro People," *Political Affairs* (October 1945): 894–901. Thelma Dale provided key leadership to the National Negro Congress and in the 1940s penned several articles for *Political Affairs*. She also contributed to *Freedom* newspaper and worked as staff with the Progressive Party. Hill, "Fosterites and Feminists," suggests that Dale was a mentor to Claudia Jones, but, in interviews, Dale Perkins recalls Jones as a strong and inspirational figure in her own political life.

99. Dale Perkins, interview with author, October 3, 2007; Biondi, *To Stand and Fight*, 213.

100. *Beah: A Black Woman Speaks*, director, LisaGay Hamilton (Women Make Movies, documentary, 2003); Mel Gussow, "Beah Richards, 80, Actress in Stalwart Role," September 16, 2000, *New York Times*, 13A.

101. Beulah Richardson to William Patterson n.d., reel 5, frame 337, part 2, CRC Papers. See Rebeccah Welch, "Black Arts and Activism in New York, 1950–1965," Ph.D. diss., New York University, 2002, for a discussion of this community of activities. Mary Helen Washington, "Alice Childress, Lorraine Hansberry and Claudia Jones," in *Left of the Color Line: Race, Radicalism and Twentieth-Century Literature in the United States*, ed. Bill V. Mullen and James Smethurst (Chapel Hill: University of North Carolina Press, 2003); Smith, *Visions of Belonging*, has a detailed chapter on Lorraine Hansberry.

102. Lorraine Hansberry, "Flag From a Kitchenette Window," *Masses and Mainstream* (September 1950): 38-40 and Alice Childress, "Conversations from Life," *Freedom*, November 1951, 8 (microfilm), Tamiment.

103. Andrea Friedman, "The Strange Career of Annie Lee Moss: Rethinking Race, Gender, and McCarthyism," *Journal of American History* 94, no. 2 (September 2007): 456.

CHAPTER 2

1. Yvonne Gregory, "Poet Demands Equality for Negro Womanhood," *Freedom*, September 1951, 7, and Beulah Richardson, "Foreword" to *A Black Woman Speaks . . . of White Womanhood, of White Supremacy, of Peace* (New York: American Women for Peace, 1951), 1, microfilm, Sc Micro F-11727, The Schomburg Center For Research in Black Culture, New York Public Library, New York.

2. Molly Ladd-Taylor and Lauri Umansky, eds., *"Bad" Mothers: The Politics of Blame in Twentieth-Century America,* (New York: New York University Press, 1998).

3. Deborah A. Gerson, "Is Family Devotion Now Subversive? Familialism against McCarthyism," in *Not June Cleaver Women and Gender in Postwar America, 1945–1960,* ed. Joanne Meyerowitz (Philadelphia: Temple University Press, 1994), 151–176. The essay highlights a clear example of this politics as women activist (including wives of CP leadership) organized to support the families and children of CP activists experiencing government harassment.

4. Elsa Barkley Brown, "'What Has Happened Here': The Politics of Difference in Women's History and Feminist Politics," in *The Second Wave: A Reader in Feminist Theory,* ed. Linda Nicholson (New York: Routledge, 1997): 275.

5. Evelyn Brooks Higginbotham, "African-American Women's History and the Metalanguage of Race," *Signs* 17 (Winter 1992): 254–255.

6. Claudia Jones, "For New Approaches to Our Work among Women," *Political Affairs* 27 (August 1948): 741.

7. Cynthia Harrison, *On Account of Sex: The Politics of Women's Issues, 1945–1968* (Berkeley: University of California Press, 1988), x.

8. For a discussion of Cold War rhetoric and the "containment" of white middle-class women, see Elaine Tyler May, *Homeward Bound: American Families in the Cold War Era* (New York: Basic Books, 1988). For how this idealized image was used to mark black women's inferiority see Patricia Morton, *Disfigured Images: The Historical Assault on Afro-American Women* (New York: Praeger, 1991), 87–98.

9. Stephanie Coontz, *The Way We Never Were: American Families and the Nostalgia Trap* (New York: Basic Books, 2000), 23–41.

10. May, *Homeward Bound,* 13.

11. Ruth Feldstein, "Introduction" to *Motherhood in Black and White: Race and Sex in American Liberalism, 1930–1965* (Ithaca: Cornell University Press, 2000).

12. Feldstein, *Motherhood in Black and White;* Ladd-Taylor and Umansky, eds., *"Bad" Mothers;* and Robert J. Corber, *In the Name of National Security: Hitchcock, Homophobia and the Political Construction of Gender in Postwar America* (Durham, NC: Duke University Press, 1993).

13. Paula Giddings, *When and Where I Enter: The Impact of Black Women on Race and Sex in America* (New York: Morrow, 1984), 252.

14. For an examination of Frazier's discussion of the "matriarchy" and this postwar shift, see Daryl Michael Scott, *Contempt and Pity: Social Policy and the image of the Damaged Black Psyche, 1880–1996* (Chapel Hill: University of North Carolina Press, 1997), 41–55 and 71–80.

15. Dorothy Roberts, *Killing the Black Body: Race, Reproduction and the Meanings of Liberty* (New York: Vintage, 1997), 15–16; Scott, *Contempt and Pity,* 41–55; E. Franklin Frazier, *Black Bourgeoisie: The Rise of a New Middle Class in the United States* (1957; reprint, New York: Free Press, 1966); Roi Ottley, "What's Wrong with Negro Women," *Negro Digest* (December 1950): 71–75.

16. For examples, see Daniel Horowitz, *Betty Friedan and the Making of the Feminine Mystique: The American Left, the Cold War and Modern Feminism* (Amherst: University of Massachusetts Press, 1998); Dorothy Sue Cobble, *The Other Women's Movement: Work Place Justice and Social Rights in Modern America* (Princeton: Princeton University Press, 2005), and Vicki Ruiz, *Cannery Women, Cannery Lives: Mexican Women, Unionization, and the California Food Processing Industry, 1939–1950* (Albuquerque: University of New Mexico Press, 1987).

17. James C. Hall, "On Sale at Your Favorite Newsstand: *Negro Digest/Black World* and the 1960s," in *The Black Press: New Literary and Historical Essays*, ed. Todd Vogel (New Brunswick, NJ: Rutgers University Press, 2001): 188–206; Robin D. G. Kelley and Earl Lewis eds., *To Make Our World Anew: A History of African Americans* (Oxford: Oxford University Press, 2000), 569. For a discussion of how these debates played out in a broad range of women's magazines with majority-white readership, see Joanne Meyerowitz, "Beyond the Feminine Mystique: A Reassessment of Postwar Mass Culture, 1946–1958," in *Not June Cleaver: Women and Gender in Postwar America, 1945–1960*, ed. Joanne Meyerowitz (Philadelphia: Temple University Press, 1994), 230–262.

18. Pauli Murray, "Why Negro Girls Stay Single," *Negro Digest* (July 1947): 4–8; Ann Petry, "What's Wrong with Negro Men?," *Negro Digest* (March 1947): 4–7; Roi Ottley, "What's Wrong with Negro Women?," *Negro Digest* (December 1950): 71–75; St. Claire Drake, "Why Men Leave Home," *Negro Digest* (April 1950): 25–27.

19. Petry was the first black woman author to have a novel sell more than one million copies.

20. Alex Lubin, ed., *Revising the Blueprint: Ann Petry and the Literary Left* (Jackson: University of Mississippi Press, 2007). "Ann Petry," in *Notable Black American Women*, ed. James Carney Smith (Detroit: Gale Research Inc., 1992), 845.

21. Petry, "What's Wrong with Negro Men?," 5.

22. Petry, "What's Wrong with Negro Men?," 4.

23. Lovestone was expelled from the Party in the late 1920s for embracing a more reformist view of building socialism in the United States. He increasingly moved toward an anti-Communist Party position and built close ties to the Socialist Party.

Pauli Murray, *Songs in a Weary Throat: An American Pilgrimage* (New York: Harper and Row, 1987), 102–104; Barbara Ransby, *Ella Baker and the Black Freedom Movement: A Radical Democratic Vision* (Chapel Hill: University of North Carolina Press, 2003), 94–97; and Winston James, *Holding Aloft the Banner of Ethiopia: Caribbean Radicalism in Early Twentieth-Century America* (London: Verso, 1998), 259, 345.

24. Murray, "Why Negro Girls Stay Single," 6, 8. Murray viewed her article in conversation with several similar articles, including Ann Petry's and an editorial written by Almena Davis.

25. Murray, "Why Negro Girls Stay Single," 6, 8.

26. For more on Cold War discourses on homosexuality and the Cold War, see David K. Johnson, *The Lavender Scare: The Cold War Persecution of Gays and Lesbians in the Federal Government* (Chicago: University of Chicago, 2004); Donna Penn, "The Sexualized Woman: The Lesbian, the Prostitute, and the Containment of Female Sexuality in Postwar America," in *Not June Cleaver: Women and Gender in Postwar America, 1945–1960*, ed. Joanne Meyerowitz (Philadelphia: Temple University Press, 1994), 358–381.

27. Pauli Murray's struggles with homosexual desire and gender identity have been documented in Doreen Drury, "'Experimentation on the Male Side': Race, Class, Gender, and Sexuality in Pauli Murray's Quest for Love and Identity, 1910–1960," Ph.D. diss., Boston College, 2001; and Glenda Gilmore, *Defying Dixie: The Radical Roots of Civil Rights, 1919–1950* (New York: W. W. Norton, 2009); see also Pauli Murray Papers, Arthur and Elizabeth Schlesinger Library, Radcliffe Institute for Advanced Study, Harvard University.

28. Murray, "Why Negro Girls Stay Single," 4–8, and Gilmore, *Defying Dixie*, 325–326.

29. William Barlow, *Voice Over: The Making of Black Radio* (Philadelphia: Temple University Press, 1998), 78–81; Michael Denning, *The Cultural Front: The Laboring of American Culture in the Twentieth Century* (New York: Verso, 1996), 316, 396; Jenifer W. Gilbert, "Ottley, Roi," American National Biography Online, February 2002, http://www.anb.org.silk.library.umass.edu:2048/articles/16/16-01243.ht.

30. Ottley, "What's Wrong with Negro Women?," 71–73.

31. Ottley, "What's Wrong with Negro Women?," 75.

32. George Clement Bond, "A Social Portrait of John Gibbs St. Clair Drake," *American Ethnologist* 4 (1988): 762–781; Peter Flint," St Claire Drake Pioneer in Black Studies Dies at 79," *New York Times*, June 21, 1990.

33. Drake, "Why Men Leave Home," 25.

34. Drake, "Why Men Leave Home," 26.

35. Kate Weigand, *Red Feminism: American Communism and the Making of Women's Liberation* (Baltimore: Johns Hopkins University Press, 2001).

36. Betty Millard, "Woman against Myth," *New Masses,* 66, December 30, 1947, 9, 7.

37. Betty Millard, "Woman against Myth II," *New Masses*, 66, January 6, 1948, 7.

38. Millard, "Woman against Myth," 7.

39. Jones, "For New Approaches to Our Work," 738–749.

40. Quoted in Harriet Hyman Alonso, *Peace as A Women's Issue: A History of the U.S. Movement for World Peace and Women's Rights* (Syracuse: Syracuse University Press, 1993), 186.

41. Amy Swerdlow, "The Congress of American Women: Left-Feminist Peace Politics in the Cold War," in *U.S. History as Women's History: New Feminist Essays*, ed. Linda K. Kerber, Alice Kessler-Harris, and Kathryn Kish Sklar (Chapel Hill: University of North Carolina Press, 1995), 296–312; Weigand, *Red Feminism*, 48–49.

42. "NNC Executive at Paris Women's Meeting" *Congress View* 9 (December 1945): 1; Thelma Dale, "The Status of Negro Women," February 3, 1947, 6, part II, reel 34, NNC Papers.

43. Dale, "The Status of Negro Women," 1.

44. Dale, "The Status of Negro Women," 4.

45. Harriet Hyman Alonso, "Mayhem and Moderation: Women Peace Activists during the McCarthy Era," in *Not June Cleaver: Women and Gender in Postwar America, 1945–1960*, ed. Joanne Meyerowitz (Philadelphia: Temple University Press, 1994), 128–150. Richardson, "Foreword" to *A Black Woman Speaks*; Claudia Jones, "Negro Women in the Fight for Peace and Freedom," *Negro History Week* (Educational Department, New York State Communist Party, 1952), Claudia Jones, Vertical File, Tamiment Library and Robert F. Wagner Labor Archives, New York University (hereafter Tamiment).

46. Alonso, *Peace as a Women's Issue*, 190–191.

47. Gregory, "Poet Demands Equality," 7.

48. Richardson, *A Black Woman Speaks*, 1.

49. Richardson, *A Black Woman Speaks*, 11.

50. Richardson, *A Black Woman Speaks*, 5.

51. Richardson, *A Black Woman Speaks*, 6.

52. Elsa Barkley Brown, "'What Has Happened Here': The Politics of Difference in Women's History and Feminist Politics," *Feminist Studies* 18 (Summer 1992): 302–307.

53. Richardson, *A Black Woman Speaks*, 6.

54. Richardson, *A Black Woman Speaks*, 2.

55. Richardson, *A Black Woman Speaks*, 11.

56. Gregory, "Poet Demands Equality," 7.

57. Alice Childress, "A Candle in a Gale Wind," in *Black Women Writers 1950–1980: A Critical Evaluation*, ed. Mari Evans (New York: Anchor Books/Doubleday, 1984), 112.

58. For a discussion of postwar gender and raced cultural politics and mass media, see George Lipsitz, *Rainbow at Midnight: Labor and Culture in the 1940s* (Champaign: University of Illinois Press, 1994), especially part 4; Meyerowitz, "Beyond the Feminine

Mystique," in *Not June Cleaver,* 229–262; May, *Homeward Bound,* 92–96.

59. Claudia Jones, "International Women's Day and the Struggle for Peace," *Political Affairs* 29 (March 1950): 35.

60. Childress, "A Candle in a Gale Wind," 112.

61. Childress, "A Candle in a Gale Wind," 115; Mary Helen Washington, "Alice Childress, Lorraine Hansberry and Claudia Jones: Black Women Write the Popular Front," in *Left of the Color Line: Race, Radicalism and Twentieth-Century Literature in the United States,* ed. Bill V. Mullen and James Smethurst (Chapel Hill: University of North Carolina Press, 2003).

62. These campaigns are discussed in more detail in chapter 3. Yvonne Gregory, "Long Distance to Life," *Freedom,* February 1951, 2; Lorraine Hansberry, "Lynchsong," *Masses and Mainstream* 4, no. 7 (1951): 31; Robert Nemiroff, "From These Roots: Lorraine Hansberry and the South," *Southern Exposure* (September-October, 1984): 32–36.

63. Robert Nemiroff ed., *To Be Young, Gifted, and Black: Lorraine Hansberry in Her Own Words* (New York: Vintage Books, 1969), 78.

64. Sidney Poitier, *This Life* (New York: Knopf, 1980), 121–122.

65. For a discussion of the CNA, see Lorraine Hansberry, "A Medal For Willie" *Freedom,* 7; Gerald Horne, *Black and Red: W. E. B. Du Bois and the Afro-American Response to the Cold War, 1944-1963* (Albany: State University of New York Press, 1986), 278; and Denning, *The Cultural Front,* 370. For the American Negro Theatre, see Alice Childress, "For a Negro Theater," *Masses and Mainstream* 4, no. 2 (1951): 61–64.

66. Washington, "Alice Childress, Lorraine Hansberry and Claudia Jones," 198.

67. Alice Childress, "Florence," *Masses and Mainstream* 3, no. 10 (1950): 34–47; Alice Childress, "Introduction," *Like One of the Family: Conversations from a Domestic's Life* (Brooklyn,

NY: Independence, 1956); Elizabeth Brown-Guillory, "Alice Childress: A Pioneering Spirit," *Sage* 4, no. 1 (Spring 1987): 68.

68. All quotes from Childress, "Florence," 34–47.

69. Edward P. Johanningsmeier, *Forging American Communism: The Life of William Z. Foster* (Princeton: Princeton University Press, 1994), 305–312.

70. Rebecca Hill, "Fosterites and Feminists, or 1950s Ultra-Leftists and the Invention of AmeriKKKa," *New Left Review* 228 (March-April 1998): 67–90; Maurice Isserman, *Which Side Were You On? The American Communist Party during the Second World War* (Middletown, CT: Wesleyan University Press, 1982).

71. Claudia Jones, "On the Right to Self-Determination for the Negro People in the Black Belt (Discussion Article)," *Political Affairs* 25 (January 1946): 72.

72. Jones, "On the Right to Self-Determination," 67, and Jones, "For New Approaches," 738.

73. Carole Boyce Davis, *Left of Karl Marx: The Political Life of Black Communist Claudia Jones* (Durham, NC: Duke University Press, 2007), 40, 56.

74. Jones, "International Women's Day and the Struggle for Peace," 35.

75. Jones, "For New Approaches to Our Work," 739.

76. Jones, "For New Approaches to Our Work," 741.

77. Claudia Jones, "An End to the Neglect of the Problems of the Negro Woman!," *Political Affairs* 28 (June 1949): 51–67.

78. Robin Kelley, "Jones, Claudia," in *Encyclopedia of the American Left,* ed. Mari Jo Buhle, Paul Buhle, and Dan Georgakas (Champaign: University of Illinois Press, 1992): 394; Buzz Johnson, "*I Think of My Mother": Notes on the Life and Times of Claudia Jones* (London: Karia Press, 1985); and Marika Sherwood, *Claudia Jones: A Life in Exile* (London: Lawrence and Wishart, 1999).

79. Thelma Dale Perkins interview with author, October 4, 2007, Chapel Hill, NC.

80. Quoted in Weigand, *Red Feminism*, 107; Hill, "Fosterites and Feminists," 68–69.

81. Jones, "An End to the Neglect," 64.

82. Jones, "An End to the Neglect," 64.

83. Millard, "Woman against Myth," 7–10; and Millard, "Woman against Myth II," 7–10.

84. Quoted in Weigand, *Red Feminism,* 60; Jones, "An End to the Neglect," 66.

85. Higginbotham, "African-American Women's History."

86. Jones, "On the Right to Self-Determination for the Negro People," 68.

87. Jones, "International Women's Day," 36.

88. Jones, "An End to the Neglect," 61.

CHAPTER 3

1. "Brief of Evidence," *The State vs. Rosa Lee Ingram, Wallace Ingram, Sammie Lee Ingram,* Ingram Case File, no. 16263, Georgia State Archives; *Ingram v. The State*, 204 GA. 164, Supreme Court of Georgia (nos. 16263, 16264, 16256).

2. "Farm Mother, 2 Sons Await Electrocution for Slaying," *Atlanta Daily World*, February 3, 1948, 1.

3. "Farm Mother, 2 Sons Await Electrocution for Slaying." In Georgia, murder carried a mandatory penalty of death unless the jury recommended mercy, which would result in life imprisonment. See Judge Harper, "Ingram Case, Commuted to Life Imprisonment," April 5, 1948; case file 16263, Georgia Archives, Morrow, Georgia.

4. *Ellaville Sun*, November 7, 1947, 2; "Rehearing for Doomed Ingrams Set March 6," *Atlanta Daily World*, February 18, 1948, 1; and "A Citizen Defense Challenge," *Atlanta Daily World*, February 4, 1948, 6.

5. *Pittsburgh Courier*, February 7, 1948, 2; Charles H. Martin, "Race, Gender and

Southern Justice: The Rosa Lee Ingram Case," *American Journal of Legal History* 29 (1985): 249–268; and Virginia Shadron, "Popular Protest and Legal Authority in Post-World War II: Georgia: Race, Class, and Gender Politics in the Rosa Lee Ingram Case," Ph.D. diss, Emory University, 1991.

6. "New Trial Hearings Set for Ingrams Thursday," *Atlanta Daily World*, March 23, 1948, 1; "Along the NAACP Battlefront," *Crisis* (April 1948): 123; and Roger Didier, "Injustice Caused Courier to Take Side of Ingrams," *Pittsburgh Courier*, September 5, 1959, 6.

7. *Daily Worker*, February 20, 1948 and "Never Heard of Her—Truman" *Daily Worker*, March 26, 1948, 1. Communist Party members provided central leadership in the CRC, although its active members, even in the midst of the anticommunist assaults, included a range of progressive activists.

8. For a discussion of this with regard to the NAACP, see John Bracey Jr. and August Meier, "The NAACP As a Reform Movement, 1940–1965: 'To Reach the Conscience of America,'" *Journal of Southern History* 59 (February 1993): 3–30; and Mark Tushnet, *The NAACP's Legal Strategy against Segregated Education, 1925–1950* (Chapel Hill: University of North Carolina Press, 1987). For a discussion of CRC organizing in the early postwar years, see Charles Martin, "The Civil Rights Congress and Southern Black Defendants," *Georgia Historical Quarterly* 7 (Spring 1987): 25–52, and Gerald Horne, *Communist Front? The Civil Rights Congress, 1946–1956* (Rutherford, NJ: Fairleigh University Press, 1988).

9. Martin, "Race, Gender and Southern Justice"; Horne, *Communist Front?* While both Martin and Horne acknowledge the importance of gender and sexuality in shaping the Ingram case and the support of black women, their studies focus more

on the overall facts of the case, the political tension that emerged between the CRC and the NAACP, and their differing organizational strategies in engaging state and federal government.

10. Richard Sherman, *The Case of Odell Waller and Virginia Justice, 1940–1942* (Knoxville: University of Tennessee Press, 1992); Eric Rise, *Martinsville Seven: Race, Rape, and Capital Punishment* (Charlottesville: University of Virginia Press, 1995); Steven Lawson, David R. Colburn, and Darryl Paulson, "Groveland: Florida's Little Scottsboro," *Florida Historical Quarterly* 65, no. 1 (July 1986); John Goodman, *Stories of Scottsboro* (New York: Pantheon, 1994); and Jacquelyn Dowd Hall, *Revolt against Chivalry: Jessie Daniel Ames and the Women's Campaign Against Lynching,* revised edition (New York: Columbia University Press, 1979, reprt. 1993): 197; Jacqueline Dowd Hall, "'The Mind That Burns in Each Body': Women, Rape, and Racial Violence," in *Powers of Desire: The Politics of Sexuality,* ed. Ann Snitow, Christine Stansell, and Sharon Thompson (New York, 1983): 328; The Scottsboro Case involved the 1931 trial of nine young black men accused of raping two white women in Alabama and produced some conflict between the NAACP and the ILD. Other "legal lynching" campaigns developed under similar circumstances but were not handled by the CP or CP-affiliated organizations; these included the Odell Waller case, led by Pauli Murray and the Workers Defense League, a Socialist Party affiliate, and the Groveland case, handled by the NAACP and its Florida chapter, led by Harry T. Moore.

11. Yvonne Gregory, "Mrs. Ingram's Kinfolk: Two Telephone Calls and a Trip to Georgia," *Masses and Mainstream* 4, no. 11 (1951): 8–13.

12. "An Outline for Some Actions and General Program to Start Ingram Campaign," n.d. (1951?), reel 8, frames 197–198, Civil Rights Congress Papers, microfilm, Manuscript, Archives, and Rare Books Division, Schomburg Center for Research in Black Culture, New York Public Library (hereafter CRC Papers).

13. For a compelling study of the ways black consensus politics often emphasize issues that affect black men as community-wide concerns while providing little space for issues that are particular to black women's experiences, see Cathy Cohen, *Beyond the Boundaries of Blackness: AIDS and the Breakdown of Black Politics* (Chicago: University of Chicago Press, 1999), esp. 10–18.

14. Ruth Feldstein, *Motherhood in Black and White: Race and Sex in American Liberalism, 1930–1965* (Ithaca: Cornell University Press, 2000); Joanne Meyerowitz, ed., *Not June Cleaver: Women and Gender in Postwar America, 1945–1960* (Philadelphia: Temple University Press, 1994); Gerald Horne, *Black and Red: W. E. B. Du Bois and the Afro-American Response to the Cold War, 1944–1963* (Albany: State University of New York Press 1996).

15. Evelyn Hammonds, "Black (W)holes and the Geometry of Black Female Sexuality," *differences: A Journal of Feminist Cultural Studies* 6 (Spring 1994): 126–145; Darlene Clark Hine, "Rape and the Inner Lives of Black Women in the Middle West: Preliminary Thoughts on the Culture of Dissemblance," *Signs* 14 (Summer 1989): 912–920. See Danielle McGuire, "'It Was like All of Us Had Been Raped': Sexual Violence, Community Mobilization, and the African American Freedom Struggle," *Journal of American History* (December 2004): 906-931, for example of African American women's refusal to be silenced during the long civil rights movement.

16. See McGuire, "It Was like All of Us Had Been Raped"; Timothy B. Tyson, "Robert F. Williams, 'Black Power,' and the Roots of the African American Freedom Struggle," *Journal of American History* 85 (September 1998): 540–570. For a discussion of the politics of protection, see Farah Jasmine Griffin, "'Ironies of the Saint': Malcolm X, Black Women and the Price of Protection," in *Sisters in the Struggle: African American Women in the Civil Rights-Black Power Movement*, ed. Bettye Collier-Thomas and V. P. Franklin (New York, 2001), 214–229.

17. While there have been several articles written on the Ingram case, most have focused on the legal aspects of the case or the conflicts between the CRC and the NAACP organizing efforts.

18. Kate Weigand, *Red Feminism: American Communism and the Making of Women's Liberation* (Baltimore: Johns Hopkins University Press, 2001) locates women activists in the CP during the 1950s as a key source of feminist theorizing. Yet, as critiques of the work highlight, Weigand only briefly discusses black women's activism and misreads their intersectional politics. See Bettina Aptheker, "Red Feminism: A Personal and Historical Reflection," *Science and Society* 66, no. 4 (2002-2003): 519–522.

19. Sara Evans, *Personal Politics: The Roots of Women's Liberation in the Civil Rights Movement and the New Left* (New York: Vintage, 1979); Winifred Breines, "What's Love Got to Do with It? White Women, Black Woman and Feminism in the Movement Years," *Signs: A Journal of Women in Culture and Society* 27, no. 4 (2002); and Winifred Breines, *The Trouble between Us: An Uneasy History of White and Black Women in the Feminist Movement* (New York: Oxford University Press, 2007). Criticisms of this framing and discussions of the development of a radically influenced black feminists politics can be found in a variety of sources, including Kevin Gaines, "From Center to Margin: Internationalism and the Origins of Black Feminism," in *Materializing Democracy: Toward a Revitalized Cultural Politics*, ed. Russ Castronovo and Dana Nelson (Durham, NC: Duke University Press, 2002): 294–313; and Ruth Feldstein, "'I Don't Trust You Anymore': Nina Simone, Culture and Black Activism in the 1960s," *Journal of American History* 91(March 2005): 1349–1379; and Kimberly Springer, *Living for the Revolution: Black Feminist Organizations, 1968-1980* (Durham, NC: Duke University Press, 2005).

20. Much of the literature on African Americans and the left, especially the Communist left, highlights the conflicts between Marxist doctrine and black equality and black nationalists politics; see Wilson Record, *The Negro and the Communist Party* (Chapel Hill: University of North Carolina Press, 1951); Wilson Record, *Race and Radicalism: The NAACP and Communist Party in Conflict* (Chapel Hill: University of North Carolina Press, 1964); Harold Cruse, *Crisis of the Negro Intellectual: A Historical Analysis of the Failure of Black Leadership* (New York: Morrow, 1967); Earl Ofari Hutchinson, *Blacks and Reds: Race and Class in Conflict, 1919-1990* (East Lansing: Michigan State University Press, 1995); and Rod Bush, *We Are Not What We Seem: Black Nationalism and Class Struggle in the American Century* (New York: New York University Press, 1999). Peniel E. Joseph, *Waiting Til the Midnight Hour: A Narrative History of Black Power in America* (New York: Holt 2006), provides a revisioning of this debate. For a discussion of this debate in terms of the "long civil rights movement," see Sundiata Keita Cha-Jua and Clarence Lang, "The 'Long Movement' as Vampire: Temporal and Spatial Fallacies in Recent Black Freedom Studies," *Journal of African American History* (Spring 2007): 265–278.

21. See Harvey Klehr, *Heyday of American Communism: The Depression Decade* (New York: Basic Books, 1984); Fraser M. Ottanelli, *The Communist Party of the United States from the Depression to World War II* (New Brunswick, NJ: Rutgers University Press, 1991); Maurice Isserman, *Which Side Were You On? The American Communist Party during the Second World War* (Middletown, CT: Wesleyan University Press, 1982); and Ellen Shrecker, *Many Are the Crimes: McCarthyism in America* (Princeton: Princeton University Press, 1998).

22. Brenda Gayle Plummer, *Rising Wind: Black Americans and U.S. Foreign Affairs, 1935–1960* (Chapel Hill: University of North Carolina Press, 1996); Penny Von Eschen, *Race against Empire: Black Americans and Anticolonialism, 1937–1957* (Ithaca: Cornell University Press, 1997); and Carol Anderson, *Eyes Off the Prize: The United Nations and the African American Struggle for Human Rights, 1944–1955* (New York: Cambridge University Press, 2003).

23. For examples, see, Meyerowitz, *Not June Cleaver*; Rebeccah Welch, "Black Arts and Activism in New York, 1950–1965," Ph.D. diss., New York University, 2002; Mary Dudziak, *Cold War Civil Rights: Race and the Image of American Democracy* (Princeton: Princeton University Press, 2000); and Michael Denning, *The Cultural Front: The Laboring of American Culture in the Twentieth Century* (London: Kennikat, 1996).

24. Dorothy Cole, "Report," March 30, 1948, reel 8, frame 185, CRC Papers; and Martin, "Race, Gender and Southern Justice," 257.

25. Audley Moore to Dear Friends, March 11, 1948, part 2, reel 6, CRC Papers and Walter Lowenfels, "Ingram Delegation Leaves Tomorrow," *Daily Worker*, March 19, 1948.

26. Cole, "Report," and Horne, *Communist Front?*, 205.

27. Harper, "Ingram Case, Commuted to Life Imprisonment."

28. "Brief of Evidence," *The State vs. Rosa Lee Ingram, Wallace Ingram, Sammie Lee Ingram*, Ingram Case File, no. 16263, Georgia State Archives; *Ingram v. The State*, 204 GA. 164, Supreme Court of Georgia (nos. 16263 16264, 16256); Harry Raymond, *The Ingrams Shall Not Die!* (New York: Daily Worker) March 1948.

29. *Ingram v. The State*, 204 GA. 164.

30. "Motion for Re-Hearing," *Rosa Lee Ingram vs. The State*, Case File no. 16263, Georgia State Archives.

31. "Map Plans for Ingram Defense," *Atlanta Daily World*, August 8, 1948, 1.

32. William Patterson to Joe (Cadden), April 5, 1948, reel 8, frame 145, CRC Papers. Martin, "The Civil Rights Congress," 34. Joseph Cadden was the executive secretary of the CRC at the time of the letter.

33. Patterson to Joe, April 5, 1948, reel 8, frame 145, CRC Papers.

34. Maude White Katz, "The Ingram Case," August 11, 1949, 2, Ingram Clipping File, Schomburg Center for Research on Black Culture; and "Freedom for the Ingram Family: The Cornerstone of Civil Rights, a Pillar of Peace," n.d., reel 8, frame 147, CRC Papers.

35. Maude White Katz to Dear Brothers and Sisters, n.d., reel 8, frame 89, CRC Papers. White Katz was one of the few black women who had been active in the CP since the 1920s.

36. A. Vivian Clarke to William Patterson, January 12, 1950 (on NCFIF letterhead), reel 8, frame 92, CRC Papers.

37. Sponsor list included in NCFIF, "Statement of Purpose," n.d., reel 8, frame 88, CRC Papers; "Mrs. Mason in City to Form Women's Ingram Defense Unit," *Atlanta Daily World*, March 21, 1948, 1; and Mary Church Terrell to Vivian Carter Mason, March 24, 1954, reel 7, frame 940, CRC Papers. Founded by Mary McCloud Bethune, the National Council of Negro Women developed into one of the largest black women's organizations in the United States.

38. NCFIF, "Statement of Purpose"; Alice A. Dunnigan, "Ingram Delegation Found Both Contempt and Courtesy on Their Southern Tour," *Atlanta Daily World,* May 18, 1949, 3; Marion E. Jackson, "Women Push Plans to Free Ingrams," *Atlanta Daily World,* April 2, 1949, 1.

39. NCFIF, "Statement of Purpose."

40. "Help Free Mrs. Rosa Lee Ingram," reel 8, frame 102, CRC Papers; Robert M. Ratcliffee, "Mrs. Rosa Lee Ingram Tells Her Own Story," *Pittsburgh Courier,* July 10, 1948, 1–2; and Joseph North, "Prison Walls Have Not Stilled Her Voice," *Pittsburgh Courier,* April 8, 1949, 1.

41. NCFIF, "Statement of Purpose"; "Petition," reel 8, frame 97, CRC Papers.

42. Maude White Katz, "Learning from History—The Ingram Case of the 1940s," *Freedomways* 19 (1979): 1.

43. Feldstein, *Motherhood in Black and White*; see Ruth Feldstein, "I Wanted the Whole World to See: Race, Gender and Constructions of Motherhood in the Death of Emmet Till," in *Not June Cleaver: Women and Gender in Postwar America*, ed. Joanne Merowitz (Philadelphia: Temple University Press, 1994): 263–303, for a discussion of ways these debates shaped black women's civil rights activism.

44. For the use of intersectional analysis in U.S. history, see Evelyn Brooks Higginbotham, "African American Women's History and the Metalanguage of Race," *Signs* 17 (Winter 1992): 251–274; and Elsa Barkley Brown, "What Has Happened Here: The Politics of Difference in Women's History and Feminist Politics," *Feminist Studies* 18, no. 2 (1992): 295–312.

45. "Ingram Brief to Be Presented UN Officials in New York Sept. 21," *Atlanta Daily World,* September 16, 1949, 1; "Ingram Committee Members Received by UN Officials," *Atlanta Daily World,* September 27, 1949, 2; White Katz, "Learning from History;" NCFIF, "Freedom for the Ingram Family," reel 8, frame 147, CRC Papers.

46. Maude White Katz to Dear Friend, April 6, 1950, reel 8, frame 92, CRC Papers.

47. William Patterson, *The Man Who Cried Genocide: An Autobiography* (New York: International Publishers, 1971), 179 and Martin, "The Civil Rights Congress," 44–48.

48. "U.S. Accused in U.N. of Negro Genocide," *New York Times,* December 17, 1951, 13; William L. Patterson, ed., *We Charge Genocide: The Historic Petition to the United Nations for Relief from a Crime of the United States Government against the Negro People* (New York: International Publishers 1951); and Horne, *Communist Front?*, 155–182.

49. For black women's organizing in these cases, see Dayo F. Gore, "'The Law. The Precious Law': Black Women Radicals and the Fight to End Legal Lynching," in *Crime and Punishment: Perspectives from the Humanities* 37 (2005): 53–83 (special issue of *Studies in Law, Politics and Society*, edited by Austin Sarat).

50. "A Call to Negro Women," 1951, 1–3, box 13, folder 3, Louise Thompson Patterson Collection, Woodruff Library Special Collections, Emory University, Atlanta (hereafter cited as LTP); and Lorraine Hansberry, "Women Voice Demands in Capital Sojourn," *Freedom,* October 1951, 6.

51. A Call to Negro Women," 1; Yvonne Gregory, "Poet Demands Equality for Negro Womanhood," *Freedom,* October 1951, 7.

52. Hansberry, "Women Voice Demands," 6.

53. Hansberry, "Women Voice Demands," 6; Horne, *Communist Front?*, 208.

54. Elwood Dean, *The Story of the Trenton Six* (New York: New Century, 1949).

55. Hansberry, "Women Voice Demands," and Horne, *Communist Front?* Each of these black leftists had come under intense government investigation and endured protracted legal battles because of their political affiliations.

56. For studies of the STJ work beyond the Ingram case, see Erik McDuffie, "'New Freedom Movement of Women': Sojourning for Truth Justice and Human Rights during the Early Cold War," *Radical History Review* (Spring 2008); and Jacqueline Castledine, "In a Solid Bond of Unity: Anticolonial Feminism in the Cold War Era," *Journal of Women's History* (Winter 2008): 57–81.

57. "Minutes of the Enlarged Meeting of the Presiding Committee of the Sojourn for Truth and Justice," November 10, 1951, 1, box 12 folder 17, LTP.

58. Claudia Jones to Beulah Richardson, September 30, 1951, box 13, folder 5, LTP; and Audley Moore (Queen Mother Moore), interview with Cheryl Gilkes, *Black Women Oral History Project from Schlesinger Library on the History of Women in America*, vol. 8, ed. Ruth Edmonds Hill (Westport, CT: Meckler, 1991), 132.

59. "Membership Card," box 12, folder 18, LTP.

60. "A Call to Negro Women," 2–3.

61. "Minutes of the Enlarged Meeting of the Presiding Committee," November 10, 1951, 1, box 12, folder 17, LTP.

62. "Draft Constitution and By-Laws of the Sojourners for Truth and Justice," 1, box 12, folder 17, LTP Collection.

63. "A Call to Negro Women," 2, box 12, folder 17, LTP.

64. This is not to imply that black women radicals did not also face anticommunist attacks and government investigation. In fact, Claudia Jones, the highest-ranking black woman in the CP, could not fully participate in the STJ because of her arrest and ensuing conviction under the Smith Act. In 1953, Jones was sentence to serve a year in prison, and in 1955, after serving more than nine months of her sentence, she was deported to England for her political activism. However, because most black women did not hold visible leadership positions, they were not often on the front lines of such government prosecutions.

65. Feldstein, *Motherhood in Black and White*; Nikhil Pal Singh, *Black Is a Country: Race and the Unfinished Struggle for Democracy* (Cambridge, MA: Harvard University Press, 2005).

66. Charlotta Bass to Beulah Richardson, September 19, 1951, box 12, folder 19, LTP. The scholar Erik McDuffie writes of Louise Thompson Patterson's memory of a heated disagreement at a STJ meeting between Richardson and Claudia Jones. It is possible that Thompson Patterson was actually remembering the conflict between Bass and Richardson or that Richardson was involved several political dispute within STJ. See McDuffie, "'New Freedom Movement of Women,'" 94.

67. Claudia Jones, "Negro Women in the Fight for Peace and Freedom," *Negro History Week* (Educational Department, New York State Communist Party, 1952), 12; Claudia Jones Vertical File, Tamiment Library and Robert F. Wagner Labor Archives, New York University (hereafter cited as Tamiment).

68. "Editorials Speaking Bitterness" *Freedom*, October 1951, 2.

69. Jones, "Negro Women in the Fight for Peace and Freedom," 12.

70. "Dear Sojourners for Truth and Justice," September 25, 1951, box 12, folder 18, LTP.

71. "Announcements and fliers," box 12, folder 18, LTP; Julia Brown to Louise Thompson Patterson, May 21, 1952, LTP.

72. Charlotta Bass, "Sojourners for Truth and Justice Bulletin" (draft), 2, box 12, folder 18, LTP. This protest never came to fruition. The Sojourners received support for their proposal from the Mississippi delegation of white women, which declared that "the real unity with you our Negro sisters, can and must lead to freedom for Mrs. Rosa Lee Ingram." See "White Women's Delegation to Sojourners for Truth and Justice," n.d., box 12, folder 18, LTP.

73. "Announcing the Eastern Seaboard Conference of the Sojourners for Truth and Justice," 3, box 12, folder 18, LTP. Capitalization is in the original.

74. "Summary Proceedings," box 13, folder 1, LTP.

75. Charlotta Bass to Walter White, April 5, 1952, box 8, folder 7, LTP.

76. Geneva Rushin to Mr. Powe, August 7, 1951, reel 8, frame 134, CRC Papers. Rosa Lee Ingram to Mr. Powe, August 8, 1951, reel 8, frame 137, CRC Papers. This was short lived. In 1954 A. T. Walden would again act as legal counsel.

77. Yvonne Gregory, "Long Distance to Life," *Freedom*, February 1951, 2.

78. Yvonne Gregory, "Mrs. Ingram's Kinfolk: Two Telephone Calls and a Trip to Georgia." *Masses and Mainstream* 4, no. 11 (November 1951): 8–13.

79. Traveling throughout the South, Wells collected and published data on lynching. See Jacqueline Jones Royster, ed., *Southern Horrors and Other Writings: The Anti-Lynching Campaign of Ida B. Wells, 1892–1900* (New York: Bedford/St. Martins, 1997), 4, and Beulah Richardson, "Victims' Kin Rebuke Tobias; Want Justice," *Freedom*, December 1951, 1.

80. Gregory, "Mrs. Ingram's Kinfolk," 8–14.

81. "An Outline for Some Actions and General Program to Start Ingram Campaign," reel 8, frames 197–198, CRC Papers. Although the memo did not list any authors, the use of language such as "black belt oppression" and the discussion of the Smith Act and Negro-white unity suggest that its authors were close to or members of the Communist Party.

82. *Women's Committee for Equal Justice*, Organizational Vertical file, Tamiment; Yvonne Gregory to Dear Friend, n.d., reel 8, frame 212, CRC Papers.

83. Mary Church Terrell to William Patterson, n.d., reel 7, frame 939, CRC Papers; William Patterson to Mary Church Terrell, March 9, 1954, reel 7, frame 935, CRC Papers.

84. "Prison Delegates Barred," *New York Times*, December 26, 1952, 8; "Segregation in Action," *New York Times*, December 27, 1952, 4; "Georgia Cops Break Word, Stop Ingram Delegation," *Daily Worker*, December 26, 1952; Martin, "Race, Gender and Southern Justice," 264.

85. WCEJ, "The Case of Mrs. Ingram," reel 8, frame 152, CRC Papers.

86. All quotes are from "A Call to the Women of the United States," reel 8, frame 180, CRC Papers. Italics are in the original.

87. WCEJ, "The Case of Mrs. Ingram."

88. For a discussion of this, see Sandra Gunning, *Race, Rape and Lynching: The Red Record of American Literature, 1890–1912* (New York: Oxford University Press, 1996).

89. William Patterson to Beulah Richardson, July 24, 1951, reel 5, frame 334, part 2, CRC Papers; *Beah: A Black Woman Speaks*, director, LisaGay Hamilton (Women Make Movies, documentary, 2003).

90. See Gregory, "Poet Demands," 7, and Richardson, "Victims' Kin Rebuke Tobias."

91. Beulah Richardson, "The Revolt of Rosa Lee Ingram," n.d., reel 15, frames 322–332, part 2, CRC Papers. A reference to Ingram being in prison for "nearly seven years" suggests that the poem was written in 1953 or 1954.

92. Loretta Waxmon to Halois Robinson, February 1,1954, reel 8, frame 2, CRC Papers. Active in the St. Louis CRC, Waxmon requested the poem for use in her discussion of the Ingram case and for the signature campaign.

93. "Talmadge States Ingram Stand," *New York Amsterdam News*, December 26, 1953, 15; Herman Talmadge to Dear Mrs. Symington, December 2, 1953, reel 7, frame 1020, CRC Papers.

94. "Rally at the State Capital" (flyer), 1953, reel 8, frame 370, CRC Papers; Women's Committee for Equal Justice, "A Report from Georgia," n.d. (circa May 1954), reel 8, frame 389, CRC Papers; "Talmadge Sulks—But Hears Pleas for Mrs. Ingram," *Daily Worker,* December 21, 1953, Ingram Clipping File.

95. William Patterson to Mildred McAdory, February 2, 1954, reel 7, frame 1015, CRC Papers.

96. Miriam B. Shultz to Dear Friends, January 27, 1954, reel 7, frame 901, CRC Papers; Viola Brown to Mr. Patterson, January 27, 1954, reel 7, frame 1018; and People's Defense Committee, "Miss Ingram Negro Mother in Prison for Life Because She Defended Her Honor," *The Defender,* February 1954, reel 8, frames 153–154, CRC Papers.

97. William Patterson to Anne Braden, April 15, 1954, reel 7, frame 896, CRC Papers.

98. Andrew Hemingway, *Artists on the Left: American Artists and the Communist Movement* (New Haven: Yale University Press, 2002), 226–227, 260–270.

99. "Dear Mr. Governor" (postcard), May 1954, reel 8, frame 380, CRC Papers.

100. Letter to Georgia Board of Pardons and Paroles, May 7, 1954, reel 7, frames 889–891, CRC Papers; WCEJ, "Prominent Americans Issue Mother's Day Freedom Appeal for Mrs. Rosa Lee Ingram," May 7, 1954, reel 8, frame 158, CRC Papers.

101. "Ingram Plea Renewed," *New York Times,* May 11, 1954, 9.

102. Ida F. Henderson to My Dear Dr. Terrell, May 4, 1954, reel 7, frame 886, CRC Papers; Mrs. G. Jones to My Dear Dr. Terrell [*sic*], May 13, 1954, reel 7, frame 885, CRC Papers;

103. Mary Church Terrell to Dear Mr. President, April 27, 1954, reel 7, frame 900, CRC Papers.

104. Talmadge to Mrs. Symington and Maxwell M. Rabb to Dear Dr. Terrell, June 1, 1954, reel 8, frame 113, CRC Papers.

105. The Provisional Committee to Free the Ingrams, "These Are the Facts of the Ingram Case," n.d., 1–4, Ingram Clipping File, Schomburg Center for Research on Black Culture.

106. "Mrs. Ingram and Two Sons Eligible for Parole Aug. 1," *Afro American,* July 16, 1955, 3; "Fight for Freedom Ingrams Still Goes On," *Afro American,* July 23, 1955, 1.

107. "Deny Parole to the Ingrams," *Chicago Defender,* September 5, 1955, 1.

108. The Provisional Committee to Free the Ingrams to Dear Friends, September 27, 1955, reel 7, frame 892.

109. The Provisional Committee to Free the Ingrams to Dear Friends, September 27, 1955, reel 7, frame 892, CRC Papers.

110. "An Evening in Honor of the 49th Birthday," reel 8, frame 375, CRC Papers. This flyer is one of the few extant records of WCEJ activities after 1954. Although it is not dated, I assume the event occurred in 1956, as Ingram was arrested in 1947 at the age of forty.

111. Federal Bureau of Investigation to Dayo Gore, September 19, 2007, in author's possession. After years of court battles and imprisonment, Claudia Jones was deported to England in 1955.

112. Trezzvant W. Anderson, "Freedom in August for Rosa L. Ingram and Her Two Sons," *Pittsburgh Courier,* June 15, 1957, 3, and "Georgia Officials Hint at Release for Ingrams," *Daily Worker,* June 13, 1957, 1.

113. Charles H. Martin, "Race, Gender, and Southern Justice: The Rosa Lee Ingram Case," *American Journal of Legal History* 29 (1985): 267. The NAACP and the CRC clashed over several "legal lynching" cases.

114. Roy Wilkins, head of the NAACP, argued that northern protests "do nothing toward getting freedom for Mrs. Ingram," while leftists protested the NAACP conservative tactics; Martin, "Race, Gender, and Southern Justice," 267.

115. "Rosa Lee Ingram, Sons, Denied Parole in Ga.," *Jet*, November 6, 1958, 10; Roger Didier, "Injustice Caused Courier to Take Side of Ingrams," *Pittsburgh Courier*, September 8, 1959, 1.

116. William Patterson, *The Worker*, September 1959,1. In this article marking the release of the Ingrams, Patterson acknowledged the impact of this claim on the work.

117. Trezzvant W. Anderson, "Will Georgia Parole Mrs. Ingram, Sons?," *Pittsburgh Courier*, August 8, 1959, 1.

118. "Georgia Ignoring Ingrams," *Pittsburgh Courier*, October 5, 1957, 1; "Freedom Is Denied to Ingrams," *Pittsburgh Courier*, November 1, 1958, 1.

119. Martin, "Race, Gender and Southern Justice," 268; Lawson, Colburn, and Paulson, "Groveland," 24–26. Odell Waller, Willie McGee, and the men of the Martinsville Seven were all executed for their crimes. Furthermore, the two surviving defendants in the Groveland, Florida, case each served more than twelve years in prison in spite of a decade-long campaign, led by the NAACP, that included the U.S. Supreme Court's overturning of the convictions and the vigilante murder of two of the four defendants.

120. "Mother and 2 Sons End Term in Killing," *New York Times*, August 27, 1959, 8; and "Now the Ingrams Have a Home," *Pittsburgh Courier*, June 25, 1960, 9.

CHAPTER 4

1. *Proceedings of the Founding Convention of the National Negro Labor Council*, 79, 1951, 8–9, box 1, folder 1, Ernest Thompson Papers, Special Collections and University Archives, Rutgers University Library (hereafter cited as ETP). Sam Parks was a former member of the Communist Party and an active member of Chicago's United Packing House Workers of America. See Randi Storch, "The United Packinghouse Workers of America, Civil Rights and the Communist Party in Chicago," in *American Labor and the Cold War: Grassroots Politics and Postwar Political Culture*, ed. Robert Cherny, William Issel, and Kieran Walsh Taylor (New Brunswick, NJ: Rutgers University Press, 2004), 78.

2. Yvonne Gregory, "Labor on the Move 1: Cincinnati Notebook," *Masses and Mainstream* 4, no. 12 (December 1951): 40–42.

3. *Proceedings of the Founding Convention*, 77.

4. See Rodger Zeiger, *The CIO, 1935–1955* (Chapel Hill: University of North Carolina Press, 1995) for a discussion of the ways the CIO leadership's embrace of anticommunist politics was shaped by efforts to align themselves with the Democratic Party and with Truman's foreign policy strategies.

5. Michael Denning, *The Cultural Front: The Laboring of American Culture in the Twentieth Century* (New York: Verso, 1996), 6.

6. For a review of some of this literature, see Eric Arnesen, "'New Graver Danger': Black Anticommunism, the Communist Party and the Race Question," *Labor: Studies in Working-Class History of the Americas* 3, no. 4 (2006): 13–52; also Ellen Schrecker, *Many Are the Crimes: McCarthyism in America* (Princeton: Princeton University Press, 1998); Ellen Schrecker, "Labor and the Cold War: The Legacy of McCarthyism," in *American Labor and the Cold War: Grassroots Politics and Postwar Political Culture*, ed. Robert Cherney, William Issel, and Kiernan Walsh Taylor (New Brunswick, NJ: Rutgers University Press, 2004); and Steve Fraser and Gary Gerstle, *The Rise and Fall of the New Deal Order, 1930–1980* (Princeton: Princeton University Press, 1989).

7. For recent scholarship that locates these pockets of resistant and gains see

Dorothy Sue Cobble, *The Other Women's Movement: Workplace Justice and Social Rights in Modern America* (Princeton: Princeton University Press, 2004) and Lisa Kannenberg, "The Impact of the Cold War on Women's Trade Union Activism: The UE Experience," *Labor History* 34 (2003): 309–323. See also Storch, "The United Packinghouse Workers of America, Civil Rights and the Communist Party in Chicago," and Margaret Miller, "Negotiating the Cold War: The Washington Pension Union and the Labor Left," both in *American Labor and The Cold War: Grassroots Politics and Postwar Political Culture*, ed. Robert Cherney, William Issel, and Kiernan Walsh Taylor (New Brunswick, NJ: Rutgers University Press, 2004).

8. Cobble, *The Other Women's Movement*, 4.

9. Cynthia Harrison, *On Account of Sex: The Politics of Women's Issues, 1945–1969* (Berkeley: University of California Press 1988), x; and Karen Tucker Anderson, "Last Hired First Fired: Black Women Workers during World War II," *Journal of American History* 69 (June 1982): 78–94.

10. Harrison, *On Account of Sex*, 5; Ruth Milkman, *Gender at Work: The Dynamics of Job Segregation by Sex during World War II* (Champaign: University of Illinois Press, 1987), 100.

11. William H. Harris, *The Harder We Run: Black Workers since the Civil War* (Oxford: Oxford University Press, 1982): 125 and 128; Anderson, "Last Hired First Fired," 84–86.

12. Cobble, *The Other Women's Movement*, 17.

13. Gerald Zahavi, "Passionate Commitments: Race, Sex and Communism at Schenectady General Electric, 1932–1954," *Journal of American History* 83 (September 1990): 514–548, argues that this shift alienated white male workers and precipitated the demise of the Communist Party and a broad-based class politics. For an analysis of the history of race politics and divisions within the labor movement, see Herbert Hill, "The Problems of Race in American Labor History," *Reviews in American History* 24 (1996): 189–208; Michael Goldfield, *The Color of Politics: Race and the Mainsprings of American Politics* (New York: New Press, 1997); and Bruce Nelson, *Divided We Stand: American Workers* (Princeton: Princeton University Press, 2001).

14. Joyce L. Kornbluh, "'We Did Change Some Attitudes': Maida Springer-Kemp and the International Ladies Garment Workers Union." *Women Studies Quarterly* 23 (1995): 41–70; Robert Rodgers Korstad, *Civil Rights Unionism: Tobacco Workers and the Struggle for Democracy in the Mid-Twentieth-Century South* (Chapel Hill: University of North Carolina Press, 2003); Martha Biondi, *To Stand and Fight: The Struggle for Civil Rights in Postwar New York* (Cambridge, MA: Harvard University Press, 2003), 17–32; Nancy Gabin, *Feminism in the Labor Movement: Women and the United Auto Workers, 1935–1975* (Ithaca: Cornell University Press, 1990); and Cobble, *The Other Women's Movement*.

15. For a discussion of women's postwar protest in the UAW, see Nancy Gabin, "Women and the UAW in the 1950s," in Ruth Milkman, *Women Work and Protest: A Century of U.S. Women's Labor History* (Boston: Routledge and Kegan Paul, 1985), 259–279; and Dorothy Sue Cobble, "Recapturing Working-Class Feminism: Union Women in the Postwar Era," in *Not June Cleaver: Women and Gender in Postwar America, 1945–1960*, ed. Joanne Meyerowitz (Philadelphia: Temple University Press, 1994), 57–83. For such efforts among black workers, see Harris, *The Harder We Run*, 138.

16. For a discussion of the shifts in demographics and policy, see George Lipsitz, *A Rainbow at Midnight: Labor and Culture in the 1940's* (Champaign: University of Illinois Press, 1994), 170–179; Cobble, "Recapturing Working-Class Feminism;" Michael Honey, *Southern Labor and Black Civil Rights: Organizing Memphis Workers* (Champaign: University of Illinois Press, 1993); Nelson Lichtenstein, "From Corporatism to Collective Bargaining: Organized Labor and the Eclipse of Social Democracy in the Postwar Era," in Steve Fraser and Gary Gerstle, *The Rise and Fall of the New Deal Order, 1930–1980* (Princeton: Princeton University Press, 1989), 133–134.

17. For a discussion of how these battles played out within the CIO, see Harvey Levenstein, *Communism Anticommunism and the CIO* (New York: Greenwood Press, 1981); Zeiger, *The CIO 1935–1955*; and Steve Rosswurm, ed., *The CIO's Left-Led Unions* (New Brunswick, NJ: Rutgers University Press, 1992).

18. Maida Springer, "The Trend in Negro Leadership," *Los Angeles Tribune*, January 26, 1946, 12.

19. Robert Korstad and Nelson Lichtenstein, "Opportunities Found and Lost: Labor, Radicals, and the Early Civil Rights Movement," *Journal of American History 75* (December 1988): 786–811.

20. Jacqueline Jones, *Labor of Love, Labor of Sorrow: Black Women, Work, and the Family from Slavery to the Present* (New York: Basic Books, 1985), 232–274. See also Tera Hunter, *"To 'Joy My Freedom": Southern Black Women's Lives and Labor after the Civil War* (Cambridge, MA: Harvard University Press, 1997), and Elizabeth Clark-Lewis, *Living In, Living Out: African American Domestics and the Great Migration* (New York: Kodansha International, 1996).

21. "Seeks to Organize Domestic Workers," *New York Amsterdam News*, March 24, 1934, 1; "Domestics Plan to Form Union,"

New York Amsterdam News, October 17, 1936, 12; and "Think Tank; Dignifying Work That's Never Done," *New York Times*, February 28, 1998, B11.

22. Ella Baker and Marvel Cooke, "The Bronx Slave Market," *Crisis* (November 1935): 330–331. Marvel Cooke, interview with Katherine Currie, November 1, 1989, Session 5, Women in Journalism Oral History Project, Washington Press Club Foundation, 27–28.

23. In 1936, DWU established the DWU Local 149-AFL. "Domestics Plan to Form Union," *New York Amsterdam News*, October 17, 1936, 12; and "Campaign to Wipe Out 'Bronx Slave Market,'" *New York Amsterdam News*, March 6, 1937, 13.

24. Ben Davis, one of the leading black figures in the CP, recruited Cooke to the party. Marvel Cooke, interview with Kathleen Currie, October 31, 1989, Session 4, Women in Journalism Oral History Project, Washington Press Club Foundation, 71–73; Mark Naison, *Communist in Harlem*, 176–177; and Daniel Leab, *A Union of Individuals: The Formation of the American Newspaper Guild, 1933–1936* (New York: Columbia University Press, 1970), 233–238.

25. Marvel Cooke, "Modern Slaves," *New York Amsterdam News*, October 16, 1937, 13–14; Marvel Cooke, "Bronx 'Slave Mart' Flourishes," *New York Amsterdam News*, July 9, 1938, 7; Marvel Cooke, "Slavery . . . 1939 Style," *New York Amsterdam News*, May 27, 1939, 17.

26. "'Slave Market' in City Protested," *New York Times*, May 19, 1938, 23; "Job Agencies to Replace Bronx Slave Markets," *New York Times*, March 20, 1941, 9; "'Slave Mart' Seen Doomed in Bronx," *New York Times*, May 2, 1941, 18.

27. "Testimony of Mrs. Marvel J. Cooke," September 1, 1953, *U.S. Congress Senate Committee Hearings, Communist Influence among Army Civilian Workers Investigation, 83rd Congress* (Washington, DC: Government

Printing Office, 1953), 4–8; Interview with Kathleen Currie, November 1, 1989, Session 5, Women in Journalism Oral History Project, Washington Press Club Foundation, 97–98. Bill Chase, "All Ears," *New York Amsterdam News*, August 1, 1942, still references Cooke as a staff member, and "Registration of Women to be Urged at Affair Held at Abyssinian Church," *New York Amsterdam News*, September 30, 1944, A10, lists Cooke as managing editor of *People's Voice*.

28. Jones, *Labor of Love, Labor of Sorrow*, 232–274.

29. Claudia Jones, "An End to the Neglect of the Problems of the Negro Woman!," *Political Affairs* 28 (June 1949): 51–67.

30. Alice Childress, "Conversations from Life," *Freedom*, September 1951, 8; Alice Childress, "Conversations from Life," *Freedom*, October 1951, 2; Alice Childress, "Conversations from Life," *Freedom*, November 1951, 1; Alice Childress, "Conversations from Life," *Freedom*, October 1952, 2; Alice Childress, *Like One of the Family: Conversations from a Domestic's Life* (Brooklyn, NY: Independence, 1956); and Mary Helen Washington, "Alice Childress, Lorraine Hansberry and Claudia Jones: Black Women Write the Popular Front," in *Left of the Color Line: Race, Radicalism and Twentieth-Century*, ed. Bill V. Mullen and James Smethurst (Chapel Hill: University of North Carolina Press, 2003), 183–204.

31. "New Paper Out Monday," *New York Times*, May 13, 1949, 17; and "New Paper Bows In," *New York Times*, May 17, 1949, 23. Marvel Cooke, interview with Kathleen Currie, November 1, 1989, Session 5, 103–105, and November 2, 1989, Session 6, 117–120.

32. Marvel Cooke, "I Was a Part of the Bronx Slave Market," *The Daily Compass* (New York), January 8, 1950, 1.

33. All quotes from Cooke, "I Was a Part of the Bronx Slave Market," 15.

34. Marvel Cooke, "The Bronx Slave Market: Where Men Prowl and Women Prey on Needy Job-Seekers," *The Daily Compass* (New York), January 9, 1950, 7; and Marvel Cooke, "'Mrs. Legree' Hires Only on the Street Always 'Nice Girls,'" *The Daily Compass* (New York), January 11, 1950, 21.

35. Cooke, "The Bronx Slave Market: Where Men Prowl and Women Prey on Needy Job-Seekers," 4.

36. Marvel Cooke, "Occupation: Streetwalker," *The Daily Compass* (New York), April 16, 1950, 2; Marvel Cooke, "Katie 'Given Away' at 3, Turned to Streets at 15," *The Daily Compass* (New York), April 17, 1950, 2; Marvel Cooke, "A Plan to Deal with Prostitution," *The Daily Compass* (New York), April 30, 1950, 6.

37. Marvel Cooke, "'Paper Bag Brigade' Learns How to Deal with Gypping [*sic*] Employers," *The Daily Compass* (New York), January 10, 1950, 21.

38. Marvel Cooke, "Some Ways to Kill the Slave Market," *The Daily Compass* (New York), January 12, 1950, 6.

39. Ted O. Thackrey, "Modern Slave Market," *The Daily Compass* (New York), January 9, 1950, 13.

40. "Expose Brings Move to Rid New York of 'Slave Markets,'" *The Daily Compass* (New York), January 18, 1950, 6.

41. "Biographical Resume," box 1, biography folder, Vicki Garvin Papers, Manuscript, Archives and Rare Books, Schomburg Center for Research on Black Culture, New York Public Library, New York (hereafter referenced as VGP); "Celebrating Women's History Month with Vicki Garvin," February 14, 1996, Women's Commission Black Workers for Justice, 4.

42. Victoria Holmes Best, "The American Federation of Labor and Social Security Legislation: Changing Policy toward Old Age Pensions and Unemployment Insurance, 1900–1932," M.A. thesis, Smith College, June 1942. Garvin went by Best, the name of her first husband, during all of her time at Smith College.

43. "Biographical Resume," VGP; "Celebrating Women's History Month with Vicki Garvin," 5; A. M. Wendell Malliet, "Race No Barrier—They Made It on Merit," *New York Amsterdam News*, January 29, 1944, 3A. For a discussion of the NWLB, see Lichtenstein, "From Corporatism to Collective Bargaining," 124–125.

44. Vicki Garvin, interview with Lincoln Bergman, tape 2; "Celebrating Women's History Month with Vicki Garvin," 6.

45. "Proceedings Eleventh CIO Convention," *Communism in America: A History in Documents*, ed. Albert Fried (New York: Columbia University Press, 1997), 372.

46. Vicki Garvin, interview with Lincoln Bergman, tape 2; Zeiger, *CIO*, 253–293; and Philip S. Foner, *Organized Labor and the Black Worker, 1619–1981* (New York: International, 1974), 281.

47. Vicki Garvin, "The Participation of UOPWA in This Conference," typed speech, n.d., 1 box 1, Trade Union Writings, VGP.

48. Thomas Richardson to Vicki Garvin, November 7, 1949, box 1, Trade Union Correspondence, VGP.

49. Vicki Garvin, interview with Lincoln Bergman, tape 2 "Vicki Garvin to David Livingston," August 29, 1951, box 1, Trade Union Correspondence, VGP.

50. "Negro Women Workers: Octavia Hawkins," *Freedom*, June 1951, 3; Childress, "Conversations from Life," *Freedom*, November 1951, 8.

51. Vicki Garvin, "Negro Women Workers: Union Leader Challenges Progressive America," *Freedom*, November 1950, 5.

52. Garvin, "Negro Women Workers." For a more detailed discussion of Claudia Jones's article "An End to the Neglect of the Problems of the Negro Woman!" see chapter 2.

53. "Initiating Sponsors" exhibit No. 148C–D, *Communist Political Subversions, Part 2: Appendix to Hearing before the Committee on Un-American Activities, House of Representatives, 84th Congress* (1956), 7366; "Harlem Trade Union Council Meet Planned," *New York Amsterdam News*, October 21, 1950,19; Foner, *Organized Labor and the Black Worker*, 294.

54. Quoted in Mindy Thompson, *National Negro Labor Council*, Occasional Paper no. 27 (New York: American Institute for Marxist Studies, 1978), 13; Yvonne Gregory, "Labor on the Move 1: Cincinnati Notebook," *Masses and Mainstream* 4, no. 12 (December 1951): 40–42; "New Council Maps Negro Jobs Battle," *New York Times*, October 29, 1951, 12.

55. Vicki Garvin, "Labor Council Links Fight of Negro People and Unions," *Freedom*, October 1951, 4.

56. Biondi, *To Stand and Fight*, 263.

57. For a discussion of NNLC connections and activism in Detroit, see Angela Dillard, *Faith in the City: Preaching Radical Social Change in Detroit* (Ann Arbor: University of Michigan Press, 2007).

58. Freedom Associates, later renamed the United Freedom Fund, was originally conceived as a fundraising and grant collective, but by 1952 it focused primarily on efforts "to raise monies for the budgets of the participating organizations." By 1952, most of these organizations shared the same housing space in Harlem. "Freedom," reel 8, frames 273–274, Paul Robeson Papers, and "Communist Come to Woo Harlem," *New York Amsterdam News*, September 29, 1951, 1.

59. *Proceedings of the Founding*, 1; Elaine Perry, interview with R. F. Prago, March 26, 1976, Oral History of the American Left, Tamiment Library and Robert F. Wagner Labor Archives, New York University (hereafter cited as Tamiment).

60. Perry recounts a telling story of her daughter being upset during a school lesson because Paul Robeson's name was not included on a list of great "Negro Leaders." Perry, interview with Prago, March 26, 1976.

61. Yvonne Gregory, "'Big Train' Speaks of the 'New Negro,'" *Freedom,* November 1951, 4; *Proceedings of the Founding Convention*; Foner, *Organized Labor and The Black Worker,* 299–300.

62. Garvin, quoted in *Proceedings of the Founding Convention,* 8.

63. *Proceedings of the Founding Convention,* 73 and 79; "NNLC Officers Elected," *Freedom,* November, 1951, 4; and "New Council Maps Negro Job Battle," *New York Times,* October 29, 1951, 12.

64. *Daily Worker,* October 25, 1951, 4; and "Labor Unit Set Up for Negro Rights," *New York Times,* March 2, 1952, 41.

65. "Labor Unit Set Up for Negro Rights," and Foner, *Organized Labor and The Black Worker,* 296, 306.

66. *Second Annual Convention Yearbook,* National Negro Labor Council, 1952, n.p., box 1, folder 2, ETP.

67. *Proceedings of the Founding Convention,* 31 and 69–71; Thompson, *National Negro Labor Council.*

68. *Brownwell Adds to Our Country's Shame,* 7, Civil Liberties Committee of the National Nero Labor Council, 1956, box 1, folder 5, ETP.

69. Jane Gilbert, "Negro Women and Jobs" (published interview with Vicki Garvin), December 23, 1951, box 1, NNLC folder, VGP.

70. Vicki Garvin, "Some Pertinent Facts on the Economic Status of Negro Women in the U.S.," box 1, Trade Union Writings, VGP; National Negro Labor Council, "The Truth about the FEPC Fight," 5, box 1, folder 5, ETP. Bill Chester to Revels Cayton, February 8, 1952, box 1, Trade Union Correspondences, VGP. Cayton was the brother of the renowned sociologist Horace Cayton Jr.

71. *Second Annual Convention Yearbook,* National Negro Labor Council, and *Brownell Adds to Our Country's Shame.*

72. "NNLC Convention," *Freedom,* December 1952, 1 and 4; *Second Annual Convention Yearbook.*

73. "Personal History Record," n.d., 3a, box 1, biographical folder, VGP.

74. Quoted in Vicki Garvin, "The Economic Status of Negro Women in the U.S.A.," n.d. (1952?), New York Job Action Conference, Hotel Theresa, box 1, speeches, VGP; "Announce Job Action Meeting for Saturday," *New York Amsterdam News,* March 8, 1952, 2; and "Labor Council Opens Job Drive in New York Area," *New York Amsterdam News,* March 15, 1952, 6.

75. "Rally March 16 for Job Rights of Negro Women," *Daily Worker* (Illinois), March 9, 1952, 8; Thompson, 28.

76. "Women Unionist Prominent in NNLC Meet," *Freedom,* December 1952, 4–5.

77. *Second Annual Convention Yearbook* and William Hood, "South: Heartland of Oppression; Land of Hope in Negro Freedom Fight," *Freedom,* December 1952, 5.

78. *Brownell Adds to Our Country's Shame,* 8–9.

79. *Brownell Adds to Our Country's Shame,* 6–7; "Summary of the Reunion of Former Leaders of the NNLC," December 12–13, 1970, 1, box 1. folder 7, ETP; "Give Us This Our Daily Bread," 1955, box 1, folder 5, ETP.

80. "The Truth about the FEPC Fight," 5, box 1, folder 5, ETP. The section included many of the same statistics and phrasing found in Garvin's *Freedom* articles and drafted speeches.

81. "Summary of the Reunion," December 12–13, 1970, 2. For a discussion of UE women's organizing, see Kannenberg, "The Impact of the Cold War," and Daniel Horowitz, *Betty Friedan and the Making of The Feminine Mystique: The American Left, the Cold War, and Modern Feminism* (Amherst: University of Massachusetts Press, 1998).

82. *Third Annual National Negro Labor Council Convention Yearbook*, 1953, 1, box 1 folder 1, ETP.

83. Vicki Garvin, interview with Lincoln Bergman, tape 3, Oak Park, IL, circa 1980, Freedom Archives Collection, San Francisco, CA.

84. "Sojourners for Truth and Justice to Vicki Garvin," n.d (1952?), box 1, folder Correspondence 1952–1992; and "Thelma Dale and C. B. Baldwin to Pearl Laws in Honor of Vicki Garvin," June 11, 1952, box 1, Congratulation Messages folder, VGP. Garvin also received congratulations from Viola Brown, Southern Regional VP of NLC, and from the American Women for Peace, which published Beulah Richardson's poem.

85. As discussed in chapter 2, Pearl Laws, Viola Brown, and Velma Hopkins all worked on the Rosa Lee Ingram case, while Laws also served with the Congress of American Women. See "Statement of Purpose," National Committee to Free the Ingram Family, n.d., reel 8, frame 88, CRC Papers; and "ALP Candidate Off for Moscow," *New York Times*, November 11, 1949, 11.

86. Vicki Garvin was not questioned about the NNLC and invoked the Fifth Amendment when questioned about the CP during her testimony before the Committee on the Judiciary Senate Hearings on the Subversive Control of Distributive, Processing and Office Workers of America. "Testimony of Vicki Garvin," February 15, 1952, *Hearing before the Subcommittee to Investigate the Administration of the Internal Security Act*, 82nd Congress (Washington, DC: Government Printing Office, 1952), 204–211, and Elie Abel, "Unionist Accused at Detroit Inquiry," *New York Times*, February 29, 1952, 6.

87. Abel, "Unionist Accused at Detroit Inquiry."

88. Luther A. Huston, "12 Groups Called Communist Fronts," *New York Times*, April 23, 1953, 1.

89. *The American Negro in the Communist Party*, December 1954, U.S. House of Representatives, Committee on Un-American Activities, Washington, DC, 11–12.

90. "Summary of the Reunion," December 12–13, 1970, 2; "NNLC Open Hearings: N.Y. Fights to End Job Bias in Hotels," *Freedom*, January 1954, 4; "Give Us This Our Daily Bread,"; and Komozi Woodard, *A Nation within a Nation: Amiri Baraka (LeRoi Jones) and Black Power Politics* (Chapel Hill: University of North Carolina Press, 1999), 37.

91. Vicki Garvin, "AFL-CIO Merger: New Hope for Negro Labor," *Freedom*, March 1955, 1 and 5; *Brownell Adds to Our Country's Shame*, 14; Vicki Garvin, interview with Lincoln Bergman, tape 4, Oak Park, IL, circa 1980, Freedom Archives Collection, San Francisco, CA.

92. Rosa Parks letter to Ernest Thompson, Chair of the National Negro Labor Council, June 15, 1956, box 1, folder 9, ETP.

93. Beth Bates, "'Double V for Victory' Mobilizes Black Detroit, 1941–1946," in *Freedom North: Black Freedom Struggles outside the South, 1940–1980*, ed. Jeanne Theoharis and Komozi Woodard (New York: New York University Press), 33, and Rosa Parks letter to Ernest Thompson, ETP.

94. *Brownell Adds to Our Country's Shame*, 16.

95. Ibid.

96. Harry Haywood, *Black Bolshevik: Autobiography of an Afro-American Communist* (Chicago: Liberator Press, 1978), 601. This reflects one of several major debates in the party, as a faction of black leftists, including Haywood, challenged this position, as well as the increasing turn away from strong support for the black national question.

97. Vicki Garvin, interview with Lincoln Bergman, tape 5, Oak Park, IL, circa 1980, Freedom Archives Collection, San Francisco, CA. Harry Haywood strongly asserts this view, particularly with regard to the NNLC, and blames "revisionism" for turning the party more mainstream and helping to destroy many of the black-led organizations in the mid-1950s. See Haywood, *Black Bolshevik*, 598–611. For a slightly different analysis of these internal struggles, see Gerald Horne, *Black Liberation/Red Scare: Ben Davis and the Communist Party* (Newark: University of Delaware Press, 1994), 270–304.

98. "Cover," *Brownell Adds to Our Country's Shame.*

99. *Brownell Adds to Our Country's Shame*, 16.

100. Vicki Garvin to Mr. Coleman A. Young, April 24, 1956, box 1, NNLC folder, VGP.

101. Vicki Garvin, interview with Lincoln Bergman, tape 2; and "Summary of the Reunion."

CHAPTER 5

1. Vicki Garvin, "Personal History—Marriage," 7, box 2, Original Drafts/Notes folder, Vicki Garvin Papers, Manuscript, Archives and Rare Books Division, Schomburg Center for Research in Black Culture, New York Public Library (hereafter cited as VGP); and Thelma Dale Perkins, interview with author, October 3, 2007, Chapel Hill, NC.

2. Vicki Garvin, interview with Lincoln Bergman, tape 4.

3. Cooke suggests that this job opportunity came about because Helen Rosen and her husband, Dr. Sam Rosen, were close friends of the Robesons and also were acquainted with Cooke's husband, Cecil. Marvel Cooke, interview with Kathleen Currie, November 2, 1987, Session 6,

Women in Journalism Oral History Project, Washington Press Club Foundation, 137–140; and Martin Bauml Duberman, *Paul Robeson* (New York: Knopf, 1988), 501–506.

4. In fact, Gregory would not reconnect with left activism after this period. Although she had struggled with mental health issues since early adulthood, in 1961 she suffered a severe "nervous breakdown" from which she would never fully recover. After living in Europe for a couple of years with her third husband, Gregory returned to the States in 1968 and died in 1971. Sheila Gregory Thomas, telephone interview with author, September 14, 2007; June Cross, *Secret Daughter A Mixed-Race Daughter and the Mother Who Gave Her Away* (New York: Viking, 2006), 165; and Yvonne Gregory Perkins, Federal Bureau of Investigation File, Department of Justice (in author's possession).

5. Robert Nemiroff, ed., *To Be Young, Gifted, and Black: Lorraine Hansberry in Her Own Words* (New York: Vintage Books, 1969); Mary Helen Washington, "Alice Childress, Lorraine Hansberry and Claudia Jones: Black Women Write the Popular Front," in *Left of the Color Line: Race, Radicalism and Twentieth-Century Literature in the United States*, ed. Bill V. Mullen and James Smethurst (Chapel Hill: University of North Carolina Press, 2003); Ira Peck, "No Time for Bitterness," *New York Times*, May 2, 1965, C5; Mel Gussow, "Beah Richards, 80, Actress in Stalwart Roles," *New York Times*, September 16, 2000, A13; and Carolyn Case Crag, *Women Pulitzer Playwrights: Biographical Profiles and Analysis of the Plays* (New York: McFarland, 2004).

6. Mark Solomon, "Rediscovering a Lost Legacy: Black Women Radicals Maude White and Louise Thompson Patterson," *Abafazi* (Fall-Winter 1995): 9.

7. In 1956, the CPUSA entered a major period of crisis and loss of members sparked by Soviet leader Nikita Khrushchev's criticism of Joseph Stalin's brutality and continuing factional debates about CPUSA policies, including its stance with regard to the "national question" and the "black belt thesis." Horne, *Black Liberation/ Red Scare: Ben Davis and the Communist Party* (Cranbury, NJ: Associated University Presses, 1994); Dorothy Healey and Maurice Isserman, *Dorothy Healey Remembers: A Life in the American Communist Party*, (New York: Oxford University Press, 1990).

8. Marvel Cooke, interview with Kathleen Currie, November 2, 1989, Session 6, 141–142; and Marvel Cooke, interview with Kathleen Currie, November 3, 1989, Session 7, Women in Journalism Oral History Project, Washington Press Club Foundation, 143–146.

9. Vicki Garvin and Maude White Katz, "Statement of General Purpose," n.d. (for May 15, 1960, meeting), 1, box 14, folder 9, LTP.

10. "Southern Boycott Spreading North," *New York Amsterdam News*, February 13, 1960, 11; "To Picket Woolworth Again," *New York Amsterdam News*, February 20, 1960, 34; "Photo and Caption," *New York Amsterdam News*, March 12, 1960, 5; Emanuel Perlmutter, "Many Here Picket at Chain Outlet," *New York Times*, March 27, 1960, 62; "Bias Foes Picket Woolworth Here," *New York Times*, June 16, 1960, 25; Garvin and White Katz, "Statement of General Purpose," 1.

11. Ibid. "Conference for Women of Africa and African Decent," 1960, box 14, folder 8, LTP.

12. Gerald Horne, *Race Woman: The Lives of Shirley Graham Du Bois* (New York: New York University Press, 2000), 156, and Duberman, *Paul Robeson*, 471.

13. "Minutes," African American Committee for Gifts, January 7, 1959, box 1, folder 3, LTP, and Blank Letterhead, "Afro

American Committee for Gifts of Art and Literature to Ghana," box 1, folder 1, LTP.

14. Shirley Graham Du Bois letter, March 23, 1960, and Shirley Graham Du Bois to Dear Members, April 28, 1960, box 14, folder 13, LTP.

15. All quotes from Garvin and White Katz, "Statement of General Purpose."

16. Esther Cooper Jackson quoted in Ian Rocksborough-Smith, "'Filling the Gap': Intergeneration Black Radicalism and Popular Front Ideals of *Freedomways* Magazine's Early Years (1961–1965)," *Afro-Americans in New York Life and History* (January 2007): 11; and Esther Cooper Jackson, "Introduction" to *Freedomways Reader: Prophets in Their Own Country*, ed. Esther Cooper Jackson and Constance Pohl (New York: Westview Press, 2000), xix–xxx.

17. Rocksborough-Smith, "'Filling the Gap,'" 23.

18. In his essay on *Freedomways*, Rocksborough-Smith convincingly makes the argument that the journal helped to sustain Popular Front–era "anticolonial, internationalist, and antiracism" activities but does not address the ways organizing for women's rights and black women's equality and articulating an intersectional politics were all central to this work, particularly for black women radicals.

19. In the early 1970s, Marvel Cooke also worked briefly with *Freedomways*, providing office support, but she never returned after an encounter with "a young black women" who worked as an "assistant in the office." Marvel Cooke, interview with Kathleen Currie, November 3, 1989, Session 7, 143.

20. All quotes from the editors, "It's a Journal!" *Freedomways* (Spring 1961): 7–9. Even in the biographies of its contributors, the editors rarely made mention of the author's past or current affiliations with CPUSA.

21. These efforts at non-partisanship did not always hold true, particularly as the 1970s split in the communist movement over the Soviet Union and Chinese relations reshaped U.S. left politics and increased tensions between black leftists and black nationalists. For example, Shirley Graham Du Bois and John Henrik Clarke both had conflicts with other *Freedomways* editors over the journal's limited reporting on black nationalist politics and international support for the anticolonial struggle in Angola. See Horne, *Race Women*, 217–223; and Elbaum, *Revolution in the Air*, 129–132, 207–221.

22. White Katz, "She Who Would Be Free-Resistance," *Freedomways* (Winter 1962): 60–71; and White Katz, "Negro Women and the Law," *Freedomways* (Summer 1962): 278–286.

23. Augusta Strong, "Southern Youth's Proud Heritage," *Freedomways* (Winter 1964): 35–50.

24. Augusta Strong, "Negro Women in Freedom's Battles," *Freedomways* (Fall 1967): 315.

25. Maude White Katz, "Learning from History—The Ingram Case of the 1940's," *Freedomways* (Winter 1979): 82–86.

26. Daniel Patrick Moynihan, *The Negro Family: The Case for National Action*, Office of Policy Planning and Research, U.S. Department of Labor, March 1965, at http://www.dol.gov/oasam/programs/history/webid-meynihan.htm.

27. Alice Childress, "Negro Woman in Literature," *Freedomways* (Winter 1966): 19.

28. Claudia Jones, "The Caribbean Community in Britain," *Freedomways* (Summer 1964): 341–357.

29. Beulah Richardson, "Victims' Kin Rebuke Tobias; Want Justice," *Freedom*, December 1951, 1 and 4.

30. Beulah Richardson, "Two Southern Cities," *Freedomways* (Winter 1964): 58–75.

31. Richardson, "Two Southern Cities," 58, 60, and 69.

32. Alice Childress, "Remembrances of Eslanda," *Freedomways* (Fall 1966): 329–330.

33. Sara Slack, "Reading, Writing and Arithmetic," *New York Amsterdam News*, April 2, 1966, 21; Maude White Katz, "End Racism in Education: A Concerned Parent Speaks," *Freedomways* (Fall 1968): 347–354.

34. "Boycott Keeps 1,450 Out of School in Harlem," *New York Times*, March 14, 1967, 49; William Jay Jacobs, "Parents and Politics," *Urban Review* 2 (December 1967): 3 and 27; Sidney Jones, "Letters: Parents and Politics," *Urban Review* 2 (April 1968): 13.

35. Jones, "Letters: Parents and Politics"; Kathleen Teltsch, "Election Splits P.S. 125 Parents," *New York Times*, May 14, 1967, 70; Sara Slack, "Now Parents Fight New Head of PA," *New York Amsterdam News*, May 20, 1967, 1.

36. Adina Back, "Exposing the 'Whole Segregation Myth': The Harlem Nine and New York City's School Desegregation Battles," in *Freedom North: Black Freedom Struggle Outside the South, 1940–1980*, ed. Jeanne Theoharis and Komozi Woodard (New York: Palgrave Macmillan, 2003), 65–91; Clarence Taylor, *Knocking at Our Own Door: Milton Galamison and the Struggle to Integrate New York City Schools* (New York: Columbia University Press, 1997); Daniel H. Perlstein, *Justice, Justice: School Politics and the Eclipse of Liberalism* (New York: Peter Lang, 2004); Jerald Podair, *The Strike That Changed New York: Blacks, Whites and the Ocean Hill-Brownsville Crisis* (New Haven: Yale University Press, 2002).

37. Quoted in Teltsch, "Election Splits P.S. 125 Parents," 70.

38. White Katz, "End Racism in Education," *Freedomways* (Fall 1968): 347–354, and Maude White Katz, "End Racism in Education: A Concerned Parent Speaks," in *The Black Woman: An Anthology*, ed. Toni Cade (New York: New American Library, 1970), 155–164.

39. White Katz, "End Racism in Education," 347–354.

40. See Tiffany Ruby Patterson and Robin D. G. Kelley, "Unfinished Migrations: Reflections on the African Diaspora and the Making of the Modern World," *African Studies Review* (April 2000): 11–45. They define diaspora as a process "constantly remade through movement, migration and travel as well as imagined through thought, cultural production and political struggle" and as a condition "directly tied to the process by which it is being made and remade," including "the context of global race and gender hierarchies which are formulated and reconstituted across national boundaries."

41. Kevin Gaines, *American Africans in Ghana: Black Expatriates and the Civil Rights Era* (Chapel Hill: University of North Carolina Press, 2004); James H. Meriwether, *Proudly We Can Be Africans: Black Americans and Africa 1935–1961* (Chapel Hill: University of North Carolina Press, 2002); George Hauser, *No One Can Stop the Rain: Glimpses of Africa's Liberation Struggle* (New York: Pilgrim Press, 1989); Ronald W. Walters, *Pan-Africanism in the African Diaspora: An Analysis of Modern Afrocentric Political Movements* (Detroit: Wayne State University Press, 1993); St. Clair Drake, "Diaspora Studies and Pan-Africanism," in *Global Dimensions of the African Diaspora*, ed. Joseph Harris (Washington, DC: Howard University Press, 1982): 341–402; Dayo F. Gore, "From Communist Politics to Black Power: The Radical Visions and Transnational Solidarities of Victoria 'Vicki' Ama Garvin," in *"Want to Start a Revolution?" Radical Women in the Black Freedom Struggle*, ed. Dayo F. Gore, Jeanne Theoharis, and Komozi Woodard (New York: New York University Press, 2009).

42. Garvin, Interview with Lincoln Bergman tape 4; Walters, *Pan-Africanism in the African Diaspora*, 101; Hauser, *No One Can Stop the Rain*, 70.

43. Vicki Garvin, interview with Gil Noble, May 23, 1999, transcript, *Like It Is* show #1153, WABC-TV, in author's possession.

44. "Ghana Notes in the 1960s," box 2, folder 26, VGP; Chief Ayo Rosiji to Victoria Holmes Garvin, February 10, 1961, box 1, Correspondence folder, VGP.

45. Vicki Garvin, "Nigeria Diary," Thursday, May 10, 1961, box 1, VGP.

46. Vicki Garvin, "Personal History—Travels," box 2, Original Drafts/Notes folder, VGP.

47. Garvin, "Nigeria Diary," 2:30 a.m., Saturday May 27, 1961.

48. George Padmore, *Pan Africanism or Communism: The Coming Struggle for Africa* (London: D. Dobson, 1956), 47; "Harlem Hails Ghanaian Leader as Returning Hero," *New York Times*, July 28, 1958, 4.

49. "Ghana Tells U.S. She Is Neutral," *New York Times*, November 21, 1960, 11.

50. A year earlier, Du Bois, with a recently approved passport in hand, had traveled to Ghana for its inauguration, in 1960, as a Republic within the British Commonwealth. In April 1962, Nkrumah also invited Robeson, who was living in England, to settle in Ghana, offering him a chair at the University of Ghana. But, recovering from a physical and mental breakdown, Robeson could not accept. Duberman, *Paul Robeson*, 508.

51. Leslie Alexander Lacy, "Black Bodies in Exile," in *Black Homeland Black Diaspora: Cross-Currents of the African Relationship*, ed. Jacob Drachler (London: Kennikat, 1975), 147.

52. Gaines argues that they viewed Ghana as "the last best hope for democracy and human freedom." See Kevin Gaines, "African-American Expatriates in Ghana and the Black Radical Tradition," *Souls* 1 (Fall 1999): 69, and Gaines, *American Africans in Ghana*.

53. Sylvie Boone to Julian Mayfield, 1966, 14, box 1, folder 8, Julian Mayfield Papers, Manuscript Collection, Schomburg Center for Research on Black Culture, New York Public Library (hereafter JMP).

54. Garvin, interview with Gil Nobel, 4; James T. Campbell, *Middle Passages: African American Journeys to Africa, 1787–2005* (New York: Penguin, 2006), 343.

55. Such radical critiques were censored from the D.C. March on Washington Movement. See Taylor Branch, *Parting the Waters: America in the King Years, 1954–63* (New York: Simon and Schuster, 1988); Alice Windom, "Account of the 1963 March on Washington Protest in Ghana," box 6, folder 21, in JMP; Walters, *Pan-Africanism in the African Diaspora,* 120; and Gaines, *American Africans in Ghana.*

56. Mary Duziak, *Cold War Civil Rights: Race and the Image of American Democracy* (Princeton: Princeton University Press, 2000), and Thomas Borstelmann, *The Cold War and the Color Line: American Race Relations in the Global Arena* (Cambridge, MA: Harvard University Press, 2002).

57. Windom, "Account of the 1963 March on Washington Protest in Ghana"; Gaines, "African-American Expatriates in Ghana," 69.

58. Garvin, interview with Gil Nobel, 4; Malcolm X with Alex Haley, *The Autobiography of Malcolm X* (New York: Ballantine Books, [1964] 1973): 353–360.

59. Horne, *Race Woman,* 187–188; Gaines, *American Africans in Ghana,* 197–201.

60. Garvin, interview with Gil Nobel, 6; X, *The Autobiography of Malcolm X,* 353; Vicki Garvin, "Malcolm X in Ghana," Session 4, "Malcolm X: Radical Traditions and a Legacy of Struggle Conference Proceedings," New York, November 1990, at http://www.brothermalcolm.net/sections/malcolm/contents.htm.

61. "Celebrating Women's History Month with Vicki Garvin," February 14, 1996, Women's Commission Black Workers for Justice, 6.

62. X, *The Autobiography of Malcolm X,* 353; and Alice Windom, "Malcolm X in Ghana," Session 4, "Malcolm X: Radical Traditions and a Legacy of Struggle Conference Proceedings," New York, November 1990, at http://www.brothermalcolm.net/sections/malcolm/contents.htm.

63. Boone to Mayfield, 14.

64. Windom, "Account of the 1963 March on Washington Protest in Ghana"; Campbell, *Middle Passages,* 342–344; Gaines, "African-American Expatriates in Ghana," 70; Lacy, "Black Bodies in Exile," 146.

65. Alice Windom to Julian Mayfield, August 23, 1966, box 6, folder 21, JMP.

66. "Celebrating Women's History Month with Vicki Garvin," 9.

67. Robert F. Williams, "N. Carolina College Youth Calls for a Militant Student Generation," *Freedom,* June 1956, 5, and "About the Author," *Freedom,* June 1956, 5.

68. Mao Zedong, "Oppose Racial Discrimination by U.S. Imperialism," in *The Political Thought of Mao Tse-tung,* ed. Stuart R. Schram (New York: Praeger, 1969), 410; Horne, *Race Woman,* 231–232; Timothy Tyson, *Radio Free Dixie: Robert F. Williams and the Roots of Black Power* (Chapel Hill: University of North Carolina Press, 1999); and Robin D. G. Kelley and Betsy Esch, "Black Like Mao: Red China and Black Revolution," *Souls* 1 (Fall 1999): 6–41.

69. Vicki Garvin, interview with Lincoln Bergman, tape 6, Oak Park, IL, circa 1980, Freedom Archives Collection, San Francisco, CA, and Mabel Williams, "Statement," Memorial Celebration of the Life and Work of Vicki Ama Garvin, September 15, 2007, The House of the Lord Church, Brooklyn, NY, recording in author's possession.

70. Vicki Garvin, interview with Lincoln Bergman, tape 6, and "Celebrating Women's History Month with Vicki Garvin."

71. Vicki Garvin, interview with Lincoln Bergman, tape 6, and "Personal History," 4a, box 1, biography folder, VGP.

72. Vicki Garvin, "China and Black Americans," *New China* (Fall 1975): 23.

73. Vicki Garvin, interview with Gil Nobel, 6.

74. "The Case of Angela the Red," *Time*, October 17, 1969; Bettina Aptheker, *Morning Breaks: The Trial of Angela Davis*, 2nd ed. (1975; reprint, Ithaca: Cornell University Press, 1999); Joy James, "Introduction" to *Angela Y. Davis Reader* (New York: Blackwell, 1998), 1–25; Angela Davis, *Angela Davis: An Autobiography* (New York: Random House, 1974).

75. Davis was also the daughter of Sallye Davis, a former member of the SNYC, and had been active in a CP youth group while attending high school in New York City.

76. Margaret B. Wilkerson, "Excavating Our History: The Importance of Biographies of Women of Color," *Black American Literature Forum* 24 (Spring 1990): 81–83; Bettina Aptheker, *Intimate Politics: How I Grew Up Red, Fought for Free Speech and Became a Feminist Rebel* (Emeryville, CA: Seal Press, 2006), 236–288.

77. Editors, "Angela Davis," *Freedomways* (Summer 197): 197; "Blacks Urged to Aid Miss Davis in Trial," *New York Times*, October 20, 1970, 27; James Baldwin, "An Open Letter to My Sister: Miss Angela Davis," *New York Review of Books* 15, no.12, January 7, 1971.

78. Stephen Ward, "The Third World Women's Alliance: Black Feminist Radicalism and Black Power Politics," in *The Black Power Movement: Rethinking the Civil Rights-Black Power Era*, ed. Peniel Joseph (New York: Routledge, 2006), 143–144.

79. Marvel Cooke, interview with Kathleen Currie, November 2, 1989, Session 6, 141–142; "Evening with Angela," *Sacramento Observer*, June 8, 1972, A2; Les Ledbetter,

"15,000 Exhorted by Angela Davis," *New York Times*, June 30, 1972, 31.

80. There are multiple spellings of her name in this chapter; I use Joan. Genna Rae McNeil, "'Joanne Is You and Joanne Is Me': A Consideration of African American Women and the 'Free Joan Little' Movement, 1974–75," in *Sisters in the Struggle: African American Women in the Civil Rights-Black Power Movement*, ed. V. P. Franklin and B. Collier-Thomas (New York: New York University Press, 2001), 259–279; James Reston Jr., *The Innocence of Joan Little: A Southern Mystery* (New York: Times Books, 1977); and Fred Harwell, *A True Deliverance* (New York: Knopf 1980).

81. Louis Burnham, "They Planted a Union—with Their Sweat—in Carolina's Boss Ridden Tobacco Empire," *Freedom*, November 1951, 3; Robert Rodgers Korstad, *Civil Right Unionism: Tobacco Workers and the Struggle for Democracy in the Mid-Twentieth-Century South* (Chapel Hill: University of North Carolina Press, 2003).

82. National Committee to Free the Ingram Family, "Statement of Purpose," n.d., reel 8, frame 88, CRC Papers; The People's Defense Committee, *The Defender*, February 1954, reel 8, frame 153, CRC papers.

83. McNeil, "'Joanne Is You and Joanne Is Me,'" 271–272; and Christina Greene, *Our Separate Ways: Women and the Black Freedom Movement in Durham, North Carolina* (Chapel Hill: University of North Carolina Press, 2005), 225–226.

84. Angela Davis, "Jo Anne Little—The Dialectics of Rape," *Ms.* 3 (June 1975): 74–77; Davis, "Jo Anne Little: The Dialectics of Rape," in *Angela Y. Davis Reader*, ed. Joy James and Angela Davis (New York: Blackwell, 1998), 149–160.

85. A student rally in New York spoke to this expansive reach as it included Gloria Steinem, Ossie Davis, Representative Bella Abzug, and Florynce Kennedy on its

speakers' list. "Students Set Little Rally,"
New York Amsterdam News, July 16, 1975,
C9; McNeil, "'Joanne Is You and Joanne Is
Me,'" 259–279; Genna Rae McNeil, "The
Body, Sexuality and Self-Defense in the
State v. Joan Little, 1974–75," *Journal of
African American History* (Spring 2008): 235
–255; Greene, *Our Separate Ways*, 225–226;
and Komozi Woodard, *A Nation within
a Nation: Amiri Baraka (LeRoi Jones) and
Black Power Politics* (Chapel Hill: University
of North Carolina Press, 1999),182–184.

86. "Fund Raising for Joanne Little," *New
York Amsterdam News*, April 30, 1975, B4.

87. Editors, "Joanne Little: America
Goes on Trial," *Freedomways* (Spring 1975):
87–88.

88. McNeil, "'Joanne Is You and Joanne
Is Me,'" 271–272 and Reston, *The Innocence
of Joan Little*, xii.

89. Cynthia Young, *Soul Power: Culture,
Radicalism and the Making of a U.S. Third
World Left (Chapel Hill, NC: Duke University
Press, 2006)*.

90. Editor, " Message to Our Readers,"
New World Review (Winter 1971): 1.

91. "The U.S.–China Peoples Friendship
Association," *New China* (Fall 1975): 47.

92. Halois Moorhead, "Peace Can Be
Ours," *New World Review* (May 1951): 31–32;
Vicki Garvin, "Our Dinner Honoring the
Robesons," *New World Review* (November
1954): 28–29; Eslanda Robeson, "Favorite
and Step-Child in the UN," *New World
Review* (October 1954) 27–31; Eslanda
Robeson, "Peace, Friendship and Progress,"
New World Review (November 1954): 29–32;
Eslanda Robeson, "UN Plus Bandung
Equals Peace," *New World Review* (June
1955): 9–14.

93. Elbaum, *Revolution in the Air*,
207–210; and Van Gosse, *Where the Boys
Are: Cuba, Cold War America and the Making of a New Left* (New York: Verso, 1993).

94. "George Murphy to Alice Childress,"
February 5, 1971, and "George Murphy

to Alice Childress," August 19, 1972,
box 4, folder 4, Alice Childress Papers,
Manuscript, Archives and Rare Books
Division, Schomburg Center for Research
in Black Culture, New York Public Library
(hereafter ACP).

95. "Alice Childress Interviewed by
Slava Tynes," *New World Review* (Fall 1971):
48–52; George Murphy to Alice Childress,
September 21, 1971, box 4, folder 4, ACP.

96. Thelma Dale Perkins, "A Letter
to Paul Robeson on Our Visit to Mt.
Robeson," *New World Review* (4th quarter
1973): 52–58.

97. George Murphy Jr. to Alice Childress,
July 10, 1971, box 4, folder 4, ACP.

98. "An Historic Event in the life of
NWR," *New World Review* (May–June
1974): 2–3.

99. Marvel Cooke, interview with
Kathleen Currie, November 3, 1989, Session
7, 143–145.

100. See various letters, in box 1, folder
Correspondence 1952–1992, VGP.

101. Elbaum, *Revolution in the Air*,
115–116. Within the U.S. left, such strong
support of China placed Garvin in the
vibrant Third World solidarity movement
and aligned her with a growing number of
Maoist organizations but also placed her at
ideological odds with the CPUSA support
for the Soviet Union as Chinese and Soviet
antagonism intensified

102. "China Journal" and "Travel to
China," box 3, folder 8, Alice Childress
Papers.

103. Alice Childress, "Salute to Paul
Robeson," *New China* (June 1976): 40–41;
and Helen Rosen, "Harry Belafonte: An
Exception Wants to Change the Rule," *New
China* (June 1976): 17–19.

104. "USCPFA News," *New China* (Summer 1975): 48.

105. Beulah Richardson to Louise
Thompson Patterson ("Beulah to Lou"),
March 6, 1976, box 11, folder 7, LTP.

CONCLUSION

1. Vicki Garvin telephone interview with author, November 14, 1999, Brooklyn, New York.

2. Thelma Dale Perkins interview with author, October 3, 2007, Chapel Hill, North Carolina.

3. Dale Perkins interview with author; Esther Cooper Jackson interview with author, May 20, 2002, Brooklyn, New York.

4. Cooper Jackson interview with author.

5. Dale Perkins interview with author, and Vicki Garvin interview with Lincoln Bergman, tape 4..

6. Augusta Strong, "Negro Women in Freedom's Battles," *Freedomways* (Fall 1967): 302–315.

Bibliography

MANUSCRIPTS COLLECTIONS AND ARCHIVAL SOURCES

Franklin D. Roosevelt Presidential Library and Museum, Hyde Park, New York
  Pauli Murray, Oral Interview, Eleanor Roosevelt Oral History Project
Butler Library, Columbia University, New York, New York
  W. E. B. Du Bois Papers, microfilm
Federal Bureau of Investigation, Department of Justice, Washington, DC
  Yvonne Gregory, FBI File
  National Committee to Free the Ingram Family, FBI File
  Sojourners for Truth and Justice, FBI File
Manuscript, Archives and Rare Books Division, Schomburg Center for Research in Black Culture, New York Public Library, New York
  Alice Childress Papers
  Civil Rights Congress Papers, microfilm
  Ewart Guiner Papers
  Vicki Garvin Papers
  Layle Lane Papers
  Julian Mayfield Papers
  Paul Robeson Papers, microfilm
Posey Library, Harvard University, Cambridge, MA
  National Negro Congress Papers, microfilm
Schlesinger Library, Radcliffe Institute, Harvard University, Cambridge, MA
  Pauli Murray Papers
  Maida Springer Kemp Papers

Manuscript, Archives, and Rare Book Library, Robert W. Woodruff Library, Emory University
  Louise Thompson Patterson Papers
Special Collections and University Archives, Rutgers University Library, New Brunswick, NJ
  Ernest Thompson Papers
Tamiment Library and Robert F. Wagner Labor Archives, New York University, New York
  American Veterans, Manuscript Collection
  Civil Right Congress, Organizational Vertical File
  Claudia Jones, Vertical File
  Communist Party USA, Organizational Vertical File
  General Photography Collection
  James Jackson and Esther Cooper Jackson, Photo Collection
  Women's Committee for Equal Justice, Organizational Vertical File

DISSERTATIONS AND THESES

Bryant, Flora Reida. "An Examination of the Social Activism of Pauli Murray." Ph.D. dissertation, University of South Carolina, 1991.
Jacqueline, Castledine. "Gendering the Cold War: Race, Class, and Women's Peace." Ph.D. dissertation, Rutgers University, 2006.
Dixler, Elsa. "The Women Question: Women and American Communist Party 1929-1942." Ph.D. dissertation, Yale University, 1974.

Drury, Doreen Marie. "'Experimentation on the Male Side': Race, Class, Gender, and Sexuality in Pauli Murray's Quest for Love and Identity, 1910–1960." Ph.D. dissertation, Boston College, 2000.

Gellman, Erik. "'Death Blow to Jim Crow': The National Negro Congress, 1936–1947." Ph.D. dissertation, Northwestern University, 2007.

Lamphere, Lawrence. "Paul Robeson, *Freedom* Newspaper, and the Black Press." Ph.D. dissertation, Boston College, 2003.

Laurent, Robert. "Racial Ethnic Conflict in the New York City Garment Industry, 1933–1980." Ph.D. dissertation, State University of New York at Binghamton, 1980.

McDuffie, Erik. "Long Journeys: Four Black Women and the Communist Party, USA, 1930–1956." Ph.D. dissertation, New York University, 2003.

Makalani, Minkah. "For the Liberation of Black People Everywhere: The African Blood Brotherhood, Black Radicalism, and Pan-African Liberation in the New Negro Movement, 1917–1936." Ph.D. dissertation, University of Illinois at Urbana, 2004.

Richards, Yvette. "'My Passionate Feelings about Africa': Maida Springer-Kemp and the American Labor Movement." Ph.D. dissertation, Yale University, 1994.

Shadron, Virginia. "Popular Protest and Legal Authority in Post–World War II Georgia: Race, Class, and Gender Politics in the Rosa Lee Ingram Case." Ph.D. dissertation, Emory University, 1991.

Shapiro, Linn. "Red Feminism: American Communism and the Women's Rights Tradition, 1919–1956." Ph.D. dissertation, American University, 1996.

Welch, Rebeccah. "Black Arts and Activism in New York, 1950–1965." Ph.D. dissertation, New York University, 2002.

ORAL INTERVIEWS AND HISTORIES

Bergman, Miranda. Telehone interview with author. June 27, 2007.

Cooke, Marvel. Interview with Kathleen Currie. October and November 1989, Sessions 1–5, Women in Journalism Oral History Project, Washington Press Club Foundation, http://wpcf.org/oralhistory/cook.html.

Cooper Jackson, Esther. Interview with author. May 20, 2002, Brooklyn, NY.

Dale Perkins, Thelma. Telephone interview with author. September 12, 2007.

Dale Perkins, Thelma. Interview with author. October 3 and 4, 2007, Chapel Hill, NC.

Garvin, Vicki. Telephone interview with author. November 4, 1999.

Garvin, Vicki. Interview with Lincoln Bergman. Circa 1980, Oak Park, IL. Tapes 1–6. Freedom Archives Collection, San Francisco, CA.

Garvin, Vicki. Interview with Gil Noble. May 23, 1999. *Like It Is*, show #1153, WABC-TV.

Gregory Thomas, Sheila. Telephone interview with author. September 14, 2007.

Moore, Audley (Queen Mother). Interview with Cheryl Gilkes. In Ruth Edmonds Hill, ed., *Black Women's Oral History Project from Schlesinger Library on the History of Women in America*, vol. 8. Westport, CT: Meckler, 1991.

Patterson, Louise Thompson. Oral interview tapes. Oral History of the American Left, 1976–1984. Tamiment Library and Robert F. Wagner Labor Archives, New York University, 1989.

Springer-Kemp, Maida. Interview with Elizabeth Balanoff. In Ruth Edmonds Hill, ed., *Black Women's Oral History Project from Schlesinger Library on the History of Women in America*, vol. 7. Westport, CT: Meckler, 1991.

White Katz, Maude. Oral Interview with Ruth Prago. Oral History of the American Left, 1976–1984. Tamiment Library and Archives, New York University, 1989.

Woodard, Komozi. Interview with author. December 21, 2007, Brooklyn, NY.

NEWSPAPERS AND JOURNALS

Advance
Atlanta Daily World
Congress View/Congress Vue
Crisis
The Daily Compass
Daily Worker
Ellaville Sun
Freedom
Freedomways
New China
New York Amsterdam News
New York Times
New World Review
Negro Digest
Political Affairs
People's Voice
Pittsburgh Courier

BOOKS

Alexander, Robert J. The Right Opposition: Lovestoneites and the International Communist Opposition of the 1930s. Westport, CT: Greenwood Press, 1981.

Alonso, Harriet Hyman. Peace as a Women's Issue: A History of the U.S. Movement for World Peace and Women's Rights. Syracuse: Syracuse University Press, 1993.

Anderson, Carol. Eyes Off the Prize, The United Nations and the African American Struggle for Human Rights, 1944–1955. Cambridge: Cambridge University Press, 2003.

Anderson, Jervis. A. Philip Randolph: A Biographical Portrait. New York: Harcourt Brace Jovanovich, 1973.

Aptheker, Bettina. Morning Breaks: The Trial of Angel Davis, 2nd ed. 1975. Reprint, Ithaca: Cornell University Press, 1999.

———. Intimate Politics: How I Grew Up Red, Fought for Free Speech and Became a Feminist Rebel. Emeryville, CA: Seal Press, 2006.

Barlow, William. Voice Over: The Making of Black Radio. Philadelphia: Temple University Press, 1998.

Biondi, Martha. To Stand and Fight The Struggle for Civil Rights in Postwar New York City. Cambridge, MA: Harvard University Press, 2003.

Borstelmann, Thomas. The Cold War and the Color Line: American Race Relations in the Global Arena. Cambridge, MA: Harvard University Press, 2002.

Branch, Taylor. Parting the Waters: America in the King Years, 1954–63. New York: Simon and Schuster, 1988.

Breines, Winifried. The Trouble between Us: An Uneasy History of White and Black Women in the Feminist Movement. New York: Oxford University Press, 2007.

Brown, Michael E. New Studies in the Politics and Culture of U.S. Communism. New York: Monthly Review, 1993.

Buhle, Mari Jo, Paul Buhle, and Dan Georgakas. Encyclopedia of the American Left. Champaign: University of Illinois Press, 1992.

Buhle, Paul. Marxism in the United States: Remapping the History of the American Left. London: Verso, 1987.

Bush, Rod. We Are Not What We Seem: Black Nationalism and Class Struggle in the American Century. New York: New York University Press, 1999.

Campbell, James T. Middle Passages: African American Journeys to Africa, 1787–2005. New York: Penguin, 2006.

Chafe, William. The Unfinished Journey: American since World War II, 2nd ed. New York: Oxford University Press, 1991.

Cherny, Robert, William Issel, and Kieran Walsh Taylor, eds. *American Labor and the Cold War: Grassroots Politics and Postwar Political Culture.* New Brunswick, NJ: Rutgers University Press, 2004.

Childress, Alice. *Like One of the Family: Conversations from a Domestic's Life.* Brooklyn, NY: Independence, 1956.

Clark, Septima Poinsette. *Ready from Within: Septima P. Clark and the Civil Rights Movement.* Trenton, NJ: Africa World Press, 1990.

Clark-Lewis, Elizabeth. *Living In, Living Out: African American Domestics and the Great Migration.* New York: Kodansha International, 1996.

Cobble, Dorothy Sue. *The Other Women's Movement: Work Place Justice and Social Rights in Modern America.* Princeton: Princeton University Press, 2005.

Cohen, Cathy. *Beyond the Boundaries of Blackness: AIDS and the Breakdown of Black Politics.* Chicago: University of Chicago Press, 1999.

Collier Thomson, Bettye, and V. P. Franklin, eds. *Sisters in the Struggle: African-American Women in the Civil Rights-Black Power Movements.* New York: New York University Press, 2001.

Coontz, Stephanie. *The Way We Never Were: American Families and the Nostalgia Trap.* New York: Basic Books, 2000.

Cooper, Frederick. *Decolonization and Africa: The Labor Question in French and British Africa.* Cambridge: Cambridge University Press, 1996.

Cooper Jackson, Esther, and Constance Pohl, eds. *Freedomways Reader: Prophets in Their Own Country.* Boulder, CO: Westview, 2001.

Corber, Robert J. *In the Name of National Security: Hitchcock, Homophobia and the Political Construction of Gender in Postwar America.* Durham, NC: Duke University Press, 1993.

Crag, Carolyn Case. *Women Pulitzer Playwrights: Biographical Profiles and Analysis of the Plays.* New York: McFarland, 2004.

Crawford, Vicki, Jacqueline Anne Rouse, and Barbara Woods,eds. *Women in the Civil Rights Movement: Trailblazers and Torchbearers, 1945–1964.* Bloomington: Indiana University Press, 1993.

Cross, June. *Secret Daughter: A Mixed-Race Daughter and the Mother Who Gave Her Away.* New York: Viking, 2006.

Cruse, Harold. *Crisis of the Negro Intellectual: A Historical Analysis of the Failure of Black Leadership.* New York: William Morrow, 1967.

Davis, Angela. *Angela Davis: An Autobiography.* New York: Random House, 1974.

———. *Women, Race, and Class.* New York: Random House, 1981.

Davis, Ossie, and Ruby D. Davis. *With Ossie and Ruby: In This Life Together.* New York: William Morrow, 1998.

Davies, Carole Boyce. *Left of Karl Marx: The Political Life of Black Communist Claudia Jones.* Durham, NC: Duke University Press, 2007.

Dean, Elwood. *The Story of the Trenton Six.* New York: New Century, 1949.

Deveaux, Alexis. *Warrior Poet: A Biography of Audre Lorde.* New York: W. W. Norton, 2004.

Denning, Michael. *The Cultural Front: The Laboring of American Culture in the Twentieth Century.* London: Kennikat, 1975.

Dillard, Angela. *Faith in the City: Preaching Radical Social Change in Detroit.* Ann Arbor: University of Michigan Press, 2007.

Drachler, Jacob. *Black Homeland Black Diaspora.* London: Kennikat, 1975.

Duberman, Martin Bauml. *Paul Robeson.* New York: Knopf, 1988.

Dubinsky, David, and A.H. Raskin. *David Dubinsky: A Life with Labor.* New York: Simon and Schuster, 1977.

Dudziak, Mary L. *Cold War Civil Rights: Race and the Image of American Democracy*. Princeton: Princeton University Press, 2000.

Elbaum, Max. *Revolution in the Air: Sixties Radicals Turn to Lenin, Mao and Che*. New York: Verso, 2004.

Evans, Sara. *Personal Politics: The Roots of Women's Liberation in the Civil Rights Movement and the New Left*. New York: Vintage, 1979.

Faue, Elizabeth. *Community of Suffering and Struggle: Women, Men and the Labor Movement in Minneapolis, 1915–1945*. Chicago: University of Chicago Press, 1995.

Feldstein, Ruth. *Motherhood in Black and White: Race and Sex in American Liberalism, 1930–1965*. Ithaca: Cornell University Press, 2000.

Foner, Philip S. *Organized Labor and the Black Worker, 1619–1981*. New York: International, 1974.

Fraser, Steve, and Gary Gerstle. *The Rise and Fall of the New Deal Order, 1930–1980*. Princeton: Princeton University Press, 1989.

Frazier, Franklin E. *The Negro Family in the United States*. Chicago: University of Chicago Press, 1939.

———. *Black Bourgeoisie: The Rise of A New Middle Class in the United States*. 1957. Reprint, New York: Free Press, 1966.

Friend, Albert, editor. *Communism in America: A History in Documents*. New York: Columbia University Press, 1997.

Freund, Bill. *The Making of Contemporary Africa: The Development of African Society since 1800*, 2nd ed. Boulder, CO: Lynne Rienner, 1998.

Gabin, Nancy. *Feminism in the Labor Movement: Women and the United Auto Workers, 1935–1975*. Ithaca: Cornell University Press, 1990.

Gaines, Kevin. *Uplifting the Race: Black Leadership, Politics, and Culture in the Twentieth Century*. Chapel Hill: University of North Carolina Press, 1996.

———. *American Africans in Ghana: Black Expatriates and the Civil Rights Era*. Chapel Hill: University of North Carolina Press, 2004.

Garfinkel, Herbert. *When Negroes March: The March on Washington Movement in the Organization Politics for FEPC*. New York: Atheneum, 1969.

Giddings, Paula. *When and Where I Enter: The Impact of Black Women on Race and Sex in America*. New York: Bantam Books, 1984.

Gilmore, Glenda. *Defying Dixie: The Radical Roots of Civil Rights: 1919–1950*. New York: W. W. Norton, 2008.

Gilroy, Paul. *'There Ain't No Black in the Union Jack': The Cultural Politics of Race and Nation*. Chicago: University of Chicago Press, 1987.

Goldfield, Michael. *The Color of Politics: Race and the Mainsprings of American Politics*. New York: The New Press, 1997.

Goodman, John. *Stories of Scottsboro*. New York: Pantheon, 1994.

Grant, Joanne. *Ella Baker Freedom Bound*. New York: Wiley, 1998.

Greenberg, Cheryl Lynn. *'Or Does It Explode': Black Harlem in the Great Depression*. New York: Oxford University Press, 1991.

Greene, Christina. *Our Separate Ways: Women and the Black Freedom Movement in Durham*. Chapel Hill: University of North Carolina Press, 2005.

Gore, Dayo F., Jeanne Theoharis, and Komozi Woodard, eds. *"Want to Start a Revolution?" Radical Women in the Black Freedom Struggle*. New York: New York University Press, 2009.

Gosse, Van. *Where the Boys Are: Cuba, Cold War America and the Making of a New Left*. New York: Verso, 1993.

Gunning, Sandra. *Race, Rape and Lynching: The Red Record of American Literature, 1890–1912*. New York: Oxford University Press, 1996.

Hall, Jacquelyn Dowd. *Revolt against Chivalry: Jessie Daniel Ames and the Women's Campaign against Lynching.* 1979. Reprint, New York: Columbia University Press, 1993.

Harris, William H. *The Harder We Run: Black Workers since the Civil War.* New York: Oxford University Press, 1982.

Harrison, Cynthia. *On Account of Sex: The Politics of Women's Issues, 1945-1969.* Berkeley: University of California Press, 1988.

Harwell, Fred. *A True Deliverance.* New York: Knopf, 1980.

Hauser, George. *No One Can Stop the Rain: Glimpses of Africa's Liberation Struggle.* New York: Pilgrim Press, 1989.

Haygood, Wil. *King of the Cats: The Life and Times of Adam Clayton Powell, Jr.* Boston: Houghton Mifflin, 1993.

Haywood, Harry. *Black Bolshevik: Autobiography of an Afro-American Communist.* Chicago: Liberator Press, 1978.

Healey, Dorothy, and Maurice Isserman. *Dorothy Healey Remembers: A Life in the American Communist Party.* New York: Oxford University Press, 1990.

Hemingway, Andrew. *Artists on the Left: American Artists and the Communist Movement.* New Haven: Yale University Press, 2002.

Herzog, Melanie Anne. *Elizabeth Catlett: An American Artist in Mexico.* Seattle: University of Washington Press, 2000.

Higginbotham, Evelyn Brooks. *Rightgeous Discontent: The Women's Movement in the Black Baptist Church, 1880-1920.* Cambridge, MA: Harvard University Press, 1993.

Honey, Michael. *Southern Labor and Black Civil Rights: Organizing Memphis Workers.* Champaign: University of Illinois Press, 1993.

Horne, Gerald. *Black and Red: W. E. B. Du Bois and the Afro-American Response to the Cold War, 1944-1963.* Albany: State University of New York Press, 1986.

——. *Communist Front? The Civil Rights Congress, 1946-1956.* Rutherford, NJ: Fairleigh Dickinson University Press, 1988.

——. *Black Liberation/Red Scare: Ben Davis and the Communist Party.* Cranbury, NJ: Associated University Presses, 1994.

——. *Race Woman: The Lives of Shirley Graham Du Bois.* New York: New York University Press, 2000.

Horowitz, Daniel. *Betty Friedan and the Making of The Feminine Mystique: The American Left, the Cold War, and Modern Feminism.* Amherst: University of Massachusetts Press, 1998.

Hunter, Tera. *To "Joy My Freedom": Southern Black Women's Lives and Labors after the Civil War.* Cambridge, MA: Harvard University Press, 1997.

Hutchinson, Earl Ofari. *Blacks and Reds: Race and Class in Conflict, 1919-1990.* East Lansing: Michigan State University Press, 1995.

Isserman, Maurice. *Which Side Were You On? The American Communist Party during the Second World War.* Middletown, CT: Wesleyan University Press, 1982.

Jackson, Walter A. *Gunnar Myrdal and America's Conscience: Social Engineering and Racial Liberalism, 1938-1987.* Chapel Hill: University of North Carolina Press, 1990.

James, Joy. *Resisting State Violence: Radicalism, Gender and Race in U.S. Culture.* Minneapolis: University of Minnesota Press, 1996.

——. *Transcending the Talented Tenth: Black Leaders and American Intellectuals.* New York: Routledge, 1997.

——. *Shadowboxing: Representations of Black Feminist Politics.* New York: Saint Martin's Press, 1999.

——, editor. *Angela Y. Davis Reader.* New York: Blackwell, 1998.

James, Winston. *Holding Aloft the Banner of Ethiopia: Caribbean Radicalism in Early Twentieth-Century America.* London: Verso, 1998.

Jennings, LaVina D. *Alice Childress.* New York: Twayne, 1995.

Johanningsmeier, Edward P. *Forging American Communism: The Life of William Z. Foster.* Princeton: Princeton University Press, 1994.

Johnson, Buzz. *"I Think of My Mother": Notes on the Life and Times of Claudia Jones.* London: Kaira Press, 1985.

Johnson, David K. *The Lavender Scare: The Cold War Persecution of Gays and Lesbians in the Federal Government.* Chicago: University of Chicago, 2004.

Jones, Jacqueline. *Labor of Love, Labor of Sorrow: Black Women Work, On the Family from Slavery to the Present.* New York: Basic Books, 1985.

Joseph, Peniel. *Waiting Til the Midnight Hour: A Narrative History of Black Power in America.* New York: Henry Holt, 2006.

———, ed. *The Black Power Movement: Rethinking the Civil Rights-Black Power Era.* New York: Routledge, 2006.

Kaplan, Amy, and Donald Pease, eds. *Cultures of United States Imperialism.* Durham, NC: Duke University Press, 1993.

Keck, Margaret, and Kathryn Sikking. *Activists beyond Borders: Advocacy Networks in International Politics.* Ithaca: Cornell University Press, 1998.

Kelley, Robin D. G. *Hammer and Hoe: Alabama Communists during the Great Depression.* Chapel Hill: University of North Carolina Press, 1990.

———. *Freedom Dreams: The Black Radical Imagination.* New York: Beacon Press, 2002.

Kelley, Robin D. G., and Earl Lewis, eds. *To Make Our World Anew: A History of African Americans.* New York: Oxford University Press, 2000.

Kerber, Linda K, Alice Kessler-Harris, and Kathryn Kish Sklar, eds. *U.S. History as Women's History: New Feminist Essays.* Chapel Hill: University of North Carolina Press, 1995.

Klehr, Harvey. *Heyday of American Communism: The Depression Decade.* New York: Basic Books, 1984.

Korstad, Robert Rodgers. *Civil Right Unionism: Tobacco Workers and the Struggle for Democracy in the Mid-Twentieth-Century South.* Chapel Hill: University of North Carolina Press, 2003.

Ladd-Taylor, Molly, and Lauri Umansky, eds. *"Bad" Mothers: The Politics of Blame in Twentieth Century America.* New York: New York University Press, 1998.

Leab, Daniel. *A Union of Individuals: The Formation of the American Newspaper Guild, 1933–1936.* New York: Columbia University Press, 1970.

Lee, Chana Kai. *For Freedom's Sake: The Life of Fannie Lou Hamer.* Champaign: University of Illinois Press, 1999.

Leffler, Melvin. *A Preponderance of Power: National Security, the Truman Administration and the Cold War.* Stanford: Stanford University Press, 1992.

Lemelle, Sidney, and Robin D. G. Kelley. *Imagining Home: Class, Culture and Nationalism in the African Diaspora.* London: Verso, 1994.

Levenstein, Harvey. *Communism, Anticommunism, and the CIO.* New York: Greenwood Press, 1981.

Lewis, David Levering. *When Harlem Was in Vogue.* New York: Knopf, 1981.

Lipsitz, George. *A Rainbow at Midnight: Labor and Culture in the 1940's.* Champaign: University of Illinois Press, 1994.

Lowe, Lisa. *Immigrant Acts: On Asian American Cultural Politics.* Durham, NC: Duke University Press, 1996.

Lubin, Alex, ed. *Revising the Blueprint: Ann Petry and the Literary Left.* Jackson: University of Mississippi Press, 2007.

Lynn, Conrad. *There Is a Fountain: The Autobiography of Conrad Lynn,* 2nd ed. Brooklyn, NY: Lawrence Hill Books, 1993.

Lynn, Susan. *Progressive Women in Conservative Times: Racial Justice, Peace and Feminism, 1845–1960s.* New Brunswick, NJ: Rutgers University Press, 1992.

Malcolm X, with Alex Haley. *The Autobiography of Malcolm X.* New York: Ballantine Books, [1964] 1973.

Marable, Manning. *African and Caribbean Politics, From Kwame Nkrumah to Maurice Bishop.* London: Verso, 1987.

———. *Race, Reform and Rebellion: The Second Reconstruction in Black America, 1945–1990,* 2nd ed. Jackson: University Press of Mississippi, 1991.

Marks, Carol. *Farewell, We're Good and Gone: The Great Black Migration.* Bloomington: Indiana University Press, 1989.

May, Elaine Tyler. *Homeward Bound: American Families in the Cold War Era.* New York: Basic Books, 1988.

Meriwether, James H. *Proudly We Can Be Africans: Black Americans and Africa 1935–1961.* Chapel Hill: University of North Carolina Press, 2002.

Maxwell, William J. *New Negro, Old Left: African-American Writing and Communism between the Wars.* New York: Columbia University Press, 1999.

Meyerowitz, Joanne. *Not June Cleaver: Women and Gender in Postwar America, 1945–1960.* Philadelphia: Temple University Press, 1994.

Milkman, Ruth. *Women, Work and Protest: A Century of U.S. Women's Labor History.* Boston: Routledge and Kegan Paul, 1985.

———. *Gender at Work: The Dynamics of Job Segregation by Sex during World War II.* Champaign: University of Illinois Press, 1987.

Morton, Patricia. *Disfigured Images: The Historical Assault on Afro-American Women.* New York: Praeger, 1991.

Moses, William Jeremiah. *The Golden Age of Black Nationalism, 1850–1925.* New York: Oxford University Press, 1978.

Mullen, Bill V. *Popular Fronts: Chicago and American Cultural Politics, 1935–1946.* Champaign: University of Illinois Press, 1999.

———, and James Smethurst, eds. *Left of the Color Line: Race, Radicalism and Twentieth-Century.* Chapel Hill: University of North Carolina Press, 2003.

Murray, Pauli. *Song in a Weary Throat: An American Pilgrimage.* New York: Harper and Row, 1987.

Myers, Constance Ashton. *The Prophets Army: Trotskyist in America 1928–1941.* Westport, CT: Greenwood Press, 1977.

Naison, Mark. *Communist in Harlem during the Depression.* New York: Grove Press, 1983.

Nelson, Bruce. *Divided We Stand: American Workers.* Princeton: Princeton University Press, 2001.

Nemiroff, Robert, ed. *To Be Young, Gifted, and Black: Lorraine Hansberry in Her Own Words.* New York: Vintage, 1969.

Noer, Thomas. *The Cold War and Black Liberation: The United States and White Rule in Africa, 1948–1968.* Columbia: University of Missouri Press, 1985.

O'Farrell, Brigid, and Joyce L. Kornbluh, eds. *Rocking the Boat Union Women's Voices, 1915–1975.* New Brunswick, NJ: Rutgers University Press, 1996.

Ogden, Frederic D. *The Poll Tax in the South.* Birmingham: University of Alabama Press, 1958.

Omi, Michael, and Howard Winant. *Racial Formation in the United States from the 1960s to the 1980s.* New York: Routledge, 1986.

Orlack, Annelise. *Storming Caesar's Palace: How Black Mothers Fought Their Own War on Poverty.* New York: Beacon Press, 2006.

Ottanelli, Fraser M. *The Communist Party of the United States: From the Depression to World War II.* New Brunswick, NJ: Rutgers University Press, 1991

Padmore, George *Pan Africanism or Communism: The Coming Struggle for Africa.* London: D. Dobson, 1956.

Patterson, William L., ed. *We Charge Genocide: The Historic Petition to the United Nations for Relief from a Crime of the U.S. Government against the Negro People.* New York: Civil Rights Congress, 1951.

Payne, Charles. *I've Got the Light of Freedom: The Organizing Tradition and the Mississippi Freedom Struggle.* Berkeley: University of California Press, 1995.

Perlstein, Daniel H. *Justice, Justice: School Politics and the Eclipse of Liberalism.* New York: Peter Lang, 2004.

Pfeffer, Paula F. *A. Philip Randolph, Pioneer of the Civil Rights Movement.* Baton Rouge: Louisiana State University Press, 1990.

Pintzuk, Edward C. *Reds, Racial Justice, and Civil Liberties: Michigan Communists during the Cold War.* Minneapolis: MEP Publications, 1997.

Plummer, Brenda Gayle. *Rising Wind: Black Americans and U.S. Foreign Affairs, 1935–1960.* Chapel Hill: University of North Carolina Press, 1996.

Podair, Jerald. *The Strike That Changed New York: Blacks, Whites, and the Ocean Hill-Brownsville Crisis.* New York: Columbia University Press, 1997.

Poitier, Sidney. *This Life.* New York: Knopf, 1980.

Ransby, Barbara. *Ella Baker and the Black Freedom Movement: A Radical Democratic Vision.* Chapel Hill: University of North Carolina Press, 2003.

Record, Wilson. *The Negro and the Communist Party.* Chapel Hill: University of North Carolina Press, 1951.

———. *Race and Radicalism: The NAACP and Communist Party in Conflict.* Chapel Hill: University of North Carolina Press, 1964.

Reston, James, Jr. *The Innocence of Joan Little: A Southern Mystery.* New York: Time Books, 1977.

Richards, Yevette. *Maida Springer: Pan-Africanist and International labor Leader.* Pittsburgh: University of Pittsburgh Press, 2000.

Rise, Eric. *Martinsville Seven: Race, Rape, and Capital Punishment.* Charlottesville, VA: University of Virginia Press, 1995.

Roberts, Dorothy. *Killing the Black Body: Race, Reproduction and the Meanings of Liberty.* New York: Vintage, 1997.

Robinson, Cedric. *Black Marxism: The Making of the Black Radical Tradition.* London: Zed, 1983.

———. *Black Movements in America.* New York: Routledge, 1997.

Robnett, Belinda. *How Long? How Long? African American Women in the Struggle for Civil Rights.* New York: Oxford University Press, 2000.

Rosen, Ruth. *The World Split Open: How the Modern Women's Movement Changed America.* New York: Penguin, 2000.

Royster, Jacqueline Jones, ed. *Southern Horrors and Other Writings: The Anti-Lynching Campaign of Ida B. Wells, 1892–1900.* New York: Bedford/St. Martins, 1997.

Roediger, David. *The Wages of Whiteness: Race and the Making of the American Working Class.* London: Verso, 1991.

Rosswurm, Steve, ed. *The CIO's Left-Led Unions.* New Brunswick, NJ: Rutgers University Press, 1992.

Ruiz, Vicki. *Cannery Women, Cannery Lives: Mexican Women, Unionization, and the California Food Processing Industry, 1939–1950.* Albuquerque: University of New Mexico Press, 1987.

Ruiz, Vicki L., and Ellen Carol Du Bois, eds. *Unequal Sisters: A Multicultural Reader in U.S. Women's History,* 2nd ed. New York: Routledge, 1994.

Sayre, Nora. *Previous Convictions: A Journey through the 1950s.* New Brunswick, NJ: Rutgers University Press, 1995.

Schrecker, Ellen. *Many Are the Crimes: McCarthyism in America*. Princeton: Princeton University Press, 1998.

Scott, Daryl Michael. *Contempt and Pity: Social Policy and the Image of the Damaged Black Psyche, 1880–1996*. Chapel Hill: University of North Carolina Press, 1997.

Scott, James C. *Domination and the Arts of Resistance: The Hidden Transcript*. New Haven: Yale University Press, 1990.

Shaw, Stephanie. *What a Woman Ought to Be and Do: Black Professional Workers in the Jim Crow Era*. Chicago: University of Chicago Press, 1996.

Sherman, Richard B. *The Case of Odell Waller and Virginia Justice, 1940–1942*. Knoxville: University of Tennessee Press, 1992.

Sherwood, Marika. *Claudia Jones: A Life in Exile*. London: Lawrence and Wishart, 1999.

Singh, Nikhil. *Black Is a Country: Race and the Unfinished Struggle for Democracy*. Cambridge, MA: Harvard University Press, 2005.

Sitkoff, Harvey. *A New Deal for Blacks: The Emergence of Civil Rights as a National Issue in the Depression Era*. New York: Oxford University Press, 1978.

Smethurst, James. *The New Red Negro: The Literary Left and African American Poetry, 1930–1946*. New York: Oxford University Press, 1999.

———. *The Black Arts Movement: Literary Nationalism in the 1960s and 1970s*. Chapel Hill: University of North Carolina Press, 2005.

Smith, Judith E. *Visions of Belonging: Family Stories, Popular Culture and Postwar Democracy, 1940–1960*. New York: Columbia University Press, 2004.

Solomon, Mark. *The Cry Was Unity: Communists and African Americans, 1917–1936*. Jackson: University Press of Mississippi, 1998.

Springer, Kimberly. *Living for the Revolution: Black Feminist Organizations, 1968–1980*. Durham: Duke University Press, 2005.

Streitmatter, Rodger. *Raising Their Voice: African American Women Journalists Who Changed History*. Louisville: University Press of Kentucky, 1994.

Sullivan, Patricia. *Days of Hope: Race and Democracy in the New Deal Era*. Chapel Hill: University of North Carolina Press, 1996.

Taylor, Clarence. *Knocking at Our Own Door: Milton Galamison and the Struggle to Integrate New York City Schools*. New York: Columbia University Press, 1997.

Taylor, Ula. *The Veiled Garvey: The Life and Times of Amy Jacques Garvey*. Chapel Hill: University of North Carolina Press, 2001.

Theoharis, Jeanne, and Komozi Woodard, eds. *Freedom North: Black Freedom Struggles Outside the South, 1940–1980*. New York: Palgrave Macmillan, 2003.

Thompson, Mindy. *National Negro Labor Council: A History*. New York: American Institute for Marxist Study, 1978.

Thompson, W. Scott. *Ghana's Foreign Policy 1957–1966: Diplomacy Ideology and the New State*. Princeton: Princeton University Press, 1969.

Trotter, Joe William Monroe, Jr., ed. *The Great Migration in Historical Perspective: New Dimensions of Race, Class, and Gender*. Bloomington: Indiana University Press, 1991.

Tyson, Timothy. *Radio Free Dixie: Robert F. Williams and the Roots of Black Power*. Chapel Hill: University of North Carolina Press, 1999.

Von Eschen, Penny M. *Race against Empire: Black Americans and Anticolonialism 1937–1957*. Ithaca: Cornell University Press, 1996.

Wald, Alan. *The New York Intellectuals: The Rise and Decline of the Anti-Stalinist Left From the 1930s to the 1980s*. Chapel Hill: University of North Carolina Press, 1987.

Walters, Ronald W. *Pan-Africanism in the African Diaspora: An Analysis of Modern Afrocentric Political Movements*. Detroit: Wayne State University Press, 1993.

Warren, Frank. *An Alternative Vision: The Socialist Party in the 1930s*. Bloomington: Indiana University Press, 1974.

Watkins-Owens, Irma. *Blood Relation: Caribbean Immigrants and the Harlem Community, 1900–1930*. Bloomington: Indiana University Press, 1996.

Weigand, Kate. *Red Feminism: American Communism and the Making of Women's Liberation*. Baltimore: Johns Hopkins University Press, 2001.

Williams, Rhonda Y. *The Politics of Public Housing: Black Women's Struggles against Urban Inequalities*. New York: Oxford University Press, 2005.

Wolcott, Victoria. *Remaking Respectability: African American Women in Interwar Detroit*. Chapel Hill: University of North Carolina Press, 2001.

Woodard, Komozi. *A Nation within a Nation: Amiri Baraka (LeRoi Jones) and Black Power Politics*. Chapel Hill: University of North Carolina Press, 1999.

Zeiger, Rodger. *The CIO, 1935–1955*. Chapel Hll: University of North Carolina Press, 1995.

PUBLISHED ARTICLES

Anderson, Karen Tucker. "Last Hired First Fired: Black Women Workers during World War II." *Journal of American History* 69 (June 1982): 78–94.

Aptheker, Bettina. "Red Feminism: A Personal and Historical Reflection." *Science and Society* 66, no. 4 (2002-2003): 519–522.

Arnesen, Eric. "'New Graver Danger': Black Anticommunism, the Communist Party and the Race Question." *Labor: Studies in Working-Class History of the Americas* 3 (2006): 13–52.

Bracey, John, Jr., and August Meier. "The NAACP as a Reform Movement, 1940–1965: 'To Reach the Conscience of America.'" *Journal of Southern History* 59 (February 1993): 3-30.

Breines, Winifred. "What's Love Got to Do with It? White Women, Black Woman and Feminism in the Movement Years." *Signs: A Journal of Women in Culture and Society* 27, no. 4 (2002): 1095-1113.

Brown, Elsa Barkley. "'What Has Happened Here': The Politics of Difference in Women's History and Feminist Politics." *Feminist Studies* 18, no. 2 (Summer 1992): 302–307.

Brown-Guillory, Elizabeth. "Alice Childress: A Pioneering Spirit." *Sage* 4, no. 1 (Spring 1987): 68–72.

"The Case of Angela the Red." *Time*, October 17, 1969: 66–68.

Castledine, Jacqueline. "In a Solid Bond of Unity: Anticolonial Feminism in the Cold War Era." *Journal of Women's History* (Winter 2008): 57–81.

"Celebrating Women's History Month with Vicki Garvin." *Women's Commission Black Workers for Justice*, February 14, 1996, 4.

Cha-Jua, Sundiata Keita and Clarence Lang. "The 'Long Movement' as Vampire: Temporal and Spatial Fallacies in Recent Black Freedom Studies." *Journal of African American History* (Spring 2007): 265–278.

Childress, Alice. "A Candle in a Gale Wind," in *Black Women Writers 1950–1980: A Critical Evaluation*, edited by Mari Evans. New York: Anchor Books/Doubleday, 1984.

Collins, Patricia Hill. "The Social Construction of Black Feminist Thought." *Signs* 4 (Summer 1989): 745–773.

Combahee River Collective. "A Black Feminist Statement." In *This Bridge Called My Back: Writings by Radical Women of Color*. New York: Kitchen Table Press, 1981.

Cooper Jackson, Esther. *This Is My Husband: Fighter for His People, Political Refugee*. Brooklyn, NY: National Committee to Defend Negro Leadership, 1953.

D'Emilio, John. "Homophobia and the Trajectory of Postwar American Radicalism: The Career of Bayard Rustin." *Radical History Review* 62 (1995): 80–103.

Drake, St. Clair. "Diaspora Studies and Pan-Africanism," in *Global Dimensions of the African Diaspora*, edited by Joseph Harris. Washington, DC: Howard University Press, 1982: 341–402.

Feldstein, Ruth. "'I Don't Trust You Anymore': Nina Simone, Culture and Black Activism in the 1960s." *Journal of American History* 91, no. 4 (March 2005): 1349–1379.

Freer, Regina. "L.A. Race Woman: Charlotta Bass and the Complexities of Black Political Development in Los Angeles." *American Quarterly* (September 2004): 607–632.

Friedman, Andrea. "The Strange Career of Annie Lee Moss: Rethinking Race, Gender, and McCarthyism." *Journal of American History* 94, no. 2 (September 2007): 445–467.

Gaines, Kevin. "African-American Expatriates in Ghana and the Black Radical Tradition." *Souls* 1 (Fall 1999): 64–71.

———. "From Center to Margin: Internationalism and the Origins of Black Feminism." In *Materializing Democracy: Toward a Revitalized Cultural Politics*, edited by Russ Castronovo and Dana Nelson. Durham: Duke University Press, 2002.

Garvin, Vicki. "China and Black Americans." *New China* (Fall 1975): 23.

Gore, Dayo F. "'The Law. The Precious Law': Black Women Radicals and the Fight to End Legal Lynching," *Crime and Punishment: Perspectives from the Humanities* 37 (2005): 53–83 (special issue of *Studies in Law, Politics and Society*, edited by Austin Sarat).

Hall, Jacqueline Dowd. "The Mind That Burns in Each Body': Women, Rape, and Racial Violence." In *Powers of Desire: The Politics of Sexuality*, edited by Ann Snitow, Christine Stansell, and Sharon Thompson. New York, 1983.

———. "The Long Civil Rights Movement." *Journal of American History* 91 (March 2005): 1233–1254.

Hall, James C. "On Sale at Your Favorite Newsstand: *Negro Digest/Black World* and the 1960s." In *The Black Press: New Literary and Historical Essays*, edited by Todd Vogel. New Brunswick, NJ: Rutgers University Press, 2001.

Hall, Stuart. "Gramsci's Relevance for the Study of Race and Ethnicity." In *Stuart Hall: Critical Dialogues in Cultural Studies*, edited by Kuan Hsing Chen and David Morley. London: Routledge, 1993.

Hamilton, Cynthia. "Women in Politics: Methods of Resistance and Change." *Women Studies International Forum* 12, no.1 (1989): 129–135.

Hammonds, Evelyn M. "Toward a Genealogy of Black Female Sexuality: The Problematic of Silence." In *Feminist Genealogies, Colonial Legacies, and Democratic Futures*, edited by Jacqui Alexander and Chandra Talpade Mohanty. New York: Routledge, 1997.

———. "Black (W)holes and the Geometry of Black Female Sexuality." *differences: A Journal of Feminist Cultural Studies* 6 (Spring 1994): 126–145.

Heger, Kenneth W. "Race Relations in the United States and American Cultural and Informational Programs in Ghana, 1957–1966." *Prologue* 31 (Winter 1999), http://www.archives.gov/publications/prologue/1999/winter/us-and-ghana-1957-1966-2.html.

Higginbotham, Evelyn Brooks. "African-American Women's History and the Metalanguage of Race." *Signs* 17 (Winter 1992): 251–284.

Hill, Herbert. "The Problems of Race in American Labor History." *Reviews in American History* 24 (1996): 189–208.

Hill, Rebecca. "Fosterites and Feminists, or 1950s Ultra-Leftists and the Invention of AmeriKKKa." *New Left Review* 228 (March-April 1998): 67–90.

Hine, Darlene Clark. "Rape and the Inner Lives of Black Women in the Middle West: Preliminary Thoughts on the Culture of Dissemblance." *Signs* 14 (Summer 1989): 912–920.

Huston, Luther A. "12 Groups Called Communist Fronts." *New York Times,* April 23, 1953, 1.

Jacobs, William J. "Parents and Politics." *Urban Review* 2 (December 1967): 3, 27.

James, Joy. "Ella Baker, 'Black Women's Work' and Activist Intellectuals." *Black Scholar* 24 (1994): 8–15.

Jones, Claudia. "Negro Women in the Fight for Peace and Freedom." *Negro History Week* (Educational Department, New York State Communist Party, 1952).

Jones, Jacqueline. "Race and Gender in Modern America." *Reviews in American History* 26.1 (1998): 220–238.

Jones, Sidney. "Letters: Parents and Politics." *Urban Review* 2 (April 1968): 13.

Kannenberg, Lisa. "The Impact of the Cold War on Women's Trade Union Activism: The UE Experience." *Labor History* 34 (2003): 309–323.

Kelley, Robin D. G., and Betsy Esch. "Black Like Mao: Red China and Black Revolution." *Souls* 1 (Fall 1999): 6–41.

———. "This Ain't Ethiopia, But It'll Do: African-Americans and the Spanish Civil War." In *Race Rebels: Culture, Politics, and the Black Working Class.* New York: Free Press, 1994.

———. "We Are Not What We Seem": Rethinking Black Working-Class Opposition in the Jim Crow South." *Journal of American History* (June 1993): 75–112.

Kornbluh, Joyce, L. "'We Did Change Some Attitudes': Maida Springer-Kemp and the International Ladies Garment Workers Union." *Women Studies Quarterly* 23 (1995): 41–70.

Korstad, Robert, and Nelson Lichtenstein. "Opportunities Found and Lost: Labor, Radicals, and the Early Civil Rights Movement." *Journal of American History* 75 (December 1988): 786–811.

Lawson, Steven, David R. Colburn, and Darryl Paulson. "Groveland: Florida's Little Scottsboro." *Florida Historical Quarterly* 65, no. 1 (July 1986).

Martin, Charles H. "The Civil Rights Congress and Southern Black Defendants." *Georgia Historical Quarterly* 7, no. 1 (Spring 1987): 25–52.

———. "Race, Gender, and Southern Justice: The Rosa Lee Ingram Case." *American Journal of Legal History* 29 (1985): 249–268.

McDuffie, Erik. "A New Freedom Movement of Women': Sojourning for Truth Justice and Human Rights During Early Cold War." *Radical History Review* (Spring 2008): 81–106.

McGuire, Danielle. "'It Was Like All of Us Had Been Raped': Sexual Violence, Community Mobilization, and the African American Freedom Struggle." *Journal of American History* (December 2004): 906–931.

McNeil, Genna R. "The Body, Sexuality and Self–Defense in the State v. Joan Little, 1974–75." *Journal of African American History* (Spring 2008): 235–261.

Murray, Pauli. "The Liberation of Black Women." In *Words of Fire: An Anthology of African-American Feminist Thought,* edited by Beverly Guy-Sheftall. New York: New Press, 1995.

Murray, Pauli, and Murray Kempton. *All for Mr. Davis: The Story of Sharecropper Odell Waller.* New York: Workers Defense League, 1942.

Nelson, Claire Nee. "Louise Thompson Patterson and the Southern Roots of the Popular Front," in *Women Shaping the South: Creating and Confronting Change*, edited by Angela Boswell and Judith N. McArthur. Columbia: University of Missouri Press, 2006.

Nemiroff, Robert. "From These Roots: Lorraine Hansberry and the South." *Southern Exposure* (September-October, 1984): 32–36.

Patterson, Tiffany Ruby, and Robin D. G. Kelley. "Unfinished Migrations: Reflections on the African Diaspora and the Making of the Modern World." *African Studies Review* (April 2000): 11–45.

Richards, Yevette. "African and African-American Labor Leaders in the Struggle over International Affiliation." *International Journal of African Historical Studies* 31 (1998): 301–334.

Richardson, Beulah. *A Black Woman Speaks . . . of White Womanhood, of White Supremacy, of Peace.* New York: American Women for Peace, 1951.

Singh, Nikhil Pal. "Culture/Wars: Recoding Empire in an Age of Democracy." *American Quarterly* 50, no. 3 (1998): 471–522.

Solomon, Mark. "Rediscovering a Lost Legacy: Black Women Radicals Maude White and Louise Thompson Patterson." *Abafazi* (Fall-Winter 1995): 6–13.

Springer, Maida. "Africans' War on Poverty, Ignorance, Prejudice." *International Free Trade Union News* 12 (July 1957): 7.

———. "West Africa in Transition." *International Free Trade Union News* 11 (April 1956): 8.

Thompson, Louise. "Negro Women in Our Party." *Party Organizer* no. 11(August 1937): 27.

Thompson, Mindy. *National Negro Labor Council.* American Institute for Marxist Studies, Occasional Paper no. 27 (1978).

Tushnet, Mark V. *The NAACP's Legal Strategy against Segregated Education, 1925-1950.* Chapel Hill: University of North Carolina Press, 1987.

Welch, Rebeccah. "Gender and Power in the Black Diaspora: Radical Women of Color and the Cold War." *Souls* 3 (2003): 71–82.

———. "Spokesman of the Oppressed? Lorraine Hansberry at Work: The Challenge of Radical Politics in the Postwar Era." *Souls* 9 (2008): 302–319.

White, E. Frances. "Africa on My Mind: Gender, Counterdiscourse, and African American Nationalism," in *Words of Fire: An Anthology of African-American Feminist Thought*, edited by Beverly Guy-Sheftall. New York: New Press, 1995.

Wilkerson, Margaret B. "Excavating Our History: The Importance of Biographies of Women of Color." *Black American Literature Forum* 24 (Spring 1990): 81–83.

Zahavi, Gerald. "Passionate Commitments: Race, Sex and Communism at Schenectady General Electric, 1932-1954." *Journal of American History* (September 1996): 514–548.

Index

Abyssinian Baptist Church, 22
Africa, 37, 29, 134, 135, 140, 144, 147, 149, 155
African American migration 15, 16, 17, 18, 20, 21, 23, 26, 36, 103, 104
African Blood Brotherhood (ABB), 28
Afro-American Committee for Gifts to Ghana, 144
All African People's Congress, 134, 144
Alligood, Clarence, 153, 154
American Federation of Labor (AFL), 20, 29, 105, 113, 118, 125
American Labor Party (ALP), 29
American League for Peace and Democracy, 22, 113
American Negro Labor Congress, 28
American Negro Theatre (ANT), 31, 52, 66
American Newspaper Guild, 23, 29, 35, 107
American Women for Peace (AWP), 42, 43, 46, 47, 48, 59, 60, 63, 64, 198n84
American Youth Congress (AYC), 24, 26, 163
anticapitalist, 20, 49, 69; capitalism, 49
anticolonial, 37, 39
anticommunism, 4, 14, 17, 35, 39, 44, 53, 59, 60, 77, 98, 125, 152, 160, 162, 163, 164, 167n4, 167n7, 171n35, 172n12, 178n93, 181n23, 184n7, 192n4, 193n13; activism, 9, 11, 131, 135, 138, 141; against black radicals, 42, 43, 66, 78, 85, 87, 96, 98, 128, 144, 188n55; Cold War, 2, 3, 5, 7, 8, 10, 11, 12, 13, 16, 40, 42, 45, 52, 54, 58, 64, 68, 78, 105, 114, 124, 126, 130, 146, 151, 161, 163, 165, 167n4, 179n95; labor, 102, 105, 103, 114, 115, 119, 120, 126, 136, 138, 164, 167n4; against leftist institutions, 10, 11, 16, 33,

40, 131; McCarthyism, 9, 14, 35, 44, 78; "positive neutrality," 146; "red scare," 2, 167n4; WWII politics, 2, 9, 101
Atlanta Daily World, 75
Austin, Warren, K. 83

Baker, Ella, 19, 23, 53, 107, 168n10
Baldwin, C. B., 124
Bass, Charlotta, 42, 85, 86, 87, 88, 89, 97, 124, 189n66
Belafonte, Harry, 31, 66, 159
Bennett, Gwendolyn, 30, 31
black culture, 28, 30, 32, 140; black arts, 31, 34; cultural resistance (activism), 28, 64-68, 139, cultural workers, 3, 12, 29, 30, 31, 65
black freedom struggle (movement), 6, 7, 9, 10, 11, 57, 122, 124, 126, 130, 131, 133, 135, 136, 137, 138, 139, 140, 149, 162; black liberation, 1, 5, 8, 21, 42, 43, 70, 68, 132, 136, 137, 144, 147, 148, 149, 150, 151, 153, 176n55
black heterosexual relationships, 49, 50, 52, 53, 54
black intellectuals, 6, 8, 17, 18, 22, 23, 29, 30, 52, 69, 146, 162
black liberation. *See* black freedom struggle
black nationalism, 6, 77, 117, 144, 154, 201n21; black power, 6, 7, 78, 143, 150, 151, 160
Black Panther, 151
black radical, 147, 148, 161, 164; exodus, 144; labor, 105; politics 10, 11, 36, 39, 136, 151, 186n20; thought, 7, 130
black self-determination, 6, 10, 28, 32, 37, 68, 69, 87, 88, 149, 164

New York Support Committee of the National Negro Congress, 55
Nigeria, 144, 145, 146
Nkrumah, Kwame, 134, 137, 146, 147, 149, 202n50
Nyerere, Julius, 137

O'Dwyer, William, 112
Ottley, Roi, 23, 52, 54, 55, 56, 63

Paderson, Irwin, 131
Pan-African, 144, 145, 146, 149
Parent Community Committee (PCC), 141, 142
Parks, Rosa, 125
Party Organizer, 33
Patterson, Louise Thompson, 1, 2, 3, 16, 18, 26, 30, 33, 42, 43, 85, 86, 97, 133, 136, 140, 144, 152, 160, 189n66
Patterson, William, 25, 26, 34, 41, 80, 84, 85, 91, 92, 152
peace, 47, 58, 59, 60, 61, 62, 64, 88, 155, 158, 159
People's Defense Committee in Winston-Salem, 95
People's Voice, 16, 23, 30, 34, 39, 52, 107
Perkins, Larry, 35, 131
Perry, Elaine, 118, 196n60
Petry, Ann, 23, 34, 39, 51, 52, 53, 55, 56, 66
Pittsburgh Courier, 75, 82, 98, 99
Poitier, Sidney, 31, 66
Political Affairs, 41, 45, 48, 68
Popular Front, 14, 16, 17, 26, 27, 28, 30, 35, 36, 37, 39, 40, 43, 52, 64, 78, 137, 159, 165, 175n48; black, 7, 8, 12, 39, 131, 135, 137, 138, 141, 178n92, 178n93, 200n18; and labor, 102, 105; people's front, 29; politics, 26, 162
Poverty, 140, 144
Powell, Adam Clayton Jr., 22, 23, 107, 133
President's Committee on Government Contracts, 123
Progressive Party, 40, 42, 89, 124, 131, 179n98
"protofeminist," 5, 70
Provisional Committee to Free the Ingrams, 96, 97, 98

Rabb, Maxwell M., 96
racism, 4, 3, 29, 53, 167n7; bias in legal cases, 21, 75, 76; increase during depression, 19; labor, 129; racial discrimination, 25, 104, 137, 146; racial equality, 5, 37, 70, 101; sexualized, 33, 76, 77; white supremacy, 17, 18, 32, 41, 46, 51, 54, 61, 62, 63, 64, 66, 67, 68, 71, 72, 91, 109, 132, 140, 144, 151
radicalism, 6, 8, 11, 16, 20, 21; activists, 6, 22, 26, 42, 137, 117, 133, 136, 137, 157, 162, 167n7; direct action, 4, 16, 97; organizations, 14, 20; politics, 9, 14, 16, 27; radical labor, 106; radical organizing, 44; women, 2, 8, 11, 58
Randolph, A. Philip, 18, 29, 37, 53, 119
reconversion, 39–40, 41, 49; and unions, 103, 104
"red scare." *See* anticommunism
resistance, 2, 8, 4, 5, 7, 18, 66, 76, 93, 105, 130, 135, 137, 160, 161; non-violent, 6, 140, revolutionary, 28, 140, 150, 155
Richards, Beah. *See* Richardson, Beulah
Richardson, Beulah (Beah Richards), 1, 5, 7, 8, 10, 14, 43, 44, 46, 47, 48, 85, 86, 87, 89, 92, 97, 130, 132, 136, 140, 159, 189n66, 198n84; "A Black Woman Speaks," 46, 61, 62–64, 138, 160
Robeson, Eslanda, 85, 95, 131, 134, 140, 156
Robeson, Paul, 3, 7, 12, 13, 34, 41, 42, 66, 74, 78, 131, 135, 140, 144, 157, 159, 161, 162, 165, 168n10, 196n60, 199n3, 202n50
Robinson, Theresa L., 81
Romero, Manuel, 142
Roosevelt, Eleanor, 83
Roosevelt, Franklin, 29
Rosen, Helen, 155, 159, 199n3

Scottsboro Boys case, 21, 29, 70, 75, 76, 163, 185n10
Sears, Roebuck and Company, 120–121
segregation, 4, 32, 38, 43, 91, 137, 143; in army, 37; in jobs, 105, 106, 119
sexual assault, 9, 92; and racial violence, 13, 76, 92, 93, 154; self-defense against, 2, 5, 13, 75, 76, 77, 79, 82, 93, 111, 153, 154, 163

About the Author

DAYO F. GORE is an assistant professor of women, gender, sexuality studies at the University of Massachusetts at Amherst. She is the co-editor of *Want to Start a Revolution? Radical Women in the Black Freedom Struggle* (NYU Press, 2009).